D0866545

BILLIONAIRES' BALL

# BILLIONAIRES' BALL

*Gluttony and Hubris in an Age*
*of Epic Inequality*

Linda McQuaig
Neil Brooks

Property oi
Baker College
of Allen Park

Beacon Press
Boston

BEACON PRESS
25 Beacon Street
Boston, Massachusetts 02108-2892
www.beacon.org

Beacon Press books
are published under the auspices of
the Unitarian Universalist Association of Congregations.

© 2012 by Linda McQuaig and Neil Brooks
All rights reserved
Printed in the United States of America

15  14  13  12    8  7  6  5  4  3  2  1

This book is printed on acid-free paper that meets the uncoated paper
ANSI/NISO specifications for permanence as revised in 1992.

Text design by Kim Arney

Library of Congress Cataloging-in-Publication Data

McQuaig, Linda.
Billionaires' ball : gluttony and hubris in
an age of epic inequality / Linda McQuaig, Neil Brooks.
p.   cm.
Includes bibliographical references and index.
ISBN 978-0-8070-0339-8 (alk. paper)
1. Wealth—United States.   2. Income distribution—United States.
3. Rich people—Taxation—United States.   4. Equality—United States.
5. Democracy—United States.   I. Brooks, Neil.   II. Title.
HC110.W4.M42 2012
339.2'20973—dc23                                    2011048724

For my precious Amy:
daughter, editor, best friend
—L. M.


To Marlane, with love
—N. B.

The disposition to admire, and almost to worship, the rich and the powerful, and to despise, or, at least, to neglect persons of poor and mean condition . . . is . . . the great and most universal cause of the corruption of our moral sentiments.

—Adam Smith, *The Theory of Moral Sentiments*

# Contents

# Return of the Plutocrats

Imagine this: you are given one dollar every second.

At that rate, after one minute, you would have sixty dollars. And after twelve days, you would be a millionaire—something beyond most people's wildest dreams.

But how long would it take to become a billionaire?

Well, at that rate, it would take almost thirty-two years.

Being a billionaire isn't just beyond most people's wildest dreams; it's likely beyond their comprehension.

Another way to grasp the sheer size of billionaires' fortunes is to imagine how long it would take Bill Gates, generally considered the world's richest man, to count his $53 billion. If he counted it at the same rate—one dollar every second—and he counted nonstop day and night, he'd have it all tallied up in 1,680 years. Still another way to look at it is this: if Bill Gates had started counting his fortune at that rate back in 330 AD—the year that the Roman emperor Constantine had his wife boiled alive and chose Byzantium as the empire's new capital—he'd just be finishing up now.

After years of basking in the glow of a flattering limelight, by the fall of 2011 the very rich were experiencing something new and altogether jarring: the glare of a harsh spotlight trained directly on them. The temptation to bark orders like: "Dim that light, or else!" was natural enough, but perhaps unwise. After all, those shining the spotlight were not their employees and were swarming in large numbers through the streets of lower Manhattan, behaving like the sort of unruly mob one finds in faraway places where the ways of the free world are insufficiently appreciated.

All of a sudden, right here in America, being wondrously, fulsomely, voluptuously rich was no longer a badge of honor, something to announce gleefully to the world by squealing the tires of one's Lamborghini at pedestrians who were in the way. Wall Street—the nexus of ambition, brains, greed, glamour, the very g-spot of the American Dream—was no longer something to be glorified, but rather occupied.

Where would it end? Could the trappings of wealth become a source of embarrassment? Could the day come when a yacht became like a fur coat—one of life's small pleasures ruined by the prospect that wearing it (or docking it) might attract a crowd of protestors? Imagine a protestor so mean-spirited that she would object to the sight of a banker lounging on a pleasure craft massively larger than the house she had once owned but that now belonged to . . . a bank.

Of course, it could be worse. Luckily for the bankers, the occupiers were a little fuzzy in their targeting, going broadly after the top 1 percent, apparently unaware that the real red meat was much higher up the food chain—the top .01 percent, the top .001 percent, or all the way up to the dizzying heights occupied (in this case appropriately so) by billionaires.

Anyway, help was on the way. Already, the lobbying industry was swinging into action. By late November 2011, one of the leading Washington lobby firms—Clark, Lytle, Geduldig & Cranford—had prepared a memo for the American Bankers Association (leaked to the press by some mean-spirited soul), which laid out a media strategy for countering the Occupy Wall Street juggernaut.

The lobbyists insisted that the answer lay in a carefully prepared counter-campaign aimed at slinging mud at the motives of the occupiers: "If we can show they have the same cynical motivation as a political opponent, it will undermine their credibility in a profound way."[1] (It's tough to imagine what cynical motivation might lead people to live in water-soaked tents for weeks on end.)

The danger was that the anti–Wall Street message, if unchallenged, could turn the big Wall Street banks into fodder for the Democratic political machine—and worse. As the memo noted: "The bigger concern should be that Republicans will no longer defend Wall Street companies—and might start running against them too."

The lobbyists even raised the prospect of the Tea Party crowd joining in some kind of a Right-Left populist free-for-all of bank-bashing: "The combination has the potential to be explosive later in the year when media reports cover the next round of bonuses and contrast it with stories of millions of Americans making do with less this holiday season." (It's gratifying to see that, even when they're plotting the destruction of a democratic movement, lobbyists now use inclusive language about the "holiday season.")

All this looming victimization was no doubt baffling to members of the financial elite, who still had trouble grasping the notion that they were somehow supposed to feel culpable for the 2008 financial crash.

That bewilderment had been evident as early as January 2009, only months after the crash, at the elite gathering in the Swiss town of Davos, where bankers, business leaders, political shakers, and other big thinkers come together every year to celebrate the globalized world of liberated financial markets, shrunken government, and reinvigorated capitalism. Of course, some bewilderment was inevitable in Davos that year, with even questions popping up about why markets had done such a poor job of policing themselves. The headline on a dispatch that appeared on the website *Slate* captured the mood: "Davos Man, Confused." Written by journalist Daniel Gross, the piece explained that, despite the confusion, there was a broad consensus at Davos that "[s]uccess is the work of Great Men and Women, while failure can be pinned on the system." Or, as another journalist, Julian Glover noted in the UK's *Guardian*: "The shock is real, the grief has hardly begun, but no one in Davos seems to think [this] means they should be less important or less rich."[2]

That would have involved a change of mindset, which was not what these economic overlords seemed inclined toward. After all, a key concept behind the economic order of the past few decades has been the central importance of individual talent—and the need to nurture it with abundant financial rewards. That way, so the idea goes, the brilliant in our midst would be lured to the top jobs that run the world. Ensuring the active participation of these giants among us was clearly understood to be worth a lot, and pay scales were adjusted accordingly, going through the roof at the upper end. Just because the global economy was now in a free fall hardly seemed like grounds to beat up the very people who'd played key roles in designing it.

So, in Manhattan, then-CEO of Merrill Lynch John Thain apparently saw no irony as he explained why he'd felt it necessary to pay $4 billion in executive bonuses to keep the "best" people on staff—right after those same overachievers had steered the company to a staggering net loss of $27 billion and, in the process, helped trigger the global economic meltdown. The decision of the Wall Street crowd to collectively pay themselves a record $140 billion in 2009—outstripping even their 2007 record—may have seemed odd under the circumstances, but then no one ever accused Wall Street bankers of being unduly modest, unassuming, or prone to self-doubt.

Away from the rarified air of Davos and Manhattan, doubts were beginning to appear. Some less-gifted types were now clamoring for change, even suggesting that cutting executive pay might induce the hypertalented to seek more socially useful employment in areas like teaching or health care. But a letter to the *New York Times* clarified the danger of this approach, making a compelling case for maintaining extravagant pay, even huge executive bonuses: "Without them, Wall Streeters will all look for other jobs. Do we really want these greedy, incompetent clowns building our houses, teaching our children or driving our cabs?"[3]

．　●　●

As a result of the dramatic increase in the concentration of income and wealth at the top during the last few decades, the United States has become an extremely unequal society.

Before going any farther, we should point out that we are not against all inequality. On the contrary, some reasonable degree of inequality is not only acceptable and inevitable but even desirable because it allows for different rewards for different levels of individual effort and contribution. But what exists today in the United States—and to a lesser extent in Britain and Canada—is a level of inequality that is extreme compared to the rest of the advanced, industrialized world. Indeed, the level of inequality in the United States today is actually more considerably extreme than what exists in many developing countries, including India, Cambodia, and Nigeria, and even in many Middle Eastern countries, such as Egypt and Tunisia, where excessive inequality is widely believed to have played a role in sparking the Arab spring uprisings of 2009–2010.[4]

Over the past three decades, virtually all the growth in American incomes has gone to the top 10 percent, with particularly large gains going to the top 1 percent and spectacularly large gains going to the top .01 percent. Between 1980 and 2008, the incomes of the bottom 90 percent of the population grew by a meager 1 percent, or an average of just $303. Meanwhile, over those same years, the incomes of the top .01 percent of Americans grew by 403 percent, or an average of a massive $21.9 million. The richest 300,000 Americans now enjoy almost as much income as the bottom 150 million.[5] These high rollers make up an enormously rich and powerful class that can best be described as a plutocracy—not unlike the plutocracy of financial interests that dominated America back in the 1920s, when the opulence of the wealthy and their disproportionate influence over the political process was particularly blatant.

America's return to plutocracy is all the more notable because, between the periods of extreme inequality of the 1920s and the extreme inequality of today, something very significant happened. During the intervening years—particularly the early postwar period, from the end of World War II until 1980—the United States achieved, as did many other industrialized nations, a degree of equality and egalitarian distribution of income rarely seen in any period of Western history. Certainly, it is striking to compare the fate of ordinary Americans in recent decades with the fate of ordinary Americans in the early decades after World War II. As mentioned in the last paragraph, the incomes of the bottom 90 percent of Americans grew by only 1 percent in the past three decades. But, in the 1950–1980 period, the bottom 90 percent did dramatically better, experiencing income growth of 75 percent, or an average of $13,222.[6] Since the 1980s, however, the revival of plutocracy has had sweeping effects, profoundly changing the nature of American society and the lives of Americans. Yet, even as this remarkable transformation took place, the issue of inequality and its negative consequences largely disappeared from public debate—until the Occupy Wall Street movement boldly pushed the subject back into the limelight in the fall of 2011.

Of the world's 1,011 billionaires, it seems fitting to begin with John Paulson, who made a fortune betting against the subprime mortgage market.

Mild-mannered, dark-suited, and with a mysterious half smile somewhat reminiscent of the Mona Lisa's—one of the few objects on the planet with arguably a higher net worth—Paulson exudes a kind of normalcy. This in itself is odd because, as the forty-fifth richest individual in the world, with a fortune of $12 billion, Paulson (no relation to former U.S. treasury secretary Henry Paulson) is certainly not average in any meaningful sense of the word. Still, there's nothing in the outward appearance of this fifty-four-year-old hedge fund manager that would suggest anything other than a middle-aged man, married with two children, quietly going about his business. Though he moves in elite circles and has all the trappings of wealth, he doesn't keep a chauffeur waiting for him and is known to travel by cab and even public transit. He doesn't appear to suffer from the syndrome that, as journalist Matt Taibbi has noted, causes some Wall Street high-rollers to "start seeing Brad Pitt in the mirror."[7] John Paulson probably doesn't much bother looking in the mirror. Why would he when he could spend that time more profitably pondering which defective subprime mortgages inside a collateral debt obligation would be most likely to yield an unconscionable rate of return?

A dedication to making a serious amount of money has always been a guiding influence for Paulson, who grew up in a middle-class neighborhood in Queens, New York, but whose family on both sides has a background in money management. Particularly influential in shaping Paulson's mindset was his maternal grandfather, Arthur Boklan, a successful Wall Street banker who, even during the Depression, managed to house his family in grand style in the elegant apartment building that still stands at 93rd Street and Central Park West.

Paulson always knew he wanted a large fortune, and he systematically went about laying the groundwork for acquiring one, applying himself sufficiently at New York University to graduate first in his finance class and then winning top honors in the Harvard MBA program. From there he soon gravitated, as water down an incline, to the money-making palaces of Wall Street, opening his own hedge fund in 1994 in order to best make use of his unusual talent for spotting the biggest money-making opportunity going. The ultimate one came his way in April 2005, when he developed a hunch that the ultra-hot subprime mortgage market was headed for spectacular collapse. Keeping that particular insight to himself, he turned his research staff loose on the problem and figured out how to make money betting that the millions of people signing up for mortgages they could only dream of actually affording would soon start defaulting. When they did, Paulson was there, watching money flood into his hedge fund with torrential force. In 2007 he personally pocketed $3.7 billion, giving him what surely must be the all-time record for financially profiting from the misery of others.

The financial crisis of 2008 produced a brief drop in income for the hedge fund industry. As the Wall Street meltdown pushed the world economy into a brutal recession in 2008, hedge fund managers' pay fell by about 50 percent. Even at that dramatically reduced level, the top twenty-five managers still earned an average of $464 million each. And, by 2009, while the world economy remained deeply mired in recession, the hedge fund industry had bounced back fully; the total pay of its top managers exceeded even the record year of 2007, when Paulson alone, in the top slot, had received $3.7 billion. The top spot was now claimed by hedge fund manager David Tepper, who collected $4 billion, basically by betting that the U.S. government would come to the rescue of the big banks (Paulson ranked fourth, with $2.3 billion). Overall, the top twenty-five hedge fund managers made $25.3 billion in 2009—averaging a little more than $1 billion each, more than double the $464 million average of the previous year. By 2010, with unemployment still gripping America, the top twenty-five hedge fund managers took home a total of $22 billion. And Paulson was back on top, exceeding his own record, with an annual income of $4.9 billion.

To put all this in perspective (as much as it's possible to put something like this in perspective), let's stack up today's top incomes against the income of John D. Rockefeller, who in his day and for many decades afterward served as the legendary Richest Man Imaginable. In 1894, at the height of the Gilded Age, Rockefeller had a staggeringly large income of $1.25 million ($30 million in today's dollars)—which was 7,000 times the average U.S. income at the time. In 2010, Paulson's $4.9 billion income was more than 100,000 times the average U.S. income.

Another way to look at it is this: Paulson, whose actions helped trigger the collapse of the global economy, received as much income in 2010 as did a hundred thousand nurses, who provided essential health care for more than eight million Americans. Fortunately we have the teachings of modern economics to help us make sense of such a gap. Otherwise, we might be left struggling to understand by what logic Paulson could possibly be worth as much as a hundred thousand nurses—or, for that matter, as much as a single nurse.

.    .    .

Paulson and Tepper vividly illustrate the sheer scope of today's top incomes, and how far they outstrip that of the very top earners of the past. Indeed, Paulson and Tepper are members of an elite group that financial historian Charles Geisst has called "the highest earners of all time."[8] As these numbers reveal, it's not just that the rich are getting richer, but that they're pulling so dramatically ahead of the rest of society. With North American workers experiencing little or no growth in their real wages over the past few decades, middle-class families now typically need two earners to keep up the material standard their parents achieved with one. So, to the extent that they're holding their ground, they're doing so by working much harder. Income growth has taken place almost entirely at the top end, and the higher one goes, the bigger the gains have been proportionately. Consider, for instance, how the pay of the average CEO compares to that of the average worker. In 1980, the gap was about 40 to 1; by 2010, it had risen to roughly 340 to 1. But even this understates the size of the gains made by the very top rung of CEOs. If we look at the average pay of just the one hundred highest-paid CEOs and compare it to the pay of the average worker, we find that the gap in the 1970s was about 45 to 1. By 2006 that gap had become 1,723 to 1.

Sometimes referred to as "Winner Take All," this gravitation of pay toward the very top has become the new normal in a wide range of fields. For athletes and entertainers, the pay at the top is now enormous. At the pinnacle of the sports world is Tiger Woods, earning $91.5 million in 2010, despite losing some celebrity endorsements after his marital infidelities. In celebrity rankings by *Forbes* magazine, more than fifty movie stars earned in excess of $20 million in 2007–2008, while Steven Spielberg made $130 million, Oprah Winfrey $275 million, and J. K. Rowling $300 million.

Then there's *Forbes'* annual list of the four hundred wealthiest Americans, ranked by net worth. In 1982, the first year the list was published, a wealthy person had to have at least $75 million to make it onto the list, which was topped by thirteen billionaires. By 2011, only billionaires made the list. The "poorest" person on the list had a fortune of $1.05 billion. Even when inflation is taken into account, the growth is staggering. In 1982, the richest person on the list was oil and shipping tycoon Daniel Ludwig, with a fortune of $2 billion—equivalent to $4.7 billion today. But on the 2011 list, that would only get him to sixty-sixth place.[9]

We can see that America's richest have weathered the 2008 financial crisis just fine. Together, they had combined financial wealth in 2011 of $1.53 trillion—up 12 percent from the year before and only slightly below their all-time high in 2007 of $1.57 trillion. Bill Gates's fortune—the world's largest for most of the past fifteen years—dropped in value from $58 billion to $40 billion on the *Forbes* 2009 list. But by 2010, it had bounced back to $53 billion and, by 2011, to $59 billion.

One can perhaps grasp the sheer size of billionaires' wealth by imagining how lavishly they are able to spend, just by living off the interest from their fortunes. If they were to indulge in the wildest orgies of consumption, diligently sustained over long periods of time, it would be a struggle for them to make even a small dent in their capital. Take Larry Ellison, CEO of business software giant Oracle, with a net worth of $27 billion in 2010. Assuming a 10 percent rate of return, Ellison could spend $51 million a week—or $303,000 an hour, every hour of the day, seven days a week—and still not dig into his principal at all. Moreover, at that same 10 percent rate of return, the taxes on Ellison's sprawling twenty-three-acre California estate could be entirely paid from his interest payments in just six hours, during one night's sleep. Nevertheless, in 2008, Ellison contested the tax bill for the estate and won a $3 million refund, which had to be repaid by local school boards and municipalities. The Portola Valley School District in northern California was ordered to repay the billionaire some $250,000, roughly the cost of hiring several new teachers. For Ellison, the tax refund was yet more pocket money—enough, for instance, to increase that week's *hourly* spending from $303,000 to $321,000.[10]

•    •    •

One striking thing about today's elite is that many of its members have made their money on their own. While inherited wealth still plays a huge role—the Walmart fortune continues to take up multiple spots on the top-ten billionaire list—there has been a dramatic rise in self-made millionaires and billionaires. Indeed, income growth among the top 0.1 percent of Americans has been strongest, not among those who live off inherited wealth, but rather among corporate and financial professionals, who presumably live by their own wits and smarts.[11] This phenomenon has led some observers to conclude that today's rich are deserving of their vast rewards, that income is now meted out in a ruthlessly competitive global economy where the best and the brightest rise relentlessly to the top on the basis of their own worth and contribution. No longer is great wealth primarily the domain of those born on the manor and raised in luxury. Today, the argument goes, we live in a "meritocracy," where talent and ability determine riches.

The notion of a meritocracy appears to provide fresh justification for the concentration of money at the top. Whatever the consequences for fairness and social justice, it is much harder to take issue with vast inequality if the rich got where they are because they are a uniquely talented and innovative bunch. Not surprisingly, the meritocracy concept has become a staple in the literature that members of the new elite rely on. In a special report in January 2011, the *Economist* heralded the rise of what it described as "the few": "Societies have always had elites. . . . The big change over the past century is that elites are increasingly meritocratic and global. The richest people in advanced countries are not aristocrats but entrepreneurs such as Bill Gates." The magazine went on to celebrate today's super-rich, arguing that "to become rich in the first place, they typically have to do something extraordinary. Some inherit money, of course, but most build a better mousetrap, finance someone else's good idea or at least run a chain of hairdressers in a way that keeps customers coming back. And because they are mostly self-made, today's rich are restless and dynamic."[12]

Similarly, a cover story in the *Atlantic* found much that was inspiring about "the new ruling class." Though writer Chrystia Freeland raised some concerns about growing inequality, she clearly accepts the notion that today's elite earns its money in a meritocracy: "Its members are hardworking, highly educated, jet-setting meritocrats who feel they are the deserving winners of a tough, worldwide economic competition." Freeland comes across as reasonable and even concerned about the potential political fallout from inequality, but she ends up largely supporting the rich in their contention that they are a deserving, exceptionally talented lot. This might have something to do with the fact that she has been invited into their inner circles, attending their conferences and events, even their dinner parties, as she has conducted her research. In a sense, she could be described as an embedded journalist, covering the story of class warfare from inside the ranks of the wealthy. Perhaps not surprisingly, she asserts: "[M]any of the plutocracy's rationalizations have more than a bit of truth in them." Freeland concludes that today's ultra-rich elite is indispensable to the well-being of the rest of us: "America really does need many of its plutocrats. We benefit from the goods they produce and the jobs they create. And even if a growing portion of those jobs are overseas, it is better to be the home of these innovators—native and immigrant alike—than not. In today's hypercompetitive global environment, we need a creative, dynamic super-elite more than ever."[13]

We disagree.

Contrary to the impressions of the rich and their admirers, we see no evidence that members of the new global elite are especially talented or indispensable—or even particularly beneficial—to society. In most cases, it appears they got rich because of brute luck, ruthlessness, connections, insider dealing, cheating, rigging the rules, all of the above, or simply being positioned well enough to redirect rewards towards themselves or to take advantage of opportunities that someone else (perhaps more talented) would have taken. Certainly, there is no evidence that members of today's elite are any more talented or hardworking than were the elite of a generation ago, who received a fraction of the pay for doing work that was at least as good and as beneficial to society.

Nor is there evidence of the most widely cited explanation of to-day's big incomes—that they are the result of globalization and skills-based technological change. Skyrocketing CEO salaries and the rise in income share going to the top have mostly occurred in Anglo-American countries (the United States, Britain, and Canada). Yet globalization and technological change have been experienced in all advanced na-tions, including European countries and Japan, where incomes are much more equally distributed.

The biggest factor in explaining today's big pay at the top isn't bet-ter performance or the effects of globalization or technological change. Rather, it's simply that our highest earners have gotten control of the agenda and rigged the rules and laws in their own favor.

A huge part of the story involves the rising power and influence of America's corporate and financial professionals—a group that now makes up 60 percent of those in the top-earning 0.1 percent.[14] In the past, such professionals were regarded as agents who managed the enterprises and money of America's owning class. In recent decades, however, these management professionals have moved centerstage, grabbing more power for themselves—and a much larger share of the financial rewards.

The result, according to John C. Bogle, founder and former chair-man of the Vanguard Group mutual fund organization, has been "grotesquely excessive compensation paid to executive chiefs"—com-pensation that is "unjustified by any remotely comparable business achievement."[15] Bogle, a longtime prominent critic, argues that the corporate world is now riddled with conflicts of interest, leaving little check on the cozy relations between CEOs and corporate directors, compensation committees and auditors that should be holding them to account. This has allowed CEOs to engage in financial sleight of hand, falsely driving up stock prices, allowing executives to then cash in extremely lucrative stock options. Continues Bogle: "The fact is that executives had created wealth for themselves, but not for their shar-eowners. Long before the stock market values melted away, executives had made a timely exodus from the market by selling much of their stock."[16] The staggering amounts that CEOs have walked off with understate their actual compensation, since the amounts don't include luxurious perks like the personal use of company aircraft, forgivable loans, and private boxes at sporting events, not to mention gold-plated termination packages. (Michael Ovitz was awarded $140 million when he was fired after a disastrous fourteen months as president of Disney.)

Inside the financial world, these sorts of problems have been all the more endemic and the impact all the more extreme. Once controlled by individual investors, the financial industry has come to be dominated by financial institutions—mutual funds, investment banks, pension funds—that control vast pools of wealth. The professionals who oversee these institutions now wield extraordinary power—and pull in extraordinary financial rewards for themselves. "More than one-fifth of the annual returns generated for investors in the financial markets—stock, bond and money market alike—have been siphoned off by fund managers," says Bogle. He insists the redirection of wealth to the tiny managerial class will get much worse if it's not corrected: "Without a major reduction in the share of market returns arrogated to themselves by our mutual fund intermediaries, more than three-quarters of the future cumulative wealth produced by stocks over an investment lifetime will be consumed by fund managers."[17]

This staggering siphoning-off of market returns by those in the financial sector is central to today's distortion of economic rewards and the gross overpayment of those at the top. The best explanation of how this has happened—and our collective blindness to the financial costs it imposes on others—probably comes from no less an authority on financial markets than the man commonly regarded as the world's smartest investor, Warren Buffett, the multibillionaire chairman of giant holding company Berkshire Hathaway. In a letter to shareholders in February 2006, Buffett noted that, throughout the twentieth century, U.S. companies overall grew at an impressive pace, delivering substantial gains to the wide array of Americans who had invested in them. But in recent years, financial professionals—collectively known as "Wall Street"—have taken on an increasingly prominent role in the investment process as intermediaries or middlemen. These middlemen carry on a whirlwind of activity—buying and selling stocks and bonds through ever more elaborate and complex financial arrangements. Ultimately, these activities, aimed at gaining an advantage over other investors, add nothing to the value of the companies, which are the true source of wealth. Indeed, the activity is mostly about structuring things so that the intermediaries are paid ever larger fees for their money management services, greatly driving up the costs of investing. Notes Buffett, "These costs are now incurred in amounts that will cause shareholders to earn *far* less than they historically have."[18]

In other words, the huge Wall Street fortunes being made are not generating new wealth but simply draining off wealth from other people, including millions of Americans whose retirement savings are invested in pension and mutual funds. The nimble-fingered deals of Wall Street financial houses do not create magical new sources of money, as it often seems. There is "no shower of money from outer space," as Buffett puts it. The shower of money raining down on Wall Street is simply the massive cut of American profits being grabbed by rapacious financial middlemen.

Buffett illustrates this by constructing a simple parable featuring an imaginary family that he calls the "Gotrocks," who own all American corporations. Over the years, the Gotrocks have grown extremely rich through steadily compounding profits. But along come some smooth, fast-talking "Helpers," who persuade the Gotrocks to allow them to handle their stock trades. This turns out to be costly, since the Helpers continually increase the volume of buying and selling. Distressed by their diminishing share of the pie, the Gotrocks become convinced they need more advisors, consultants, managers. Eventually, some *really* smooth, fast-talking Helpers strut onto the scene, assuring the frustrated Gotrocks that the problem is that they haven't been paying high enough fees. "The more observant members of the family," writes Buffett, "see that some of the hyper-Helpers are really just manager-Helpers wearing new uniforms, bearing sewn-on sexy names like HEDGE FUND or PRIVATE EQUITY." Nonetheless, family members sign up. "And that's where we are today," notes Buffett. "A record portion of the earnings that would go in their entirety to owners—if they all just stayed in their rocking chairs—is now going to a swelling army of Helpers."[19]

All this frenzied activity today results in some $40 trillion worth of stock market trades a year. Bogle notes that only a small fraction of this amount—about $200 billion—is involved in carrying out the function that financial markets are supposed to perform: ensuring that capital is allocated to the most promising business enterprises. The rest—more than $39 trillion a year—is purely speculative trading activity with, therefore, negative value, according to Bogle. "The cost of capital allocation is one-two-hundredth of the speculative cost." There are winners and losers on each side of every trade, Bogle insists, "but the guy in the middle always wins."[20]

And the biggest of these middlemen winners are the hedge fund managers. Hedge funds, which are restricted to wealthy investors, have become the ultimate symbol of the new Gilded Age. While they barely existed before 1980, they've become key vehicles for a new financial world in which long-term investing has been mostly replaced by financial speculation at whirlwind speed. At the end of the 1990s, there were 515 of these funds, managing $500 billion; by 2005, there were 2,200 funds, handling almost $1.5 trillion. By the spring of 2011, with the world economy still reeling from the financial collapse, hedge funds continued to grow, managing $2.02 trillion in assets for the world's wealthy elite. And nowhere has the money grab by the managerial class been more evident than in hedge funds, whose managers have become among the richest people in the world. These individuals have catapulted themselves into a stratosphere of income compensation that is in a league all its own, vastly higher than even the wildly extravagant CEO pay levels at leading corporations.

This has been largely accomplished by self-serving financial maneuvering. What makes hedge funds so spectacularly lucrative for their managers is the way they're structured. Fund managers take a percentage—generally 2 percent of the money they manage and

20 percent of the profits. Considering the vast sums they manage, this allows pay packages for the very top managers to reach *above $1 billion in a single year.* (In 2010, the average income of the top-paid twenty-five hedge fund managers was $880 million *each.*) Some observers have noted that hedge funds aren't so much an investment strategy as a compensation strategy.

Indeed, devising new ways to collect ever bigger personal rewards is pretty much the limit of Wall Street innovation. Complex financial instruments have made hedge fund managers fabulously wealthy, but, says Bogle, they have "absolutely nothing to do with creating value for society."[21] Former Federal Reserve Board chief Paul Volcker made the same point: "I wish somebody would give me some shred of evidence linking financial innovation with a benefit to the economy." Volcker went on to suggest that the only really worthwhile financial innovation of the past twenty-five years was the ATM machine. "It really helps people, it's useful."[22]

But if hedge funds have offered no useful innovation to the economy—and, in fact, on some occasions greatly contributed to financial instability—the compensation packages have provided a tiny crowd of fund managers a chance to grab a significant piece of the world's treasure, without even taking any risks. If things turn out well, the manager gets a huge cut of the profits; if things go badly, the Gotrocks alone take the hit. It's perhaps not surprising that the hedge fund crowd, having talked their way into deals this sweet, feel a certain swaggering self-confidence in dealing with the world. That self-confidence apparently leaves them feeling entitled to a tax loophole that allows them to pay tax at an exceptionally low rate on their mega-earnings—a loophole that they've fought bitterly to keep. (More on this later.)

Given all this, it seems odd to consider the enormous amassing of wealth in a few hands as the product of mysterious forces arising from the global economy and technological change. Rather, the growing concentration of income and wealth is largely the product of deliberate changes affecting the corporate and financial world—changes that became law because of the lobbying efforts of an unusually aggressive and grasping new elite. The enormous CEO compensation packages of recent years were largely the product of wildly generous stock options, and attempts by regulatory authorities to rein in these options were blocked by corporate lobbyists and their allies in Congress. Similarly, the rise of a rapacious industry of financial intermediaries has been greatly facilitated by the dismantling of financial regulations that were wisely put in place in the 1930s, following the 1929 Wall Street crash. The dismantling of these controls can be directly attributed to massive lobbying campaigns by those who ended up benefiting from the changes.

And no discussion of how the rich manage to rig the rules in their own favor would be complete without mentioning their role in convincing governments to reduce their tax burden. In 1955, the four hundred richest Americans actually paid taxes that amounted to 51.2 percent of their total incomes (and they still felt immensely rich compared to everyone else, no doubt). By 2007, the four hundred richest Americans paid taxes that amounted to just 16.6 percent of their total incomes. If the four hundred richest Americans in 2007 had paid tax at the 1955 rate, they would have contributed an additional $47.7 billion to the national treasury—all that from just four hundred individuals![23] For that matter, some wealthy Americans manage to pay no income tax at all. Los Angeles Dodgers owner Frank McCourt and his then-wife, Jamie, arranged their finances so that between 2004 and 2009 they paid no federal or state income tax on total income of $108 million—a detail that emerged in their divorce proceedings.[24]

Along with their intensive lobbying of politicians, the elite have managed, through a massive propaganda campaign, to convince the public that the huge redirection of rewards to the top is simply not an issue. This pervasive campaign—reflected in the media and in public discourse—has effectively changed social norms and expectations, silencing the popular outrage that would surely have otherwise accompanied such a massive heist of national income by the richest members of society. In the past, there was a largely unspoken agreement in society as to the acceptable levels of remuneration for jobs at all levels, including at the top. Executives and their peers on corporate boards were therefore constrained in how much they could collude in granting excessive compensation to themselves out of fear of a public backlash.

Those social constraints have been all but wiped away. The propaganda campaign selling the virtues of unbridled acquisitiveness seems to have convinced large segments of the public that excessive greed is acceptable or at least an inevitable not-to-be-resisted aspect of the postmodern age. With public outrage largely muted or deflected onto other things, there has been little to deter those at the top of the corporate and financial world from dipping ever deeper into the till, with the active cooperation of lawmakers (whose campaigns they largely fund).

The implications of this—for social equity and harmony, for the well-being of the nation's citizens, and for American democracy itself—are enormous. But let's at least start with some clarity about what's taken place and not be sidetracked by construing as a "meritocracy" a system that is delivering the largest rewards in history to a group whose only distinguishing characteristic is an unusually fierce determination for self-enrichment.

Of course, not all of today's top earners (those in the top 0.1 percent) are corporate CEOs, managers, or financial professionals—the crowd that has particularly benefited from stock options, financial deregulation, and the elimination of the restraint on greed.

Perhaps if we look beyond this crowd, we will see some more deserving types. The next largest group, comprising 6.3 percent of top earners, consists of individuals who aren't working (this includes members of the leisure class living off dividends). Next, making up 6.2 percent are lawyers, who we may safely assume, are mostly corporate and tax lawyers protecting the property rights of the well-to-do. Next, comprising 4.7 percent of top earners are those who make money through real estate, many of whom likely profited from the subprime mortgage fiasco. Finally, we come to entrepreneurs—the group most commonly associated with extremely high incomes. Yet entrepreneurs make up just 3.6 percent of this very high-end crowd.[25]

Finally, then, we are in the territory of Bill Gates and Mark Zuckerberg—innovators who have changed the way we live. Surely no one would question their right to their massive fortunes?

Actually, we do.

Bill Gates may be the toughest case to contest, given that he is credited with nothing less than making the computer revolution accessible to billions of people and having donated billions of dollars to worthwhile causes. We will look at him in more detail later. For now, though, let's take a quick look at Mark Zuckerberg, already a self-made multibillionaire at the age of twenty-eight, whose invention of Facebook has been celebrated in the immensely popular Hollywood movie *The Social Network*.

In questioning the legitimacy of Zuckerberg's fortune, our point is simply to note that he has received a staggering amount of money—$13.5 billion—for producing a product in which his role was, by any reasonable measure, fairly marginal. Certainly, Zuckerberg couldn't have made that $13.5 billion all on his own, or even remotely on his own. He made it, as a mere university student, by taking advantage of the enormous technological inheritance provided by all those who had developed the Internet and, before that, the personal computer and, before that, the mainframe computer and, before that . . . all the way back to the invention of the wheel.

Indeed, it's estimated that about 90 percent of any wealth generated today is due to this "knowledge inheritance" of the past. If this sounds unlikely, imagine whether Zuckerberg could have created the Facebook empire if he had, say, been a student thirty years ago in the pre-Internet age, or if he hadn't attended college in the early 2000s, when computer advances had reached a certain stage of sophistication. Given these advances, he and a number of other bright students spotted the opportunity to develop a social networking program. If Zuckerberg hadn't got Facebook off the ground in early 2004, any of his competitors would have soon got theirs off the ground and gone on to dominate the field.

So who does the massive knowledge inheritance that made Facebook possible logically belong to? We argue that a much larger portion of it belongs to society and that society should capture its rightful share through a progressive tax system.

It could be added that a more progressive tax system would have done little to discourage Zuckerberg's enterprise. While he was scrambling to develop Facebook, it's unlikely that he was devoting much time to worrying about what taxes he might eventually pay if he were to become phenomenally, incomprehensibly rich. It's certainly hard to imagine him simply abandoning his quest had he thought that success might leave him with an after-tax fortune of only, say, $5 billion—or, for that matter, just $5 million. And if he had abandoned the quest, his competitors, hot on the same entrepreneurial trail, would have happily finished the job.

With or without Mark Zuckerberg, we would all today be experiencing the benefits of social networking.


Before we go on to probe the problems created by the dramatic rise in inequality, it's worth taking one last look at just how wildly unequal things have become.

The actual dollar amounts become numbing after a while. To get a clearer sense of how very rich the top income-earners have become—and how dramatically they've pulled ahead of the population at large—it's helpful to create a visual image. To do so, we've borrowed a concept created by Dutch statistician Jan Pen. Pen's idea was to present the distribution of income as a national parade in which everyone in the country marches. The height of the marchers is determined by their incomes. The entire parade takes one hour, during which time the entire nation marches by very quickly, in order of height, starting with the shortest marchers (the lowest income earners) at the front and ending with the tallest ones (the highest income earners) at the rear.

The parade demonstrates inequality, and it can be adapted to show the level of inequality in any country at any time. So, before we take a look at the U.S. national income parade today, let's put things in a really broad context by looking at what a national income parade would have looked like in preindustrial Britain. There's a tendency to think of extreme inequality as a thing of the past, a relic of a less advanced time. But while kings and nobles of preindustrial times enjoyed a standard of living that was wildly lavish compared to the poor in their day, that gap was actually considerably smaller than what exists today between billionaires and the homeless living on the streets of major U.S. cities. The lives of the destitute probably haven't changed that much over time, but the rich have become vastly richer than their preindustrial counterparts. Here, then, is what the national income parade would look like for England in the late seventeenth century (1688, to be exact).[26]

At the outset, we'd see some very tiny characters—vagrants, gypsies, rogues, vagabonds—who manage to collect about 2 pounds a year, begging or performing magic tricks for village gatherings. These extremely small people are followed by a large number of paupers and cottagers, who are still very low to the ground. Following close behind, about fifteen minutes into the parade, are household servants and common laborers, with incomes of about 15 pounds a year, measuring about two feet tall.[27] Eventually, we start to see the "middle class"—blacksmiths, silversmiths, masons, tinkers, tailors, weavers, cobblers, cordwainers (leather workers), all earning about 38 to 40 pounds a year and standing about normal height. Just slightly taller are prosperous shopkeepers, ale-sellers, and innkeepers. Finally, there are naval officers, about 10 feet fall. Only in the last few minutes do we see some giants—successful merchants and sea traders, measuring about 50 feet. Then in the last second, a cavalry of heavily armored knights appear, 108 feet tall (without their horses). Behind them, in heavy church garb, are pious-looking archbishops and bishops, earning 1,300 pounds a year and soaring up to 175 feet, even as they proclaim that the poor will inherit the earth. Finally, a couple dozen magnificently attired dukes and earls, with income above 6,000 pounds, stretch a lordly 815 feet into the air.

Now let's have a look at the height discrepancies in the U.S. national income parade of today.[28]

For the first six minutes of the American parade, we see nothing but very tiny people—less than a foot tall. This low-income crowd, all earning less than $7,000 a year, includes welfare recipients, part-time workers, and senior citizens on fixed incomes. The height of the marchers rises ever so gradually. After about fifteen minutes, there are fast-food workers, retail clerks, and parking-lot attendants, all less than three feet tall. Eventually, slightly taller receptionists, factory workers, and truck drivers appear, but they're still awfully short, none measuring more than four feet. Their ranks seem never-ending.

The parade goes on for almost forty minutes before we start to see people of normal height, reflecting average income levels in the $30,000 to $35,000 range.[29] It is only in the last ten minutes that really tall people start to appear. These are typically high-income professionals—architects, accountants, engineers—and they stand well above the crowd, seven or even eight feet in height. In the last six minutes, the marchers are much taller still—surgeons, lawyers, advertising executives—standing over fourteen feet tall.

Just before we come to the end of the parade, let's recall that we're measuring income inequality. (If we were measuring wealth inequality, the size differences would be even more dramatic.) The size differences in this parade reflect the differences in what Americans earn in a year as they go about working and contributing to the overall economy. Clearly, some individuals work much harder than others or are much more talented than others, but for the most part, everybody works and contributes in some way. Yet, as the parade shows, the rewards individuals receive for their efforts are wildly different—particularly at the very end. While the vast majority of Americans in the parade so far have been dwarves or people of regular height, we are about to encounter some startlingly huge giants towering above their fellow Americans.

So let's pick up the end of the one-hour parade, with about half a minute to go. All of a sudden, the marchers have soared to more than 30 feet, and we begin to spot some very famous faces in the crowd. Look, there's Wolf Blitzer of CNN ($3 million annual income) measuring a massive 820 feet tall. Moments later we see Stephen Colbert of *The Colbert Report* ($4 million) soaring to 1,093 feet, but quickly overshadowed by *Daily Show* host Jon Stewart ($14 million), who, although he looks short on TV, rises a striking 3,826 feet above ground. Then there's basketball star Gilbert Arenas ($17.7 million), standing a gigantic 4,838 feet tall, and Robert Stevens, CEO of military powerhouse Lockheed Martin ($19 million), measuring a full 5,193 feet. Now, in the last few seconds, we need binoculars to see the faces appearing: Donald Trump ($42 million), stretching about two and a quarter miles off the ground; Philippe Dauman, CEO of Viacom ($84 million), 4.3 miles high; Lady Gaga ($90 million), 4.6 miles; Tiger Woods ($91 million), slightly taller at 4.7 miles; Jerry Bruckheimer, creator of the hit TV series *Without a Trace* and *CSI: Crime Scene Investigation* ($145 million), 7.5 miles high.

As the very end approaches we get a glimpse of the hedge fund crowd—or at least of their feet. Their bodies stretch so far above us that we can't really make them out. Then, finally, there he is—John Paulson, the very tallest person in the parade. With an income of $4.9 billion, the man who helped bring the world economy to its knees stretches a staggering 254 miles into the sky, an infinite distance above the billions of people still mired in recession back on the ground. A high-flying airplane dashes past him, at the level of his ankles. Paulson's head, well beyond view even with high-powered binoculars, juts more than 180 miles into outer space.[30]

# CHAPTER 2

# Why Pornography Is the Only True Free Market

For the most part, Western governments did little to clip the wings of bankers, who continued to reward themselves exorbitantly even after they'd devastated the global economy in 2008. The one exception was Britain. After bailing out its banks for more than $1.6 trillion, Britain's Labour government slapped a 50 percent tax on bank bonuses in the fall of 2009. The move prompted howls of protests from the banking elite, including foreign banks operating in Britain.

As the furor grew, Goldman Sachs, the legendary Wall Street firm, quietly informed a key British media outlet that it was considering re-locating its massive London operation to Geneva, signaling that its top officials had no intention of submitting to higher taxes. Goldman CEO Lloyd Blankfein, who received $73 million in compensation in 2007 and had amassed some $500 million in Goldman stock, revealed how little the crash of 2008 had affected bankers' perception of themselves and their role in society. In an interview with the *Sunday Times* of London, Blankfein steadfastly defended his company and himself, ex-plaining that he was just a banker "doing God's work."[1]

Britain's tax on bank bonuses was actually its second move to raise taxes on the rich in the wake of the 2008 crash. In the spring of 2009, the government had raised the marginal tax rate[2] on high-income earners from 40 to 50 percent, prompting similar howls of protest and threats from the rich that they would abandon Britain. Theatre impresario

Andrew Lloyd Webber appealed to the public to reject what he characterized as a tax increase on those who create wealth: "The last thing we need is a Somali pirate-style raid on the few wealth creators who still dare to navigate Britain's gale-force waters." Film star Sir Michael Caine, seventy-six, echoed the outrage, threatening to leave Britain if taxes at the upper end went even one percentage point higher. In a sympathetic article about Caine's tax complaints, journalist Iain Martin noted that Caine, the son of a charlady and a porter in London's fish market, personified the rags-to-riches success the government should be trying to encourage. What we need is not higher taxes, Martin asserted, but to clear "the rubble of the interfering state out of the way."[3]

In fact, Martin—and just about every other critic of high taxes on the rich—conveniently overlooks one key fact: without "the rubble of the interfering state," the rich would have nothing.

It's a simple and unassailable point, but it's almost always ignored: it is only possible for anyone to own anything—money, land, jewelry, yachts—if there is a state to create laws and enforce those laws. This is the logical starting point for any serious discussion about income and wealth and who is entitled to what.

Without government, there would be chaos and anarchy, or what seventeenth-century English philosopher Thomas Hobbes called "a war of all against all." Not only would life under such circumstances be rough and disorderly—or, in Hobbes's words, "nasty, brutish, and short"—but there would be no reliable way to enforce ownership. As another English philosopher, Jeremy Bentham, succinctly put it: "Take away the laws, all property ceases." Under such conditions, everyone's welfare would be fairly minimal—and roughly equal. Accordingly, philosophers Liam Murphy and Thomas Nagel argue that it is wrong to "pretend that the differences in ability, personality, and inherited wealth that lead to great inequalities of welfare in an orderly market economy would have the same effect if there were no government to create and protect legal property rights."[4]

By imagining the complete removal of government, we can quickly dispose of the notion that the "interfering state" has been hard on the rich. On the contrary, that interfering state has been their best friend. Without it, they'd be scrounging around in the bush with the rest of us, worried about when the next marauding gang was going to pounce on the buffalo they had just speared in an attempt to feed their children. Only with the complex set of laws governing property, inheritance, contracts, banking, stock exchanges, and other commercial relations—not to mention criminal prosecution of those trying to seize their buffalo— can the rich be secure in holding their possessions and enjoy the comfortable lives that come with those possessions.

Indeed, a government-enforced system of property rights, while theoretically benefiting all, provides far greater benefits to the rich than to the rest of us. As American legal scholar Robert Hale put it: "One owner, as the result of the entire network of restrictions inherent in property rights, gets the benefit of finding that liberty to use a particular ragged suit of clothes will not be interfered with by the acts of non-owners. Another owner gets the liberty of wandering over a large estate and using a large number of automobiles without interference from others. . . . The benefits conferred by these rights are not equal in any important sense."[5] It could be added that the police would likely respond somewhat differently to a call from the homeless man saying that someone was making off with his ragged suit than they would to a call from the estate owner reporting that his mansion was being robbed. While the state theoretically serves us all, it serves some more readily and fully than others.

In fact, those who lack resources will quickly find the state and all its resources lined up against them. Hale notes that while no law forbids a man to eat food, "there is a law which forbids him to eat any of the food which actually exists in the community—and that is the law of property." Unless the individual has the money to afford the food available, he will have to go without. Similarly, he can't take possession of the delightful swing set in someone's yard and then tell the police that he was simply exercising his right to acquire private property. Private property is a special privilege, backed up by state power, conferred exclusively on those who have control over sufficient resources.

Of course, the rich have no quarrel with government interference when it comes to enforcing property rights. They are only irked when the government interferes by imposing taxes on their incomes, particularly when those taxes are progressive, that is, impose a higher marginal rate on higher levels of income. But in protesting this taxation as unjust—in suggesting that it amounts to a "Somali pirate-style raid"—the rich are implying that the income they received before tax was somehow just. There they were, minding their own business, receiving their just compensation due to their talent and effort, and then along came the tax system and disturbed this otherwise intrinsically fair distribution. The assumption is that the way the "market" distributes income is fair.

This assumption is based on the notion that the market operates according to basic, natural principles—supply and demand—that are not subject to the sort of human whims that shape the tax system. In other words, the market is what would just happen if the interfering hand of government were removed, if things were simply allowed to happen, free of human interference. Hence, the term *laissez-faire* ("let act" or "leave alone"). In fact, this is a bit of fiction. The "market" is a creation of the state every bit as much as the tax system is. Both are based on an elaborate series of laws devised by humans and enforced by governments.

The profit level of a company, for instance, is determined by a whole range of laws: environmental laws that determine how much it may pollute or what fines it will face if it exceeds those levels, labor laws that determine whether its employees are allowed to form a union and whether they are permitted to withdraw their services, contract laws that determine what it can collect from a client who fails to live up to the terms of an agreement or what it must pay a landlord if it wants to break the lease held on its factory. After these (and many other) laws determine the company's profit level, there is a whole different set of laws governing how owners of the company will transfer those profits to themselves—what rights shareholders have in determining how the profits will be divided, who will get paid and who won't in the case of the corporation's bankruptcy, and so on. (The very existence of the company, for that matter, is made possible by laws that allow for incorporation, thereby limiting the personal financial vulnerability of the company's officers and owners in the event of a lawsuit.)

Once a shareholder is allotted his share of the company's profits, he may perhaps invest some of this money in bonds. Once again, the hand of government will be involved in determining how much he will profit from his investment, since the return he receives on his bonds will be determined by interest rates, which are determined by the actions of government-appointed central bankers. Their decisions affecting interest rates will hinge on whether they (and, ultimately, the government that appointed them) give priority to controlling inflation (as wealth-holders tend to want) or to encouraging employment (as those without wealth tend to want).

For that matter, lawyers, doctors, accountants, engineers, architects, and other professionals enjoy elevated incomes because of laws that give these groups monopoly power over their occupations. By giving them the legal power to license those practicing in their fields, governments enable these professionals to restrict the number of participants, thereby ensuring high demand and high prices for their services. While such laws may be necessary to protect the public from quacks and charlatans, they also clearly bolster the incomes of a small group of professionals. Certainly, these professionals are operating in tightly controlled situations governed by a set of laws—far from what is conjured up by the expression "free market."

The point is that there's no simple, natural thing called "the market." The market is the result of the complex set of laws that regulate commerce and financial exchange in a particular jurisdiction. It can take any number of forms, depending on decisions made by government officials and parliamentarians who design, approve, and implement those laws. If the government tilts toward the interests of business owners, it may ensure strong property rights by, for instance, enacting laws that make it very difficult for workers to unionize or that make work stoppages or strikes illegal. In doing so, the government is not simply letting

Property oi
Baker College
of Allen Park

nature take its course, as implied by the phrase laissez-faire; rather, it is actively intervening in a way that restricts the rights of workers, preventing them from combining with other workers or from withdrawing their labor in order to maximize their bargaining power.

If a new government takes over and tilts more toward workers' interests, it might revise those laws to ensure the right to unionize, thereby strengthening the bargaining power of labor in its struggle with business owners. There is a wide range of legal possibilities just on issues dealing with unionization—and unionization represents just one area of the vast array of laws that determine how any particular "market" will operate. All these variations represent ways that the goalposts can be moved around and each variation will produce a different result, with different winners and losers.

So, for instance, the stagnation in workers' wages in recent decades is largely due to the enactment of conservative policies that have tilted the playing field against labor, by weakening laws protecting workers' incomes and their right to unionize and strike, and by strengthening laws protecting corporate rights. At the same time, changes in other laws—particularly ones governing financial regulations and taxation—have made it possible for those at the top to earn vastly more than was possible for their counterparts to earn a few decades ago.

How much less, for instance, would Goldman CEO Lloyd Blankfein have earned in 2007 had there been a different set of laws governing financial markets?

To answer this question, it's useful to briefly review some recent history. Only a few decades earlier, financial markets had been much more carefully regulated. Financial houses were subjected to stricter capital requirements, greatly limiting the amount they could leverage in financial deals and therefore limiting their potential rewards.

For that matter, it was because of changes in the rules governing the financial marketplace that the big Wall Street firms grew to become such colossal—and wildly profitable—giants in the last decade. In the early postwar period, the major Wall Street firms were considerably smaller, because they were restricted to operating as private partnerships. This meant that a firm was owned by its senior partners, who shared all the profits, but who also were jointly responsible for all the firm's debts and liabilities. As a result, the partners were careful in their investing practices, knowing that they would personally be on the hook in the event of big losses. They also held each other in check, since the reckless behavior of one individual could lead to losses that affected all the partners in the firm.

But things began to change after 1970—because the rules governing the marketplace changed. Up until 1970, the New York Stock Exchange had prohibited investment banks from becoming public corporations listed on the stock exchange, effectively limiting them to the partnership model. When this ban was repealed, the major investment banks began to switch over to the public model. Merrill Lynch went public in 1971, followed by Bear Stearns in 1985, Morgan Stanley in 1986, Lehman Brothers in 1994, and Goldman Sachs in 1999.

As public corporations, investment banks were now able to raise money from investors through the stock exchange. This gave them access to far more cash and enabled them to grow into much bigger operations. By the time Lehman Brothers went bankrupt in September 2008, it had amassed $600 billion in debt—an amount far greater than anything it could have accumulated as a partnership. The change also meant that the senior executives of the investment banks were no longer personally liable for their firms' debts. When individuals within a firm—or whole trading divisions—indulged in rogue behavior in pursuit of ever-bigger profits, there was none of the vigilance that existed in the days when the fate of all the firm's partners was on the line. Now bankers could use other people's money to award themselves massive pay packages even as they gambled recklessly, without facing any personal risk.

There were other advantages to the investment banks' new status as public corporations. Their bigger size and the fact they were dealing with the public's money meant that government now deemed them "too big to fail." If their irresponsible behavior risked undermining the stability of the entire financial system, government would have to step in and bail them out. For the bankers, it was a dream world: they could take enormous risks, knowing that whatever gains they made would be theirs alone, while any losses they suffered would be assumed by the taxpayers.

All this suggests that the more stringent laws that governed financial markets in the early postwar period had been eminently sensible, and their removal greatly contributed to the 2008 financial crash. The point is that today's plutocracy earns much of its income in ways that would simply not have been possible under the particular set of market rules that existed only a few decades ago. Without a whole new set of manmade laws governing the financial marketplace, Lloyd Blankfein would undoubtedly have earned considerably less than $73 million in 2007, and his Goldman Sachs stock would be worth a lot less than $500 million today—probably hundreds of millions less.

Indeed, under the laws of the early postwar era, doing "God's work" would have been a lot less profitable.

We may never know how well Sir Michael Caine would have fared had he become a porn star, but his income would have certainly been smaller.

This is relevant because it helps unpack the mythology that allows Caine, Andrew Lloyd Webber, and other big earners in the entertainment world to believe that their large incomes are simply the result of the exercise of their talents in the free market. Make no mistake about it: their good fortune has come about because of government intervention in the marketplace. And no, we are not talking about government subsidies for the arts but rather something much more basic and enriching—the elaborate set of copyright laws that allow artists and performers to receive royalties for their creative efforts. Without these laws, the movies Michael Caine appears in could be copied and sold to people all over the world, without Caine receiving a penny. Under such a wide-open system, no movie production company would be willing to pay Michael Caine a huge fee for his performance, or much of a fee at all.

This indeed is the fate of porn stars. No matter how great their talent, porn stars earn far less than stars in the regular movie business. That's because the porn business, which by its very nature operates outside legal boundaries restricting sexually explicit material, isn't able to take advantage of the huge protection the state offers moviemakers and other creative artists in the form of copyright laws. If a porn producer contacted police to report that his videos were being reproduced without permission, the police might chuckle before arresting him for violating laws against displays of nudity and sexually explicit behavior. As a result, porn producers don't bother reporting cases of copyright infringement, and porn videos are freely ripped off by others. The Internet abounds in freely available pornography. This unregulated system is closer to what an actual "free market" in the movie industry would be like.[6]

But it's not a market that allows performers to get rich, as American economist Dean Baker has noted. The huge incomes enjoyed by stars like Michael Caine and Andrew Lloyd Webber would be impossible without an elaborate set of government laws that provide them with property rights over their own artistic works—rights that are enforced by police and the courts. Baker notes that copyrights and patents are really government-granted monopolies, and that they have their origins in the feudal system of guilds.

It's straying a bit from our point, but it's worth briefly noting that it would be possible to do without copyright and patent laws, which form a large part of our legal system. The justification for these laws is that, without them, there would be little investment of time and money in creating new works of music, film, or writing—or, for that matter, developing new pharmaceutical drugs. But, as Baker argues, there are other forms of government intervention that could ensure adequate investment in these areas, while creating fewer negative consequences due to the monopoly power of copyrights and patents. For instance, Canadian laws permitting generic equivalents of brand-name drugs to be produced under license have helped restrain brand-name manufacturers from using their monopoly power to earn astronomical profits on drugs badly needed by the public. The consequences of monopoly power are less serious in the field of the creative arts, but Baker argues that the monopolies created by copyright laws are enormously costly to enforce, and becoming more so as the technology for video and music reproduction becomes ever easier. He proposes instead a system of individual vouchers, under which each taxpayer would be given a fixed sum that he or she would pass on to individual artists each year through the tax system. That may sound like it would involve a great deal of government intervention, but then so does the system of copyright and patent laws.

The point here is that government intervention in the form of copyright laws benefits stars like Michael Caine and Andrew Lloyd Webber. They have gotten rich, not by exercising their talents in some mythical "free market" but by exercising those talents within a tightly regulated, government-enforced monopoly, heavily enforced at great cost by police and the courts. Without the interfering rubble of this aspect of the modern state, Caine and Webber would be no richer or more famous than the giants of the porn world, no matter how much natural talent they were endowed with.

So it is bizarre to isolate the possible tax increases faced by Lloyd Blankfein, Michael Caine, or Andrew Lloyd Webber and condemn them as the actions of an interfering government. The market is nothing but a complex web of government interventions. The income-tax hike stands out in these people's minds only because it's an intervention that goes against their interests, whereas so many of the other laws and government policies favor them. As Murphy and Nagel wryly put it, "[P]eople care more about what unjustly harms them than about what unjustly benefits them."[7] The favorable interventions tend to become invisible to their beneficiaries, as if they were just part of the natural order of things.

The notion that it should be possible to become a billionaire is rooted in the idea that there are some uniquely talented people whose contribution is so great that they deserve to be hugely, fabulously rewarded. Some fabulously wealthy individuals, such as American businessman Leo J. Hindery Jr., have articulated this point themselves. Hindery, whose contribution was to found a cable television sports network (a clear example of a government-granted monopoly, by the way), put it this way: "I think there are people, including myself at certain times in my career, who because of their uniqueness warrant whatever the market will bear."[8] Similarly, Lew Frankfort, chairman and chief executive of the high-end handbag company Coach, argues that today's extraordinary pay packages can be justified because of the extraordinary skills required by the individuals running corporations in the "technological age." As he told the *New York Times* in 2007, "To be successful, you now needed vision, lateral thinking, courage, and an ability to see things, not the way they were but how they might be." Sanford I. Weill, long a towering figure on Wall Street, is also impressed with the contributions of billionaires like himself: "People can look at the last twenty-five years and say that this is an incredibly unique period of time. We didn't rely on somebody else to build what we built."

What is so striking about such statements, beside the absence of modesty, is the lack of acknowledgment of the role society plays in the accumulation of any great fortune. These men apparently fail to see society's role in constructing a market that favors their interests. More broadly, they seem unaware of the pervasive role played by society in general (as well as by specific other people) in every aspect of their lives—in nurturing them, shaping them, teaching them what they know, performing innumerable functions that contribute to the operation of their businesses and every other aspect of the market and indeed every part of life around them.

Those justifying large fortunes tend to see the individual in splendid isolation, achieving great feats on her own. In fact, no such reality exists. There is no such thing as the "self-made man." Humans are, above all, social beings who make their way in the world with the assistance and involvement of countless others who play roles of varying importance. This point is so obvious that it seems ridiculous, even trite to mention it. Yet it is typically left out of the formulations of those invoking the inherent right of individuals to accumulate large fortunes.

Philosophers have conjured up the notion of the individual, alone in a state of nature, choosing to enter into a contract with society. But this is clearly a metaphor with no basis in reality. No individual ever existed first in a state of nature and then decided to join society. Her involvement with society came first and, except in the most unusual circumstances, continued throughout her life. The primacy and ubiquity of society—so casually erased by billionaires and others justifying their fortunes—must be restored if we are to have any meaningful discussion of income and wealth, and where an individual's claim ends and society's begins. The restoration of society into the equation allows us to meaningfully explore the question of the proper relationship between the individual and the community—and who owes what to whom.

One of the crucial ways that society assists individuals in their ability to generate wealth lies in the inheritance from previous generations. This inheritance from the past is so vast it is almost beyond calculation. It encompasses every aspect of what we know as a civilization and every bit of scientific and technological knowledge we make use of today, going all the way back to the beginning of human language and the invention of the wheel. Measured against this vast human cultural and technological inheritance, any additional marginal advance in today's world—even the creation of a cable television sports network—inevitably pales in significance.

The question then becomes this: who is the proper beneficiary of the wealth generated by innovations based on the massive inheritance from the past—the individual innovator who adapts some tiny aspect of this past inheritance to create a slightly new product, or society as a whole (that is, all of us)?

Under our current system, the innovator captures an enormously large share of the benefits. Clearly, the innovator should be compensated for his contribution. But should he also be compensated for the contributions made by all the other innovators who, over the centuries, have built up a body of knowledge that made his marginal advance possible today?

It is our position that society—and, by extension, all of us—should be entitled to a much larger share of the benefits. This could be accomplished through a decision to raise taxes at the upper end, thereby adjusting the economic goalposts—a decision no more arbitrary than the decisions that determined the current location of the goalposts.

Some will protest that raising taxes on the rich isn't worth the effort, since the extra revenues collected would, in the grand scheme of things, be trivial. In fact, this isn't true. The sums involved are potentially immense. Virtually all the economic gains of the past few decades have gone to the top; that's where the money is. But even so, the goal is not just to find a new revenue source. The goal here is more basic: to determine a morally valid basis for the distribution of income, rather than accepting on faith the moral validity of the way income is distributed by the set of manmade laws that make up the current version of the "market."

We will return to this important subject later in the book. But for now, we want to emphasize that the need for a goalpost adjustment is particularly compelling today when huge amounts of the wealth currently being generated stem from the enormous technological gains of the past. Technological breakthroughs related to the development of the computer in the past half century account for a large part of the spectacular fortunes accumulated today by those selling the information-age products that flood our consumer markets.

For example, a large number of today's successful entrepreneurs became fabulously wealthy building businesses based on the technological advances related to the Internet. An equally impressive set of technological breakthroughs related to the development of the internal combustion engine occurred early in the 1900s, paving the way for a similarly lucrative payoff with the rise of a consumer market for cars and airplane travel following World War II. The difference was that, back in that early postwar era, the enormous economic gains that resulted were more widely shared, due to the more egalitarian ethos and a more equitable tax system. Today, the stupendous gains made possible by the technological advances of the information age have been almost entirely captured by a tiny elite.

So we take issue with Lew Frankfort, the CEO of Coach, who argued that today's billionaires deserve their fortunes because they had "vision, lateral thinking, courage and an ability to see things" in the "technological age." We think he's got things fundamentally backwards. The enormous pay at the top hasn't come about because today's elite has been particularly innovative in adapting to the technological age. Rather, the technological age has unleashed spectacular gains, and the elite has been adroit at seizing a particularly large portion of these gains.

Today's gigantic fortunes seem to be less a reflection of the innovative genius of current billionaires and more a reflection of how exceptionally adept they've been at elbowing their way to the front of the trough.

As mentioned, the level of inequality in America in recent years is extreme by historical standards. The last time income was distributed this unequally was in 1929.

It's striking to note that the two moments of greatest income concentration in America over the last century came just before the two infamous Wall Street crashes. Indeed, even the extent of the income concentration immediately preceding 1929 and 2008 is virtually the same. In both years, the top-earning 1 percent of Americans captured almost 24 percent of the national income. (By comparison, during most of the intervening postwar period, the share of national income captured by the top 1 percent dropped dramatically to about 10 percent.)

Could it be that the rise of a fabulously rich super-elite was the real cause of the recent Wall Street crash, with its devastating and lingering economic impacts for just about everyone in the world? In our attempt to probe the dangers of extreme income concentration, this seems like a good place to begin.

# CHAPTER 3

# Millionaires and the Crash of 1929

There was more than the usual secrecy as Frank Vanderlip and Henry P. Davison arrived at the White House on a cool evening in the fall of 1911. The men were two of Wall Street's most senior figures, and their meeting with President William Howard Taft was to be strictly confidential. A conservative Republican, Taft was known to have close ties to members of America's economic elite. But his advisors were constantly urging him to be careful not to appear too accommodating to the wealthy. So it was considered best that the public know nothing about this meeting. After all, Vanderlip and Davison were top officials in the nation's leading banks, and they were there representing two even more wealthy and powerful men, John D. Rockefeller and J. P. Morgan, who not only ran the banks but, between them, exercised control over just about every corner of the American economy.

On the agenda at that White House meeting was a matter of considerable concern to the banking interests of Rockefeller and Morgan: the Taft administration was on the verge of shutting down "bank securities affiliates." These were companies set up by banks to get around restrictions that barred banks from becoming involved in the risky business of trading in stocks and bonds. Taft's solicitor general, Frederick J. Lehmann, after a review by his department, had concluded that these affiliates violated the nation's banking laws. Spotting the potential for them to become vehicles for dangerous speculative ventures, Lehmann had notified the banks that he was planning to shut them down.[1]

Lehmann's decision had come as a surprise to Rockefeller and Morgan, who were used to getting their way in political matters. When Taft had taken office in 1909, a top Morgan official had wired Morgan, then vacationing with a massive entourage in Egypt, to confirm that the new Taft cabinet was in line with the recommendations made by the Morgan empire: "Franklin MacVeagh Chicago has been selected for Secretary of the Treasury. Wickersham will be Attorney General and other places are filled to our entire satisfaction."[2]

But now it seemed that one of those cabinet members, Frederick Lehmann, had proved too zealous in pursuing his duties. The only remedy at this point was to appeal to the president himself. Taft was someone they presumed they could prevail upon—even though they were aware that he was sensitive about appearing too close to the powerful—something even his wife advised him against. While Taft golfed with the influential industrialist Henry Clay Frick, he drew the line at playing a round with the even more powerful oil magnate John D. Rockefeller. Similar discretion was required in his dealing with banking colossus John Pierpont Morgan, who quietly visited Taft's stately summer home in Beverly, Massachusetts, on a number of occasions without the visits becoming public. Taft's prudence in these matters was understandable. The public was agitated about the extraordinary clout wielded by these titans, and the president felt it necessary to at least appear intent on breaking up their giant monopolies or "trusts"— just as his popular predecessor, Theodore Roosevelt, had been. As with Roosevelt, there was a lot of antitrust talk and some antitrust action during the Taft administration, but also a lot of accommodating the business tycoons.

Certainly Taft had a freer hand to accommodate members of the elite when the issues were less in the public eye, as in the case of this "bank securities affiliates" matter. While the issue of trusts was highly controversial, much talked about in Congress and the press, bank affiliates were really on nobody's mind, except the bankers'. So when Taft met at the White House with Vanderlip, president of the Rockefeller-controlled National City Bank, and Davison, a high-ranking partner in J. P. Morgan & Company, the president knew he had some leeway. If he were to acquiesce to their demands, the public wouldn't have to know. He didn't need to fear that loudmouths like Congressman Charles A. Lindbergh (father of the famed future aviator) would have another opportunity to denounce the "Money Trust" as the most sinister power of all, or that muckraking journalist Lincoln Steffens would spot another chance to decry Pierpont Morgan as "the boss of the United States." No, what happened at this meeting—even the fact that it ever took place—would never have to become public.

And so it was that the stout, moustached Taft, all three hundred pounds of him, settled comfortably into a large, sturdy chair. In the cozy secrecy of the White House, he assured Vanderlip and Davison that he would overrule his own solicitor general, thereby handing his guests—and, beyond them, the potentates for whom this bone was really intended—the power to wreak havoc in the financial markets for almost two decades.

In many ways, the seeds of the 1929 Wall Street crash were sown in that quiet White House meeting. What the president agreed to—in overruling his prescient solicitor general—amounted to a significant deregulation of the financial markets. The restrictions that kept banks out of trading in stocks and bonds had been a crucial pillar of the post–Civil War banking system. Given their important role in handling the public's savings, banks had been considered too central to the economy to be allowed to play in the notoriously fast-and-loose trading world, which more closely resembled the world of gambling. Taft's decision to allow banks into this lucrative area essentially eliminated a deliberate safeguard that had been built into the 1864 U.S. National Bank Act, which had been modeled on British banking practices.

Not only did Taft's decision to free up banks to use their vast deposits in risky ways, but it also allowed the banks to raise even more money from members of the public by selling them stocks and bonds. Ordinary citizens were much more likely to trust a securities firm connected to a well-established bank than a lesser-known player in the securities field—a field that was known to be full of shady characters. This greater public confidence in the banks (which turned out to be undeserved) helped draw many unsophisticated investors into the financial marketplace, fuelling what became a gigantic speculative bubble in the late 1920s.

But it's important to note that this key act—Taft's willingness to allow banks to venture into stock trading—came about because of the immense political power of a few extremely rich financiers. That Rockefeller and Morgan were able to get the president to agree not to enforce the nation's banking laws was a reflection of the extent to which control over the nation's wealth had become highly concentrated in a very small number of hands.

Certainly, the country of small yeoman farmers that had existed in colonial times and that the founding fathers had envisioned as a permanent feature of American democracy had largely disappeared by the early decades of the 1900s. Instead, the United States had become a highly stratified, top-heavy society dominated by a few dozen incredibly wealthy "robber barons." Ferdinand Lundberg captured the extent of the economic concentration that prevailed in the early years of the twentieth century in the title of his book on the phenomenon: *America's 60 Families.* It was an age of stunning, conspicuous inequality, with grand, ornate mansions rising along Fifth Avenue and the ultra-wealthy occupying a world of their own, whiling away their time in luxuriant splendor on sprawling country estates, waited on by legions of servants, or congregating for glittering costume balls at the glamorous Waldorf-Astoria Hotel.

Part and parcel of this concentration of wealth was the emergence of a dominant banking elite, personified by the rise of John Pierpont Morgan. The son of a banker who had made a fortune raising British capital for American industrial expansion, Morgan ended up becoming America's richest and most powerful banker. An intense and domineering man who barked orders at underlings and vacationed with members of the British royal family, he became a symbol of the growing concentration of money and power in banking.

Morgan's reach extended far beyond what he actually owned. Through dominant positions on boards and executive committees, he and his close associates eventually controlled some thirty-five banks and insurance companies and sixty nonfinancial institutions, including such diverse corporate giants as the United States Steel Corporation, American Telephone and Telegraph, the Chesapeake and Ohio Railroad, the General Electric Company, International Harvester Company, Consolidated Edison Company, the Niagara Hudson Power Corporation, Standard Brands Incorporated, and the United Gas Improvement Company. In all, Morgan effectively controlled companies worth a total of $17 billion—equivalent to about $370 billion today. And there were dozens more financial and nonfinancial entities in which Morgan was a dominant influence, even without holding direct control. Writer Anna Rochester compared his sprawling empire to a medieval fortress whose "inner stronghold is surrounded by open stretches on which maneuvers can take place only with the knowledge and goodwill of the ruling lord."[3]

Indeed, Morgan had all the imperiousness of a medieval lord. In open defiance of the nation's antitrust laws, he and Rockefeller had brazenly created a giant holding company that knit together all their interests, raising fears that the entire American economy could end up under the control of one corporation. When Theodore Roosevelt's administration initiated an antitrust action against the holding company in 1902, Morgan was highly annoyed, telling guests at a dinner party he had been assured that the new president, for all his trust-busting talk, would do the "gentlemanly thing." Morgan appears to have regarded the antitrust action almost as a matter to be sorted out privately by two equally powerful potentates. Meeting with Roosevelt at the White House, he reportedly told the president: "If we have done anything wrong, send your man to my man and they can fix it up." Although the antitrust case did proceed (and eventually resulted in the dissolution of the holding company), the president assured Morgan at the White House meeting that Morgan's many other monopoly interests were safe from government intervention.[4]

Along with Morgan, two other banking interests had come to dominate Wall Street early in the twentieth century—National City Bank, controlled by Rockefeller (with J. P. Morgan the second largest stockholder), and First National Bank of New York, controlled by financier George F. Baker, the eleventh-richest man in the country. Concern over the influence of these three enormously potent banking interests prompted a 1912 congressional investigation. Led by Congressman Arsène Pujo of Louisiana, the lengthy probe documented the extraordinary financial reach of this banking triumvirate: together, their principals held 341 directorships in 112 corporations, with aggregate resources or capitalization of $22 billion ($482 billion in today's dollars). This gave this inner circle of Wall Street interests a degree of control over the economy that was shocking even to an American public that had become used to the power wielded by the big industrial monopolies of the time—the oil trust, the railroad trust, the steel trust, the copper trust, the sugar trust, and so on. The Pujo committee charged that, of all the trusts, this one—the "money trust"—was the most threatening to the public welfare: "Far more dangerous than all that has happened to us in the past in the way of elimination of competition in industry is the control of credit through the domination of these groups over our banks and industries."[5]

The clout of the House of Morgan was most nakedly displayed in the infamous "Bankers' Panic" of 1907. After a series of moves that suggested Morgan may have deliberately created a panic in the markets, President Theodore Roosevelt put $25 million in treasury funds under the control of J. P. Morgan & Company, hoping that the banker would use it to calm down the markets. When the market tumult continued, Roosevelt realized Morgan wanted more from the White House—specifically, approval for U.S. Steel to absorb Tennessee Coal and Iron, a takeover that would amount to a serious violation of the Sherman Antitrust Act. As the Wall Street panic grew, the president met with high-level Morgan emissaries at the White House and assured them his administration would take no action in the event of a Tennessee Coal takeover. Calm was very quickly restored to the markets, for which Morgan was widely credited. Roosevelt delivered on his end of the implicit deal as well; U.S. Steel was permitted to take over Tennessee Coal while frustrated government antitrust lawyers were obliged to look the other way.[6]

In the wake of the Bankers' Panic, the power of the moneyed interests had become so flagrant that there were widespread calls for something to be done. Congress set up a commission to consider banking reforms—only to have Morgan interests quickly capture control of it. Indeed, from the outset, the commission was effectively under the thumb of the House of Morgan. It was chaired by Republican senator Nelson Aldrich, a wealthy Rhode Island financier who moved in elite business and social circles and whose daughter Abby had married John D. Rockefeller Jr. As a senator, Aldrich was known for vigorously championing the causes of the wealthy, and he immediately appointed Henry P. Davison, a trusted Morgan associate, as his advisor on the banking commission. (Davison was the banker who would later represent Morgan in the 1911 meeting with Taft at the White House.) This meant that Davison would have ample opportunity to influence the Aldrich commission in the direction favored by Morgan and the Wall Street clique—a clique that Aldrich was already closely allied to. As a cable sent to Morgan from one of his officials noted: "It is understood that Davison is to represent our views and will be particularly close to Senator Aldrich."[7]

The key reform to be considered by the Aldrich commission was the creation of a central bank. The House of Morgan had effectively been operating as one, but it was now widely appreciated that this gave Morgan far too much clout over the American economy. The important question for the commission was what form such a bank would take. Should it be under the control of private interests, similar to the Bank of England, or under government control? Some reformers, notably the farmer-dominated Populist movement, weren't keen on a central bank at all, fearing it would end up dominated by Wall Street, no matter who technically ran it.

But among the small group of insiders with input into the Aldrich commission, the matter was never in doubt. In 1910, Senator Aldrich, along with his close advisor Henry Davison and a small cabal of Wall Street bankers, departed for a secret retreat at the Jekyll Island Club, a favorite Morgan hideaway off the coast of Georgia. There, in secluded splendor, ostensibly on a duck-hunting vacation, they devised a plan for a fully private central bank, involving a system of private regional reserve banks to be governed by a board of private bankers.

When Aldrich presented his plan, it was widely denounced as a Wall Street scheme and blocked by Democrats in Congress. Several years later, the Democrats brought forward legislation for the Federal Reserve System, a central banking system modeled along the lines of the Jekyll Island plan but with the modification that the private regional banks be placed under the authority of a government-appointed board based in Washington. Although the creation of the Federal Reserve System in 1913 was aimed at limiting Wall Street's power, in reality, things turned out much as the Populists had feared. Despite the government board at the top, the New York Reserve Bank dominated the system, largely setting the nation's monetary policy to suit Wall Street interests. Benjamin Strong, who served for many years as governor of the New York Reserve Bank, was a Wall Street banker who had been part of the Jekyll Island cabal. Author Ron Chernow argues that, far from seeing its power diminished, the House of Morgan was able to "skillfully harness the Fed and use it to amplify its powers."[8]

By the 1920s, the power of the financial elite had become even more entrenched than it had been in the preceding decades. The labor and agrarian protest movements that had sprung up in the late nineteenth and early twentieth centuries had largely petered out as a significant force in American politics. Their leader, William Jennings Bryan, had proved unable to win the White House, despite three attempts as the Democratic presidential nominee. By 1924, the badly divided Democrats abandoned any pretense of being a reform-oriented party and, on the 103rd ballot at their convention, selected as their leader John W. Davis—a senior attorney for J. P. Morgan.[9] Meanwhile, wealthy interests unabashedly dominated the Republican Party. As Lundberg wryly noted, the contest between Herbert Hoover and Andrew Mellon for the 1928 Republican presidential nomination "was strictly one between Morgan finance capital and Mellon finance capital."[10] Indeed, with no pressure from the left, the Republicans happily drifted even further to the right. After two decades of feeling the need to at least appear concerned about the problems posed by the giant monopolies, the three Republican presidents who held office in the 1920s—Warren Harding, Calvin Coolidge, and Herbert Hoover—settled into the comfortable niche of simply accommodating the interests of the wealthy.

Nowhere was this more evident than in the area of tax policy. Arguably more important than the rather lackluster Republican presidents themselves was Andrew Mellon, a wealthy Pittsburgh banker who served as treasury secretary in all three Republican administrations of the 1920s, and whose extensive financial and business holdings made him the fifth-richest man in the nation. Mellon used his position and personal influence to work tirelessly to reduce taxes on the well-to-do. Although opposition from progressives in Congress thwarted some of his early attempts, Mellon succeeded in pushing through a 1926 revenue bill that dramatically cut taxes on the rich. Under the bill, someone earning $1 million a year saw his tax bill plummet from $600,000 to $200,000.[11] Mellon also brought down taxes on estates to a maximum of 20 percent, a rate that kicked in only on estates worth more than $10 million (equivalent to $121 million today).[12]

Not content to massively reduce their taxes in the present and the future, Mellon reached back into the past as well, quietly signaling to wealthy taxpayers (particularly Republican friends) that the Treasury Department would happily review any requests they might have for reductions in their taxes going back to 1917. (It was Mellon's view that the rich had paid too much tax on the enormous wartime profits they'd made during World War I.) Not surprisingly, wealthy people and corporations responded keenly to the offer and, before long, some 27,000 lawyers and accountants were presenting tax rebate cases to the Treasury.[13]

Under Mellon's guiding hand, the Treasury proved very accommodating to the desires of the rich to get back whatever financial contribution they had made to the war effort. The list of tax refunds eventually totaled $1.27 billion and filled some twenty thousand pages. Incredibly, $7 million went to Mellon himself and $14 million to his corporate interests.[14] Altogether, between the reduced tax rates and the refunds, Mellon's Treasury Department handed over an astonishing $6 billion to the wealthiest Americans—equivalent to $72 billion today—a massive windfall that was to act like gasoline in fueling the stock market bubble of the late 1920s.

As the nation's elite devoured an ever-larger share of the national income, far below them, the majority of Americans lived extremely modest, austere lives with little political power. Unionization efforts had been fiercely opposed by the great industrial titans of the late nineteenth and early twentieth centuries, with strikes ruthlessly suppressed, often with state support. Workers returning from the battlefields of World War I came home to high unemployment and stagnant or falling wages. With union power on the decline, dissenters within union ranks turned to radicalism and even anarchism, making it easier for authorities to vilify and clamp down on labor.

So, although the 1920s proved to be a decade of significant technological advances, workers were in such a weak bargaining position that they were unable to demand a meaningful share of the gains. From 1919 to 1929, worker output in manufacturing rose by 43 percent, but wages by only by 8 percent. With the costs of production falling and workers getting only a small share of the benefits, most of the gains of this improved productivity flowed into corporate coffers. As John Kenneth Galbraith noted, "The rich were getting richer faster than the poor were getting less poor."[15]

This left vast segments of the working population unable to afford the amazing new consumer goods that technological advances were making possible—notably cars, refrigerators, radios, and vacuum cleaners. The more prosperous workers could only afford these luxuries by buying them on credit through popular, new installment plans. With consumer demand constrained by the limited buying power of the masses, there was little incentive for corporations to invest their huge profits in expanding their factories. Those factories were already highly productive, efficiently manufacturing as much as could be sold to a population whose appetite for the new consumer items far outstripped its ability to pay for them.

This left corporations looking for other places to invest their surplus funds. Like wealthy individuals, whose pockets were also bulging after Mellon's generous 1926 tax cut, corporations increasingly directed their funds toward Wall Street. There was certainly money to be made there. Corporate stocks, reflecting the substantial productivity gains, were rising impressively. For instance, shares in Radio Corporation of America (RCA) shot up from $85 to $420 in the course of 1928, feeding the notion that Wall Street was a place where money quickly multiplied. As more and more money flowed in, stock prices rose ever higher with seemingly unstoppable momentum.

The glittering lives of the very rich and the upward surge of the stock market set the tone for the era, creating the impression that getting rich quick was just another exciting feature of the Roaring Twenties. Middle-class Americans who had been weaned on ideologies of hard work, honest effort, and doing without were suddenly mesmerized by the thought that, by investing just a little bit, they too could get wildly rich. Speculation pushed up Florida land prices to feverish heights in the mid-1920s, with investors snapping up unseen swamp properties far from any beach—only to have the market come crashing down, in part because of a brutal 1926 hurricane. Undeterred by the sobering losses, the focus of the speculative fever simply moved elsewhere. Wall Street bankers fanned the flames, and the press, much of it owned by the wealthy Hearst and Pulitzer families, helped out with their own keen promotion of the wealth-making possibilities on Wall Street. Even the Democratic Party, having abandoned any pretense of being a promoter of progressive causes, pushed Wall Street schemes as the solution to the nation's problems. Writing in *Ladies' Home Journal* in 1929, Democratic national chairman and prominent financier John J. Raskob expressed the new zeitgeist of the party in an article full of investment tips, under the title "Everybody Ought to be Rich."

It was an almost irresistible notion, made tantalizingly possible by Wall Street's offer of allowing investors to buy largely on credit. This was a variation of the installment plans being peddled to middle-class consumers to help them afford cars and appliances. Just as they could put down a little money toward buying a car, Wall Street was inviting them to put down a little money toward getting very rich, offering to sell them stocks "on margin" for a fraction of the price. With just $10, it was possible to buy an $85 share in RCA at the beginning of 1928, with the remaining $75 provided by the Wall Street broker in the form of a loan. By the end of the year, the share was worth $420. So, after repaying the broker's loan with interest, the purchaser was left with a whopping profit of about $330—all from a mere $10 down.

Wall Street was keenly peddling endless variations of this sort of scheme. But while there were real opportunities to make a lot of money quickly, the risks were also tremendous. One obvious risk was that the stock price would fall, leaving the investor in considerable trouble. If he'd put up $10 to buy the $85 RCA stock, and the stock fell to $60 by the end of the year (instead of rising to $420), he would lose his initial $10 and also owe another $15 (plus interest) to the broker for his loan.

But this less attractive scenario was far from the minds of those playing in the giant gambling parlors of Wall Street. As the market kept rising and more and more money flowed in, there was an eagerness to believe that this cornucopia was real and had only to be seized. And so caution was largely thrown to the wind. The miracle profits that were possible by buying on margin were only the beginning. These profits could be infinitely multiplied by adding layer upon layer of investments—all bought on margin. This was accomplished through "investment trusts"—paper companies that did nothing but hold stock in other companies. A purchaser could buy a share in an investment trust, which would then, on margin, buy stock in another investment trust, which would then, on margin, buy stock in yet another investment trust, and so on. A giant pyramid could be constructed without investors ever actually putting down much real money. As long as the stock prices kept rising, the profits simply multiplied. On the other hand, if prices were to collapse, the whole edifice would come tumbling down, and the investors would owe a great deal of money to those providing the loans.

The nation's leading banks, liberated by President Taft from their legal responsibility to stay out of this world of gambling, had jumped in fully. Their presence only helped drive the frenzy. After all, the major Wall Street banks seemed to know what they were doing. So, for instance, the public was inclined to trust the National City Company, a securities affiliate of the powerful National City Bank, which was controlled by Rockefeller with a major share held by J. P. Morgan. At the height of the boom, National City Company had some 1,900 salesmen out aggressively selling its financial products, including some highly risky Latin American loans that were offered to the public as largely risk-free bonds. Whereas potential investors would have ordinarily been skeptical of bonds offered by unknown dealers from Brazil, Chile, or Peru, they put aside such fears and eagerly bought up the near-worthless bonds when they were offered by an affiliate of the prestigious National City Bank, with its top-drawer Wall Street pedigree.

The banks were only too pleased to take advantage of such trusting naïveté, selling shares in investment trusts to the investing public at greatly inflated prices. In 1927, the public bought more than $400 million worth of stock in investment trusts; in 1929, that number rose to $3 billion. The ultimate scam, launched in the final gasp of market frenzy leading up to the crash, involved a Morgan-sponsored investment trust known as Alleghany Corporation that sold shares in a holding company that went on a massive binge of railroad and real-estate takeovers.[16] The company created a giant pyramid scheme in which each new purchase was used as collateral for the next. The scam was made all the more curious by the fact that the holding company was managed by two Cleveland real estate brokers, Otis and Mantis Van Sweringen— strange, inseparable brothers who lived in a sprawling empty mansion where they slept in the same bedroom. The brothers ended up as fig- ureheads of a giant railway conglomerate worth $3 billion. In fact, the real owner of the company was J. P. Morgan & Co., which, it was later revealed, had cheated public investors out of $16 million. Meanwhile, a select group of Morgan associates and friends had been allowed to buy shares at a heavily discounted advance price, providing these insiders with instant profits when the shares were offered to the public. Among those who cashed in on such windfalls as part of the Morgan "preferred list" were a host of political figures from both parties, including just- retired president Calvin Coolidge.

As the stock market rose to dizzying heights, funds flowed in from around the United States and even from around the world. All this had a choking effect on the "real" economy, as money was sucked from corporate coffers and the bank accounts of the wealthy into the speculative bubble. Much of the money lent to investors essentially for gambling purposes actually came from the treasuries of major corporations. By late 1928, as the Fed pushed up interest rates in a belated attempt to cool the dangerously overheated market, the go- ing rate for these loans to the "call market" shot up to 12 percent—a rate of return that was almost impossible to achieve by investing in the actual production of goods but which speculators, anticipating mammoth returns, were willing to pay. By 1929, many of the lead- ing corporations—including Standard Oil, Bethlehem Steel, United Gas Improvement Company, General Foods, General Motors, and the Chrysler Corporation—had made multimillion-dollar loans in the "call market," seeing that as the most profitable place to put their money. The involvement of such major companies in the Wall Street markets was unprecedented.[17]

The relationship between the financial world and the broader econ- omy had been turned upside down. No longer was there any notion that the financial community was performing the useful function of acting as the brains of the economy, directing capital to where it could be most productively employed and helping to spread risk in the process. Instead, the financial markets were sucking money directly out of productive places and feeding it into a giant speculative bubble—a bubble that would eventually burst, with devastating repercussions for the whole economy.

When a sweet-looking, thirty-two-year-old female midget crawled into the lap of banking magnate Jack Morgan, the 1933 Senate hearings into the banking disasters of the previous decade almost literally turned into a circus. Jack Morgan wasn't quite the legendary character his father had been, but as head of the sprawling financial empire built by his father, he had emerged as a famous and feared Wall Street titan in his own right. He was even called J. P. Morgan, just as his father had been, providing a continuity that helped perpetuate the dominance of the Morgan dynasty. So the stunt, dreamed up by newsmen covering the hearings to provide them with a dramatic photo, caught the reserved, middle-aged banker completely off-guard and somewhat flustered. As the professional circus performer planted herself firmly on Morgan's knee, photographers got their dream photo, and the broader public saw for the first time a scene in which the usually imposing and haughty head of the House of Morgan was no longer calling the shots.

In many ways, the moment dramatically captured a power shift that was underway in America. For the first time, the head of the most powerful set of money interests was being forced to submit to something almost completely unfamiliar to him: public authority. The 1929 Wall Street crash and the painful downturn that followed had fundamentally altered the political landscape. By 1933, there were 13 million unemployed (about 25 percent of the labor force), with thousands of homeless men riding the rails searching for work. The enraged American public was not only hungry for food, but also hungry for answers about what had gone so terribly wrong.

The bank hearings, held right after Franklin D. Roosevelt took office in March 1933, served up the villains that angry citizens were looking for. Conducted by a tough, uncompromising former New York prosecutor named Ferdinand Pecora, the hearings pried open the lid on the scheming world of Wall Street. Even the grand, graciously chandeliered House of Morgan at Wall and Broad streets was obliged to open its doors to Pecora's inquisitive agents, giving the public its first real look inside the highly secretive world. With the public intently following the hearings, which were covered in salacious detail by the scandal-mongering press, Pecora unveiled just how elitist these aristocratic banks truly were. They didn't handle just anybody's money, but rather regarded a Morgan account as a privilege to be bestowed only upon those inside their social circle. Duncan Fletcher, the powerful chairman of the Senate Banking and Currency Committee under whose auspices the hearings were being held, prodded Morgan with questions about his bank's aloofness. Morgan simply confirmed that, no, the bank would not accept deposits from strangers. Frustrated, Fletcher pressed on: "I suppose if I went there, even though I had never [seen] any member of the firm, and had $100,000 I wanted to leave with the bank, you would take it, wouldn't you?"

"No we should not do it," Morgan calmly replied. "Not unless you came in with some introduction, Senator."[18]

Public rage grew as the hearings wore on. The unrelenting, cigar-smoking Pecora, who had grown up poor as an Italian immigrant in New York, unearthed the fact that President Taft had met secretly with the Rockefeller and Morgan representatives in 1911 and promised them he wouldn't enforce the ban on bank securities affiliates. There were revelations that the banks, through these securities affiliates, had been involved in more than four hundred stock pools—syndicates that actively manipulated stock prices, often with the help of publicity agents or even financial reporters taking bribes. Perhaps the most egregious fact unveiled by the relentless Pecora hearings was that Jack Morgan—who in the midst of the Depression still took home a princely salary of $5 million a year, lived on a lush, 250-acre island estate, and sailed on the world's most elaborate yacht—had paid absolutely no federal income tax in 1930, 1931, or 1932. (For that matter, none of the twenty wealthy Morgan partners had seen the need to pay any income taxes in 1931 or 1932.) With so many Americans destitute, this was the final straw. When headlines about "tax evasion" blared across the country the next day, the stage was set for a historic move aimed at bringing Wall Street to heel.

Barely a month later, in June 1933, President Roosevelt signed a bill that had been working its way through Congress. Known as the Glass–Steagall Act, after sponsors Senator Carter Glass and Representative Henry Steagall, the legislation restored the safeguard that President Taft had so cavalierly tossed aside in 1911. Banks were once again to be kept out of the volatile, speculative arena of stock trading. A strict wall of separation was erected to separate investment houses from commercial banks, which handled the savings of the public. Wall Street fiercely protested the move. But this time, with an irate public watching closely, the bankers weren't able to prevail. Despite his wealthy pedigree and past employment at a Wall Street firm, Roosevelt did not capitulate.

Indeed, the following year, Roosevelt angered Wall Street further by appointing maverick Utah banker Mariner Eccles to be chairman of the Federal Reserve. Eccles believed in Keynesian-style economic stimulus as a cure to the Depression—an approach that was anathema to conservative Wall Street bankers. Worse still, from Wall Street's point of view, Eccles encouraged an overhaul of the Federal Reserve Act that transferred power from the New York Fed to the Federal Reserve Board in Washington, stripping Wall Street of its effective control over the nation's central bank. The best-laid plans of the Jekyll Island banking clique lay in ruins. Wall Street had been reduced to a faint shadow of its former self.

# CHAPTER 4

# Billionaires and the Crash of 2008

The humbling of Wall Street in the 1930s was a key part of the sweeping changes that significantly reduced the power and wealth of the very rich in the decades that followed. As a result, the United States became a considerably more egalitarian society dominated by a large and thriving middle class.

Of course, many racial, ethnic, and gender prejudices remained, blocking a number of groups—notably blacks and women—from sharing fully in the move toward economic equality. Still, overall, the change from the pre-1929 Gilded Age was striking, remaking America in ways that would have been barely imaginable a few decades earlier. And, as Nobel Prize–winning economist Paul Krugman has noted, the rise of a significant middle class in these postwar decades wasn't a gradual process that evolved due to market forces, but rather a sudden development that had more to do with the changing balance of power.[1] Widespread anger at Wall Street for bringing on the Depression had brought an end to public resignation about the privileges of the rich. There was now a determination that wealth and power should be more broadly shared with the rest of society.

The once-cozy relationship between Wall Street and the White House had been severely strained, as the Roosevelt administration now promised a "New Deal" that would include ordinary Americans. At a speech at Madison Square Garden in 1936, President Franklin

Roosevelt unabashedly expressed antagonism toward the wealthy interests that had brought chaos to Wall Street: "Never before in our history have these forces been so united against one candidate as they stand today. They are unanimous in their hate for me—and I welcome their hatred." His secretary of the interior, Harold Ickes, described America as locked in a struggle between the power of money and the power of the democratic instinct: "This irreconcilable conflict, long growing in our history, has come into the open as never before, has taken on a form and an intensity which makes it clear that it must be fought through to a finish—until plutocracy or democracy—until America's sixty families or America's 120 million people win."[2]

With strong public backing, the Roosevelt administration took steps that greatly strengthened the hand of organized labor, bringing an end to the days when government automatically sided with the corporate elite. FDR signaled the beginning of a new labor-friendly era in 1935 by signing the Fair Labor Relations Act, a far-reaching bill aimed at ensuring workers the right to organize and bargain collectively, and giving government a role in enforcing those rights. During World War II, Roosevelt used the sweeping powers of the National War Labor Board to raise wages, particularly for the lowest-paid workers, in a range of industries. With government actively backing unions and pushing up pay, unionization increased dramatically, almost tripling from 12 percent of the workforce in 1935 to 35 percent a decade later.

In the new climate, unions flourished, winning deals at the bargaining table from employers who now saw cooperation with their workforces as the sensible approach. In a precedent-setting 1949 deal dubbed the Treaty of Detroit, the United Auto Workers (UAW) and General Motors agreed to labor peace in exchange for workers receiving wage hikes and benefits in line with productivity gains. The deal set the tone for labor relations in the postwar years, allowing the gains of the UAW to push up wages across the economy. Among other things, this meant that workers came to form a vast consumer block with considerable buying power. As a result, corporations had plenty of incentive to invest in making products to sell to these eager consumers, rather than directing their capital into the speculative dens of Wall Street.

As the middle class became more prosperous, there was a relative decline in the fortunes of the rich. Indeed, as mentioned, the share of national income going to the top 1 percent fell from 24 percent to about 10 percent. To some extent, the rich had lost ground as a result of the financial cataclysm of 1929 and the severe downturn that followed. However, even when the rest of the economy bounced back robustly after 1945, they didn't recover their former predominance. As economists Thomas Piketty and Emmanuel Saez have shown, the declining fortunes of the wealthy were due in part to government action.[3] Among other things, Washington dramatically increased taxes on the rich.

In the 1920s' heyday of pro-rich tax policies under Andrew Mellon, the top marginal tax rate had been a mere 24 percent. But Roosevelt pushed that top rate up to 63 percent, and then to 79 percent. As this more egalitarian ideal became the established norm in the postwar years, successive governments—even Republican ones—followed suit. Under the Eisenhower administration, the top marginal rate rose to a striking 91 percent. (Some commentators try to dismiss the significance of these high rates, suggesting that loopholes allowed the wealthy to avoid paying them. While the rich certainly did take advantage of loopholes, the simple truth is that, in the early postwar era, they paid a significantly larger share of their incomes in tax than they did in earlier times, or than they do today.) Estate taxes followed a similar pattern, with the top rate rising from 20 percent in the 1920s to 77 percent in the 1950s, making it more difficult for the ultra-wealthy to perpetuate family dynasties. There were still rich people who lived very comfortable lives, but the super-rich—the ones living fairy-tale lives on sumptuous estates groomed by armies of servants—were increasingly relics of bygone days.

The overall result was a more egalitarian society, as the wage increases of working people and heavier taxation of the rich led to greater equality in income distribution. The egalitarian reality also contributed to a new ethos of equality, fairness, and public empowerment. This was reflected in support for government, which was called upon to defend and promote the public interest. No longer regarded as simply an instrument for protecting the interests of a small wealthy class with which it had been so closely allied, government was now seen as an institution with a duty to represent the interests of the population at large. Having proved itself capable and effective in defending the population in fighting the war and pulling the country out of economic depression, government came to enjoy respect as a central and beneficial force in society.

The very notion that there was such a thing as a public interest, and that government had an obligation to serve it, was part of a profound change in attitudes. Among other things, the new mood removed the well-to-do from their protected bubble at the top of society and brought them more into the mainstream. They were now subject to economic as well and social constraints, facing greater regulation in their business affairs, heavier taxation of their incomes, and public disdain for any behavior that seemed excessively self-interested or greedy. Under the new social contract, everyone was expected to contribute to the community. J. P. Morgan had once famously said, "I owe the public nothing."[4] In the egalitarian heyday of the early postwar years, the self-centered banker would have been regarded as the crassest of boors.

The new era cast a pall over Wall Street. In line with the Glass–Steagall Act, commercial banks were now required to divest themselves of their lucrative investment divisions, which were sold as separate investment banks. The idea was that commercial banks, which received deposits from the public, were to be subject to a tight new set of regulations. In exchange, they were to be protected from bank failure by government, which would provide insurance covering deposits, so that members of the public wouldn't rush to pull their money out in the case of a financial panic. There was thus a trade-off for the commercial banks: although they were now subjected to strict regulation, they got the full protection of government, ensuring they wouldn't fail.

Commercial banks were also prevented from holding significant equity stakes in companies. Along with these new restrictions, higher estate taxes clipped the wings of the banking elite's favored clientele. As Ron Chernow notes, "The glue that compressed companies, banks, and rich families into a coherent financial class was coming unstuck."[5]

For those who had enjoyed great clout, the restrictions no doubt felt like a blow. But for all the bemoaning and the vilification of FDR as an enemy of his class, the big Wall Street banks and investment houses continued to function and even thrive. What had changed was that they were now performing the function they were supposed to perform: raising and allocating capital so that the economy could operate efficiently. In Chernow's words, investment banks in the postwar era "functioned according to a textbook model in which capital was tapped for investment, not financial manipulation."

The result was an era of remarkable financial stability, with the lowest level of bank failure in American history.[6] In the ten years of the 1970s, only seventy-nine banks failed—compared to two thousand during the seven-year period between 1985 and 1992.[7] Indeed, banking was transformed into a fairly dull, predictable enterprise. "Postwar commercial banking became similar to a regulated utility, enjoying moderate profits with little risk and low competition," noted economist Simon Johnson and analyst James Kwak.[8] The lack of excitement in the banking world was captured in what became known in banking circles as the "3–6–3 rule": pay depositors 3 percent, make loans at 6 percent, and hit the golf course by 3 P.M.[9]

But while the financial world may have lacked glamour and drama in the early postwar years, bankers were performing their proper role as intermediaries, connecting capital to the real economy. As a result, American industrial interests in automobiles, steel, aluminum, and oil took center stage, providing the basis for a period of strong, sustained economic growth—and one in which labor was allowed to share. This early postwar era—an era of restrained banking, reduced incomes for the rich, and a rising middle class—was also a time of extraordinary economic growth and prosperity. It should be acknowledged that the rapid growth of those decades proceeded with little attention to the severe environmental consequences that were unfolding. (By stressing the prosperity of the period, we don't mean to minimize the seriousness of this environmental degradation, but simply to note that it is a separate issue.)

However, there were always those who wanted to unravel the postwar deal. On Wall Street, the yearning for the old days remained alive. And with the rise of less-regulated financial markets in Europe (Euromarkets) in the early 1960s, there was increasing resentment in New York toward the restrictions imposed by the Glass–Steagall Act. By investing in these overseas markets, banks got a taste of being able to operate freely again, tossing aside bothersome New Deal rules requiring them to hold mandatory reserves and pay deposit insurance premiums.

The appetite for such freedom only grew as time went on, particularly with the innovation of leveraged buyouts (LBOs) in the 1980s. A throwback to the pyramid-style holding companies championed by J. P. Morgan & Company in the 1920s, LBOs made Wall Street bankers key players in corporate takeovers. Typically, bankers would provide funding to a company's management team and a group of outside investors who were trying to take control of the firm, using the company's own assets as collateral for the loans. The deals were incredibly dangerous to the health of the targeted company, which would be left holding high levels of debt after the takeover, but not very risky for the bankers and its takeover partners, who put up only a small part of the money. As merger mania spread through the corporate community, bankers were transported back to the heady world of the 1920s—playing lucrative self-enriching games with other people's assets, and shifting the risk onto others.

Meanwhile, the emergence of the new discipline of academic finance seemed to provide an intellectual basis for a return to a more freewheeling era. Economists and finance professors at the leading universities started developing arcane new financial innovations—using high-yield debt, securitization, arbitrage trading, and derivatives— based on highly complex mathematical models that gave a scientific veneer to the old game of gambling. Out of this new discipline came the Efficient Market Hypothesis, which seemed to prove that markets are always right, and that there is therefore little need for regulation. Those who mistrusted the new theories and products were dismissed as Luddites unable or unwilling to seize the exciting new wealth-making opportunities.

This blind faith in the market was highly reminiscent of the irrational Wall Street confidence of the late 1920s. But whether or not the dangers had been properly appreciated in the twenties, they should have been clearly evident by the 1980s. A number of meticulous investigations—most notably those headed by Congressman Pujo and former New York prosecutor Pecora—had left little doubt what the banking world would do if given the freedom to indulge in risky, unregulated behavior. The need to hold the line would seem obvious, but the forces pushing to knock down the barriers that penned in Wall Street had gained strength. Indeed, the reemergence of an aggressive Wall Street was part of a broader resurgence of wealthy interests, whose influence was enhanced by the 1980 election of Ronald Reagan.

Although packaged to the public as a folksy straight-talker, Reagan had elevated himself from B-movie-star status mostly on the basis of his Hollywood union-busting. His rise had been championed by business and conservative forces anxious to roll back the restraints and egalitarian policies of the postwar era. These wealthy interests had never given up resisting the New Deal. After failing dismally in their bid to put conservative extremist Barry Goldwater in office in 1964, they became more focused and better organized, bankrolling an array of Washington think tanks that aggressively attacked liberalism and promoted ideologies favoring less regulation of business. They finally scored with Reagan, whose down-to-earth manner connected with voters. And Reagan delivered for them. From his early move to crush the air traffic controllers' strike to his massive tax cuts for the rich—reducing the top rate from 50 to 28 percent—Reagan's message of "morning again in America" was a sweet one for the country's financial and corporate elite.

The Reagan era brought significant change to America—notably a dramatic rise in inequality and an ethos that supported this increased inequality. Indeed, it's hard to identify which came first—the inequality or the ethos that made it palatable to the public. They clearly worked in tandem, reinforcing each other like a vicious circle. The more tax rates were cut and the rich became richer, the more money flooded into think tanks promoting new conservative ideas, and the more the corporate-owned media felt comfortable promoting these ideas to the public. As the new conservatism took hold, creating a culture of rewarding "success," there was increased momentum for changes favoring corporate America.

The result was a significant decline in the clout and income of workers. The captains of the corporate world, empowered in the new environment, adopted a more adversarial approach toward organized labor, and successfully pressured government to let labor protections lapse and the minimum wage languish. As a result, unions were no longer able to ensure their members a share of productivity gains, and the positive ripple effects of unionization once felt by the broad middle class diminished. This in turn led to a decline in unionization, as well as a stagnation in the real wages of American workers and a decline in their income security. The middle class managed to retain some of its buying power after 1980, largely thanks to the Federal Reserve's looser monetary policy, which kept real interest rates low and made borrowing more affordable. But easier credit simply encouraged the middle class to fall deeper and deeper into debt, with many living on their credit cards or borrowing against the equity in their homes. All this made ordinary Americans particularly vulnerable to a serious downturn. It also meant that there was less incentive for corporations to invest in products to sell to middle-class consumers, whose incomes were mostly stagnating.

The bleak prospects for the middle class were spelled out in a newsletter that Citibank sent out to its well-heeled clients in 2005. The newsletter noted that the United States, Britain, and Canada had become "plutonomies"—economies where financial growth is largely restricted to the rich. The Citibank analysts who wrote the newsletter actually expressed surprise at their findings. They said that they'd been shocked to discover the level of income concentration at the upper end—a level that they noted was matched by only a few other epochs in history (one of them being the Roaring Twenties in America). But their point wasn't to criticize or provoke controversy; certainly not to suggest the need for any income redistribution. On the contrary, it was simply to advise their wealthy clients to focus their investment strategies on products catering to the rich—the only markets where the analysts foresaw substantial growth. (One of the analysts, Ajay Kapur, later left Citibank to start his own hedge fund.)[10]

But of course the rich, even though they take consumption very seriously, can only consume so much. Even if every wealthy family buys ten or twenty cars—plus similar numbers of high-end barbecues, walk-in refrigerators, or massive flat-screen TVs to grace their multiple homes—there simply aren't enough wealthy families to keep up consumer demand. And with limited prospects for consumer spending among the masses, American business responded by ceasing to invest in its own expansion. James Livingston, a historian at Rutgers University, notes that through the years of George W. Bush's administration, business invested less than its retained earnings for a period of six years—the longest stretch since World War II.[11] Instead, as in the 1920s, the action drifted to Wall Street. Whereas the financial sector accounted for just 2 percent of the economy in the early postwar years, by 2006 it had grown to 8 percent. Similarly, while the financial sector attracted only 5 percent of Harvard undergraduates in the 1960s, it was enticing more than 20 percent of them by the mid-2000s.[12]

Wall Street was both the beneficiary of the new conservatism and an active promoter of its agenda. With the wind at its back, it pushed more aggressively to dismantle the regulatory controls of the New Deal. Up until the Reagan years, banks had tried to undermine regulations by essentially ignoring them, carrying on forbidden banking activities in the hope that regulators and Congress would turn a blind eye. But now the bankers felt emboldened to try to actually get the controls removed. Not surprisingly, the House of Morgan was in the forefront of the attack, laying out its case in 1984 in a pointed document called "Rethinking Glass–Steagall."[13] A key player in the campaign was Alan Greenspan, then a Morgan director as well as the former chairman of President Gerald Ford's Council of Economic Advisers (and later, of course, chairman of the Federal Reserve).

This was just the opening salvo of a massive and abundantly funded campaign for financial deregulation that was to become part of the vicious circle favoring the wealthy. As the rich became richer, they became bolder and more confident in their demands, and put more and more money into achieving them. And as they won more tax reductions for themselves, they had yet more money to sink into lobbying and campaigning. Between 1998 and 2008, financial companies donated $1.7 billion to federal political campaigns and spent another $3.4 billion on lobbyists. That's more than $5 billion in a war chest dedicated to dismantling decades-old regulations aimed at protecting the public from manipulation and speculation by the financial industry.[14]

Emboldened by the new political environment, Wall Street became more flagrant in its violations of Glass–Steagall. In 1998, financial services giant Travelers Group bought out Citibank, creating a sprawling conglomerate combining banking and insurance, and openly defying Glass–Steagall. The following year, Congress passed legislation, championed by then Texas senator Phil Gramm, to repeal key sections of Glass–Steagall, making the Citibank merger retroactively legal. Gramm followed up soon after with the Commodity Futures Modernization Act, which made it impossible to regulate the exploding and highly speculative market for the new craze—credit default swaps (CDS)—which now, thanks to the repeal of Glass–Steagall, were being eagerly bought up by regular banks. The floodgates were open. Things had come full circle back to 1911, when Morgan and Rockefeller interests had managed, in one secret meeting with the president, to overturn long-standing rules barring banks from participating in high-risk ventures.

Deregulation mania raged for the next decade, liberating every corner of the American financial industry from what were patently sensible regulations aimed at protecting the public from reckless bankers, speculators, hucksters, and just the blind, stupid greed of the herd on a rampage. The phenomenon can't simply be chalked up to the alleged imperatives of globalization or the existence of freer financial markets offshore. There were international efforts to rein in the financial anarchy, but instead of joining them—even taking a leadership role—the U.S. government actively resisted attempts to bring order and caution to the markets. When the European Union tried to bring the foreign operations of America's five big investment banks under stricter European regulations in 2004, the Bush administration helped ward off such interference, siding with the banks' request to be left alone to decide how best to regulate their own risky behavior.

Indeed, with billions of dollars of deals being made daily on Wall Street, regulation largely disappeared. And so it was that AIG, a global insurance colossus holding insurance policies for millions of people and businesses, ended up being regulated by the modestly equipped Office of Thrift Supervision (OTS). (In a fit of deregulation mania, Congress had passed legislation that enabled certain kinds of companies to choose the patently inadequate OTS as their regulator.) It's a bit understated to note that the OTS was understaffed; its one insurance specialist, C. K. Lee, later acknowledged that he had been wrong in assuming that AIG's $500 billion worth of credit default swaps, backed up by nothing of real value, were "fairly benign products." Surveying the damage in March 2009, U.S. Treasury Secretary Timothy Geithner observed that there had been a serious lack of "adult supervision."[15]

What Geithner did not point to was the role played by extreme inequality.

As in the 1920s, the enormous concentration of income and wealth after 1980 placed a stunning degree of power in the hands of a small crowd of financiers, and they used this power to, among other things, shape the financial landscape to suit their interests. Indeed, as the rich have become richer in the past three decades, they have attained a virtual stranglehold over the domain most important to them: the financial sector. Simon Johnson has noted, the rising wealth of the rich in America in the past twenty-five years has enabled them to consolidate political power, giving the United States not just the most advanced economy, military, and technology in the world, but also "its most advanced oligarchy"—similar to the extremely powerful financial elite of the early part of the last century.

This extraordinary political clout has enabled the wealthy few to effectively disable government when it comes to regulating financial markets. So when Brooksley Born, head of the U.S. Commodity Futures Trading Commission, tried in the late 1990s to bring greater oversight to the wildly gyrating derivatives market, she was stopped in her tracks. It was almost inevitable that her efforts would be defeated, since she was opposed by the three most powerful government officials in the financial domain: Treasury Secretary Robert E. Rubin, Securities and Exchange Commission Chairman Arthur Levitt Jr., and Federal Reserve Chairman Alan Greenspan. Significantly, these men had all earned their wealth via Wall Street and all were dedicated to the Wall Street creed of deregulation. Indeed, as noted, Greenspan, in his days as a J. P. Morgan director, had played a pivotal early role in the campaign for the repeal of Glass–Steagall.

In fact, by the early 1990s, prodigies of Wall Street had effectively taken over government by being appointed to its top economic management positions. A virtual revolving door now connects the power corridors of Wall Street and Washington, with Goldman Sachs practically serving as a training school for those running the U.S. Treasury. Robert Rubin spent twenty-six years at Goldman Sachs, rising to cochairman of the firm before becoming Treasury secretary under Bill Clinton; Henry Paulson, a one-time Goldman CEO, became George W. Bush's Treasury secretary. Then there's Lawrence Summers, formerly Barack Obama's top economic advisor, who earned $5.2 million in 2008 from hedge fund D. E. Shaw. And Greenspan left the Federal Reserve to become a financial consultant to Pimco, a key player in international bond markets. Given these interconnections—which are multiplied at lower levels as Wall Street titans bring their associates and bright underlings with them to fill positions throughout the Washington bureaucracy—it's not surprising that the two worlds now share a mindset and a worldview, built around freeing up the market and loosening controls on financial capital. And it's not hard to imagine how this nexus of power between Wall Street and Washington filtered down to encourage a "belief system," as Simon Johnson puts it, that gave Wall Street's power and influence a legitimacy throughout the broader culture.

It's been said that much of the foolishness and excess on Wall Street in 2008 happened out of ignorance, that few players even understood the nature of the bets they were taking and the extent of the gambles they were making with other people's money. But that could never be said of Angelo Mozilo, the garrulous and cocky former CEO of Countrywide Financial Corporation—a company close to the center of the financial crisis. Countrywide was one of the leading peddlers of subprime mortgages, offering the treacherous loans to thousands of Americans who, by any reasonable measure, couldn't possibly make the payments they were signing up for. If Mozilo didn't know the details of every case, he certainly knew the broad arc of the problem he was instrumental in creating. He knew that some of Countrywide's mortgages were, as he described them in internal e-mails, "poison," "toxic," or, not to put too fine a point on it, "the most dangerous product in existence."[16]

What makes the Mozilo story particularly interesting is not just his role so close to the epicenter of the meltdown, but his apparent reluctance to be there. In the early 1990s, Mozilo, perhaps heeding the wise counsel of his longtime business partner, David Loeb, and perhaps his own inclinations, resisted the temptation to take Countrywide into the lucrative subprime market, sensibly steering clear of a product that was a danger to his company as well as to homeowners who would soon be defaulting on their payments. But his resistance only lasted so long.

As the market heated up in the late 1990s, and his partner retired in 2000, Mozilo saw his chance to finally make it into the top banking circles he'd always felt excluded from. Wall Street was hungry for the risky subprime mortgages, with their obscenely high interest rates that only clicked in after months of rock-bottom "teaser" rates, and that were only spelled out in very fine print. Mozilo moved aggressively into the subprime market, setting up a subsidiary specializing in them with thirty offices across the country and even cloaking the company's blatant opportunism in the mantle of social activism. "Homeownership is not a privilege but a right," he declared in a speech in Park City, Utah, as he peddled "the most dangerous product in existence" to tens of thousands of unsuspecting, low-income folks. So, while Countrywide had insisted on 20 percent down on mortgages a few years earlier, it was now offering them for zero down—and to people who had no proof of having any sort of income. The full tragedy of the situation—beyond the fact that people who could barely afford a trip to the laundromat were being lulled into believing that they too could own a home of their own—was the fact that some borrowers with good credit ratings were redirected into the subprime market, where they ended up losing homes they could have afforded. This was done because it offered more profit for the likes of Mozilo and the Wall Street clan.

Countrywide became a stunning success story. By 2003, Mozilo had a personal compensation package of $33 million. He had more than realized his dreams of acceptance and achievement, being welcomed into the ranks of the big bankers. In 2005, Countrywide made it onto *Fortune*'s list of "Most Admired Companies." Mozilo—whose Italian immigrant father had hoped his son would someday take over his butcher shop—was now being identified by *Barron*'s as one of the thirty best CEOs in the world.

It's easy (and appropriate) to condemn Mozilo for his seemingly bottomless greed. But it might be more useful to try to understand him as a cultural phenomenon—a product of a culture (or even a cult) of greed in which, over the past few decades, the desire for material accumulation has been applauded, fanned, and stimulated to an extraordinary extent. Wall Street has been the engine room of the cult, a kind of hothouse of avarice, an experimental lab in which the normal restraining impulses—caution, prudence, common sense, not to mention common decency—were sliced and diced along with the toxic assets being peddled, and everyone was urged to join in a wild, rapturous romp aimed at snagging an ever-bigger pot of gold.

The ability to set cultural norms and attitudes is part of the power wielded by the dominant forces of society. In times of great wealth concentration, the financial elite not only captures political control of the mechanisms of government, but also more broadly establishes the tone and defines the mores of the era. In both the pre–1929 period and in recent decades, a culture celebrating greed and wealth accumulation dominated, with notions of social responsibility and public spiritedness shunted to the sidelines, even sneered at as a kind of political correctness. Wall Street traders routinely boasted about "ripping the face off" clients, an expression that meant making profits by selling derivative deals so complicated the buyers couldn't possibly understand them.[17] Such indifference to clients, let alone other members of the public, promoted an ethos in which greed and an obsessive focus on self-interest were considered normal and acceptable, even laudable and beneficial. It was this deadly combination—a political agenda controlled by the rich, reinforced by a culture celebrating greed and saluting billionaires—which encouraged thousands of apparently normal people to take part in the subprime mortgage scam, either as participants preying on the vulnerable or as political authorities failing to stop the brazenly predatory behavior.

It could be argued that, in a more egalitarian era, a different group—perhaps the middle class or, more specifically, organized labor—captures control of the political agenda and sets the tone of the times. There's some truth to this, although conservative commentators generally exaggerate the amount of power ever wielded by labor. The notion of labor as a powerful "special interest" has been used to justify anti-union attacks in recent decades. In reality, workers are always at a disadvantage to corporate interests, which, by definition, have power over their employment. Even in the heyday of labor power in the early postwar decades, corporations remained enormously potent and there was considerable inequality. Back then, CEOs weren't earning the massive incomes they are today, but they were still bringing in about thirty times more than the average worker, allowing them to enjoy substantially more comfortable lives. So to the extent that labor wielded some power in the 1940s, '50s, and '60s, this provided nothing more than a bit of healthy rebalancing, tipping the scales less overwhelmingly in favor of corporate interests, which had called all the shots before 1929.

In any event, the point at issue here is the role extreme inequality played in the stock market crashes of 1929 and 2008. Income inequality hasn't generally been considered a factor in the 2008 crash. Nor has it attracted much attention as a factor leading to the 1929 crash and the Great Depression. Indeed, income inequality doesn't figure at all in the explanation of the Great Depression that has been most widely accepted in mainstream circles in recent years. The dominant thesis is the one put forward by Milton Friedman and Anna Jacobson Schwartz, who blame the Depression on inappropriate actions by the Federal Reserve, particularly the contraction of credit between 1930 and 1932, which they believe turned what would have been just another downturn in the business cycle into a full-fledged depression. This theory, embraced by current Federal Reserve chairman Ben Bernanke, considers management of the money supply the key to managing the economy, and has led to the notion that the Fed can ward off depressions through sensible policies. As Bernanke, then a member of the Fed board, told the crowd at a ninetieth birthday party for Friedman in 2002: "I would like to say to Milton and Anna, regarding the Great Depression: You're right. We did it. We're very sorry. But thanks to you, we won't do it again."

But the notion that things would have worked out fine back in the 1930s if only the Fed had properly managed the money supply seems less convincing in the wake of the 2008 Wall Street collapse, which happened despite the apparently greater sophistication of those running the Fed today, who had the benefit of hindsight. Rather, the striking similarity in the inequality levels in both 1929 and 2008—and the lack of financial crises in the more egalitarian intervening decades—suggest a causal relationship between inequality and financial crashes. For that matter, while the Friedman–Schwartz thesis has become the dominant view in recent years, there have always been analysts who pointed to inequality as the key factor in the 1929 crash. In his book *The Great Crash 1929*, economist John Kenneth Galbraith identified five factors he considered had a particular bearing on the 1929 disaster, the first one being "the bad distribution of income." Historian Robert S. McElvaine agrees. "The causes of the Great Depression were many. . . . In the end, though, the greatest weight must be assigned to the effects of an income distribution that was bad and getting worse," McElvaine wrote in *The Great Depression.* "Maldistribution was only one among many roots of the Great Depression, but it was the taproot."[18]

Recently, a number of analysts have also pointed to the significance of inequality as a factor in the 2008 crisis. "The real cause of the crisis," wrote World Bank economist Branko Milanovic in the spring of 2009, "is not to be found in hedge funds and bankers who simply behaved with the greed to which they are accustomed (and for which economists used to praise them). The real cause of the crisis lies in huge inequalities in income distribution which generated much larger investable funds than could be profitably employed."[19] Historian James Livingston has also pointed to the similar patterns of extreme income concentration in the late 1920s and the run-up to the 2008 collapse. Livingston, rejecting the Friedman–Schwartz thesis, argues that the "underlying cause" of the Great Depression "was not a short-term credit contraction engineered by central bankers . . . [but] a fundamental shift in income shares away from wages/consumption to corporate profits that produced a tidal wave of surplus capital that could not be profitably invested in goods production." He notes that in the past twenty-five years, there has been a similar shift away from wages and consumption and toward corporate profits. For a while, government transfer payments offset wage stagnation, but this only delayed the gathering storm, according to Livingston, who teaches at Rutgers University. "The moment of truth reached in 1929 was accordingly postponed. But then George Bush's tax cuts produced a new tidal wave of surplus capital, with no place to go except real estate."[20]

The evidence suggests that a high level of inequality sets up a dynamic that contributes to financial instability. Lack of buying power on the part of the mass of citizens leads to a lack of good investment opportunities in the real economy, driving capital toward the financial sector and concentrating wealth and power in the hands of financiers. This elite uses its clout both to create a social ethos that condones greed and to directly shape the political agenda to facilitate the amassing of great fortunes. A crucial element in this political agenda is the freeing up of financial markets for lucrative speculative activities. While these speculative activities are clearly orchestrated by the financial elite, segments of the broader public are drawn in, and they bear most of the risks and the ultimate costs of a financial collapse.

By contrast, when income is more widely dispersed, as in the early postwar era, there is strong consumer demand for goods and services, attracting capital into the real economy. Political power is also more widely held. Middle-class citizens and organized labor aren't inclined to use their political clout to press for freer financial markets, but rather to protect and enhance their own incomes and buying power. This creates a political agenda and a social ethos that has a restraining effect on financial markets. As we've seen, Wall Street investment banking continued to function in the more egalitarian postwar era, but it did so as it should have—as a vehicle for raising and allocating capital for the broader economy, and not as a vehicle for highly destabilizing financial speculation.

It could perhaps be added that eras of extreme inequality have a certain zesty drama about them that may seem lacking in more egalitarian times, with their textbook virtue, restraint, and rule of law. "Money has lost its mystique and banking, therefore, has lost a bit of its magic," wrote Chernow almost wistfully at the end of his massive 1990 history of the J. P. Morgan empire, apparently saddened by the idea that "there will never be another barony like the House of Morgan." True, a larger-than-life financial titan vacationing with royalty and whipping presidents into line does provide a lot of color—as do today's rogue billionaires accumulating the riches of kings even as they fleece society's most vulnerable citizens. On the other hand, a little less drama in the lives of bankers might be a reasonable trade-off for a lot less devastation in the lives of millions of others.

# CHAPTER 5

# Why Bill Gates Doesn't Deserve His Fortune

Bill Gates's fortune is worth well over $50 billion.

One of the key arguments of this book is that Gates, like other billionaires, only "deserves" a fraction of his fortune. Of course, even if his fortune were much smaller—say, just a couple of billion—Gates would still be a fabulously wealthy man, and his other billions could be spent in ways that would dramatically improve the lives of millions of others.

Let's start by noting that there's a difference between the concept of what one deserves and the concept of what one is legally entitled to. Presumably, Bill Gates has good tax lawyers, so he probably hasn't broken any tax laws. And if he were to run afoul of any tax or other laws affecting property, the matter would be sorted out through proper legal channels. Therefore we can assume that his billions are legitimately his, under the law. So he is entitled to them. But the question remains: Does he deserve them? The question is essentially a moral one, a question about what society considers fair.

Gates is, in many ways, a good test case for the question of whether billionaires deserve their fortunes because he sets the bar high. As billionaires go, he seems like a rather deserving one. He didn't just inherit a fortune; he went out and made one on his own in the marketplace. He not only has great natural talents, but, by all accounts, worked extremely hard to get where he is, making full use of his abilities and every opportunity he encountered. Furthermore, his accomplishment is nothing less than coming up with the operating system for the personal computer—the most widely used innovation of the past century and one that few of us would want to do without. So Gates has made a substantial contribution to society. And, to top it off, he's become one of the world's foremost philanthropists, donating $28 billion to the Bill and Melinda Gates Foundation, which has directed huge sums of money to help truly needy people, like African victims of AIDS and other diseases. It wasn't surprising then that *Time* magazine elevated him to one of the one hundred most influential people of the twentieth century, and in 2005 chose him (along with wife, Melinda, and rock star Bono) as Person of the Year. If there's anyone who seems to deserve his fortune, it's Bill Gates.

Indeed, at first glance, he's just about a perfect role model—lots of talent and effort, a major social contribution, and a generosity toward the needy. Not surprisingly, Gates has become an almost mythical character, one who makes wealth accumulation look justified. He's a kind of poster boy for billionaires.

Like most legends, of course, there's more to the story. Certainly the point has been made, including by Malcolm Gladwell in his best-selling book *Outliers*, that Gates's success was dependent on luck, which immediately makes him seem less heroic. Indeed, Gates had the great luck of being born into a well-to-do family, opening up possibilities that would almost certainly not have been available to a child of low-income parents. His father was a successful Seattle lawyer, and his maternal grandfather a rich banker. As a result, he was sent to a private school, Lakeside, which happened to have a computer club—something unusual in the late 1960s. A fund-raising drive by the savvy mothers of Lakeside students didn't just raise chump change for hockey sweaters or school outings. Rather, drawing on the school's wealthy clientele, they raised enough money—and were sufficiently forward-looking—to buy a $3,000 computer terminal for the school. This made Lakeside one of the few high schools in the country, and probably the world, with a computer terminal in the 1960s. And it was a particularly good one. Bill Gates, who hadn't been very interested in schoolwork, took readily and enthusiastically to the technology and was soon spending all of his time in the school basement playing with the exciting new machine.

As it turned out, his timing was perfect. Society was on the cusp of a revolution that would shortly bring computers into the lives of millions of people. Decades of technological advances had led to the development of giant IBM mainframe computers, which had spectacular powers but were enormously costly and big enough to fill a room. By the late 1960s, the technology was evolving rapidly. In particular, a project that had been done for the U.S. Air Force in the early 1960s, called "Augmenting Human Intelligence," made possible the development of miniature computers that could be programmed to process data in response to commands. This created the possibility that, in addition to giant machines used by government and the military, computers could be personal devices used by individuals in their own lives. The prospects were breathtaking. Bill Gates, just thirteen years of age and in grade eight, was getting ample access to rare and expensive computer time, enabling him to experiment for hours on end with a technology that was about to change the world.

Over the next few years, Gates got a number of important lucky breaks that greatly helped him get a grounding in the emerging technology. The mother of one of the Lakeside boys happened to be involved in computer programming at the University of Washington. She and some colleagues had set up a small business developing software for sale to companies wanting to lease time on the university computer. They decided to let the students in the Lakeside computer club come down to their office and test out the company's software programs after school and on weekends.

That meant more access to free computer time, and Gates and the others grabbed the opportunity. Soon they had an even better deal with another Seattle company, Information Services Incorporated (ISI), which had its own mainframe and was willing to give them free time in exchange for testing out software it was developing for processing company payrolls. In addition, the Lakeside gang discovered that they could get free time on the computer at the University of Washington in the middle of the night. Again, they jumped at the chance, becoming regular nocturnal visitors.

The ISI connection proved crucial. When Gates was in his final year of high school, a company looking for programmers to help it develop a computer system for a state power station approached ISI. The assignment required experience with a particular type of software—software now very familiar to Gates after hours of work on the ISI computer. He managed to convince the teachers at Lakeside to let him move to the southern part of the state to work on the power project as an independent study program. The following year, Gates went off to Harvard, where computers remained his obsessive focus. After a couple of years there, he dropped out and, in 1975, set up Microsoft with former Lakeside computer pal Paul Allen.

For the first few years, Microsoft was a relatively small, aggressive technology company with several dozen employees—one of a number of such companies working in the emerging field of desktop computers. At this point, these were fairly primitive machines and hard to operate, and the market for them, while growing, was still limited. Gates was successful in the field, but not a leading figure. He was certainly far behind Gary Kildall, a brilliant computer innovator thirteen years his senior who had already developed an operating system, known as Control Program for Microcomputers or CP/M, which was the most widely used operating system for desktops at the time. Kildall's company, Digital Research, had sold hundreds of thousands of copies of CP/M, and was pulling in revenue of more than $100,000 a month. Microsoft's main business was selling computer-programming language that ran on Kildall's CP/M.

But Microsoft caught a huge break in 1980 that was to launch it into the stratosphere of corporate success as the dominant force in the computer industry. That year, IBM had set up a secret internal task force, code-named Project Chess, to consider developing a desktop computer for the mass market. Crucially, the company would need an operating system for its new minicomputer. By any logic, the task force should have turned to Kildall, who was the acknowledged leader in the field. As writer Harold Evans puts it: "Everybody in the computer field knew that Kildall had created CP/M—everybody, it seems, except the biggest beast in the mainframe jungle, in which personal computers had hitherto been invisible." Instead, oddly, the IBM task force headed to Seattle to see a secondary player, Bill Gates.[1]

Gates received members of the IBM team enthusiastically, but when they tried to buy the license for CP/M from him, he told them that it wasn't actually his. Gates referred them to Kildall, whom he knew personally; he'd been to dinner with Kildall and his wife at their home in Monterey, California. The IBM project team flew down to see Kildall the next day to negotiate a licensing deal. There's some dispute over exactly what happened when they showed up at Kildall's office. Kildall later claimed that there'd been an agreement in principle that day, confirmed by a handshake. However, there were no follow-up negotiations. Instead, the IBM team was soon headed back to Seattle, where Gates now assured them that Microsoft would be able to come up with an operating system to meet their requirements. He then quickly bought the rights to another operating system—an adaptation of Kildall's CP/M developed by Tim Paterson and produced by a Seattle company.

Gates flew down to IBM's southern headquarters in Boca Raton, Florida, to meet with the IBM project team for lunch. The meeting went well. Project leader Don Estridge told Gates that the new IBM chief executive, John Opel, was delighted to hear that the company might be doing a deal with Gates, whose mother he knew personally. (Opel sat on the board of the United Way with Mary Gates.) Certainly Bill and his mother fit much more comfortably into the upscale corporate culture of IBM than did the hippie-like and free-spirited Gary Kildall.

In the end, IBM did a deal with Gates—even though Kildall's system was clearly superior. Indeed, Kildall, who was years ahead of everyone else in the field, had already developed the capacity for multitasking—a function that it would take another decade for IBM and Microsoft to come out with. According to Evans, Kildall was "the true founder of the personal computer revolution and the father of PC software."[2] But of course it was Gates who was to get the credit, and in the process become one of the world's most famous and celebrated men—and the richest person on the planet.

But does he deserve that fortune?

Although Gates was a go-getter who maximized every opportunity that came his way, he wasn't the actual inventor of the operating system of the personal computer, as he's often celebrated for being. If anyone deserves that title, it's Gary Kildall. Of course, this is by no means the first time an actual inventor has been nudged aside by a rival who was simply more adept at maneuvering himself to the front of the line. The history of inventions is full of such stories. But the point isn't that Gary Kildall should have ended up with $50 billion (in fact Kildall, although not in the same league as Gates, did do very well financially). Rather, the point is to question whether anyone should end up with such a vast fortune as a reward for inventing a system that was in fact developed through the collective contributions of many, many people.

Our culture inculcates us with the notion that important advances are the product of individual genius. We tend to see the development of human civilization over the centuries as the history of spectacular achievements by individuals, virtually eliminating the role that society plays. This notion gives credibility and legitimacy to the accumulation of vast fortunes. If Bill Gates—or for that matter, Gary Kildall—was responsible all by himself for an invention that changed the world, then our winner-take-all system of rewards might make sense. But the personal computer didn't just spring whole from either of their brains. On the contrary, it was the product of a long series of technological developments going back decades (or even centuries), each one making possible the advance of science to the point that the next breakthrough became possible, indeed almost inevitable.

In many ways, the story of the personal computer begins in France in the early 1800s with the invention of a superior loom for weaving silk. The intricately brocaded fabrics that were fashionable at the time could be produced by an instrument known as a drawloom, but only with extremely difficult and complex hand-weaving. Joseph Marie Jacquard, the fifth of nine children of a master weaver from Lyons, devised a loom that allowed the weaving function to be done without manual effort. The key to his invention was a series of punched cards. These were inserted into the loom, where metal rods attached to individual threads would hit against them. If a rod encountered a hole in a card, it would activate a thread; if it encountered solid card, it would do nothing. So the actions of the loom were determined by the placement of a series of holes in the punched cards. With the insertion of the cards, the loom could effectively be programmed to carry out the complex weaving tasks on its own. The Jacquard loom, notes technology historian James Essinger, "was a machine of a caliber and sophistication that had never been seen before. In fact, when it was patented in 1804, it was unquestionably the most complex mechanism in the world."[3] Its punched-card technology was the germ of the idea for the computer. (Indeed, the first computers Bill Gates worked on as a student still used punched cards.)

Jacquard's loom was the inspiration for an ambitious calculating machine that is now considered to be a Victorian-age "computer." Developed by British scientist and mathematician Charles Babbage, the machine was an attempt to adapt the punched-card technology of Jacquard's loom for the tedious task of mathematical calculation.

At the time, for instance, tables used to calculate the movement of stars and planets were prepared slowly and painstakingly by clerks who were known, interestingly enough, as "computers." Babbage wanted to create a machine that would avoid this time-consuming manual process, and also produce more reliable results. In the same way that Jacquard had used punched cards to control the metal rods on his loom, Babbage's machine used punched cards to control metal rods that in turn activated cogwheels carrying out calculating functions. His "Analytical Engine" even had a memory, which he called "the store," and a processor, which he called the "mill." Babbage openly acknowledged that his idea was derived from Jacquard, even displaying a magnificent portrait of the French weaver in his home, made of silk using the Jacquard loom. While Babbage developed highly sophisticated portions of his machine, as well as detailed plans and drawings for its completion, he failed to actually make it operational. More than a century and a half later, in 2004, scientists built a full model of his extraordinary apparatus—with eight thousand parts and weighing five tons—based faithfully on his drawings. Babbage is now considered the father of the modern computer.

The next key step was taken by Herman Hollerith, an American engineer who used the punched-card technology of Jacquard's loom to create a machine that was actually able to process information. Hollerith originally developed his machine, known as the "tabulator," to simplify the massive task of processing data gathered by the U.S. census. Hollerith had some success adapting his machine for commercial purposes, and his company later merged with three others and surfaced under a new name in 1911: International Business Machines, or IBM. It was under IBM, and specifically its high-powered, sales-oriented president, Thomas John Watson, that Hollerith's punched-card tabulating machine became a widely used business tool. By the 1930s, IBM had developed an advanced automatic tabulation machine and was manufacturing some fifteen hundred of them a year. The Depression hurt sales, but the introduction of the Social Security Act in 1935 as part of the New Deal created a bonanza for IBM. Suddenly, the U.S. government needed to automate the employment records of the entire nation, and it soon ordered five hundred machines from IBM.

IBM got even more help from the government during World War II, when the U.S. Army funded it to carry out special projects. In January 1943, IBM produced its first real computer—the first automatic digital calculating device—for use by the U.S. Navy. The device consisted of a massive steel frame fifty-one feet long and eight feet high containing five hundred miles of wire and three million wire connections, but it was still based on the central punched-card technology.

Meanwhile, two engineers from the University of Pennsylvania, J. Presper Eckert and John Mauchly, again with funding from the U.S. government, succeeded by the late 1940s in developing an all-electronic computer. It could carry out five thousand operations per second—compared to just three thousand for IBM's wartime computer. The development of transistors in the late 1940s allowed computers to get more powerful still, and they could soon perform up to one hundred thousand tasks per second. At the same time, the devices were getting smaller.

By 1955—the year Bill Gates was born—the computer revolution was well underway, drawing the intense interest of some fifteen thousand enthusiasts intent on devising ways to develop and widen the use of these powerful machines. It was this loose group of computer professionals and hobbyists that Gates would join in the early 1970s. But before he had finished kindergarten, there were a whole host of advances that set the stage for his upcoming role in the rise of personal computers. Almost all these advances were the result of work funded by the U.S. government and military, and most were the result of teamwork, with individual contributions often hard to identify. Notes Essinger: "Ever since the late 1950s, this has tended to be the pattern for breakthroughs in computing: they have been the result of collaborative and joint effort by large teams composed of often anonymous people rather than by individual pioneers."[4]

Some individual pioneers do stand out, most notably Douglas Engelbart, a visionary engineer driven by a desire to develop computers to help solve the urgent problems facing humanity, rather than just as commercial tools enabling people to work faster. With funding from the U.S. Air Force in the early 1960s, Engelbart, along with engineer Bill English, invented some of the key features that we associate with personal computers today, such as the mouse.[5] Up until this point, computers, though immensely powerful, were essentially inaccessible to humans, except to a few initiates possessing sophisticated programming skills. Engelbart and others got around this problem by devising ways for people to interact with these potent machines—through the keyboard, the screen, the mouse, the menu, and other items of what's known as the graphical user interface (GUI)—so that individual users could easily instruct computers to carry out specific tasks.

These devices—absolutely essential in transforming the computer into the ubiquitous machine that is central to the lives of hundreds of millions of people today—were developed by Engelbart and dozens of others, long before Apple Computer (and, later still, Microsoft) simply repackaged them for the mass market. (Before Microsoft developed Windows, it used MS-DOS—short for Microsoft Operating System—a much less user-friendly system in which users typed command words on the keyboard.) In a 1994 interview with *Playboy* magazine, Bill Gates acknowledged that one of the keys to Microsoft's incredible success was "committing to the graphics interface"—an array of tools developed not by him but by many others, who remain largely obscure and considerably less rich. Engelbart, who has been sadly disappointed by the commercial direction of the computer revolution, held the patent for the mouse, although he never actually received any royalties for it because he allowed it to expire in 1987, on the cusp of the desktop revolution.

So if we were to present the story of the development of the personal computer as a stage play, it would be a rich and complex drama with a long list of characters. From early scenes featuring Joseph Marie Jacquard and his punched-card technology, the play would go on to include starring roles for Charles Babbage, Herman Hollerith, Thomas John Watson, J. Presper Eckert, John W. Mauchly, Douglas Engelbart, and Bill English, with a host of other largely unidentified characters playing crucial supporting roles onstage and off. Toward the end of this rather long drama, there'd be an intriguing subplot about how technological innovator Gary Kildall thought he had a deal with IBM, only to discover his friend Bill Gates had sold IBM an adaptation of Kildall's own operating system for the first mass-market personal computer. Indeed, it would only be at this point late in the final act that we'd get our first sight of Gates, and he wouldn't come across as a particularly heroic character. Certainly, as the curtain came down at the end of the production, it would be hard to imagine Bill Gates getting a curtain call or stealing the lion's share of the applause, let alone walking away with the entire box office.

Among other things, the story of the personal computer suggests that inventions and innovations are the result of an evolutionary process involving many players, rather than being the product of one brilliant individual. As Isaac Newton famously remarked in a letter to scientific rival Robert Hooke: "What Descartes did was a good step. You have added much several ways. . . . If I have seen a little further it is by standing on the shoulders of Giants."

Indeed, an invention typically occurs when the scientific body of evidence has accumulated to the point that the breakthrough is almost apparent—at least to the scientists closely engaged in the field. Political economists Gar Alperovitz and Lew Daly put it this way: "What commonly happens is that a field of research reaches a certain point in time when 'the next step' is obvious to insiders—and because it is obvious, it is also inevitable that somebody, or more likely many somebodies, will take the step. Someone will connect the dots (but only, it is important to note, when the requisite dots have developed to the point where they can be connected.)"[6]

This truth is illustrated by the fact that a number of major inventions appear to have been "invented" by different individuals at virtually the same moment. One striking case is that of Alexander Graham Bell, forever credited with inventing the telephone. Bell did file a patent on February 14, 1876, but that same day, an American electrical engineer named Elisha Gray filed a caveat—a statement of intent to patent—for a similar apparatus. In the log book at the patent office, Bell was no. 5, while Gray was no. 39, which would seem to suggest Bell won the race to develop a telephone, if only by a hair. But two things throw that claim into question. Many of the patents were received by mail, and it's not clear from the patent office logs at what point in the day on February 14, 1876, the submissions by Bell and Gray were received. More importantly, it turned out that the mechanism outlined by Bell in his original patent wouldn't have actually worked—he had to file another patent soon afterward, correcting some of his design problems—while Gray's original submission would have worked. After years of unsuccessful litigation by Gray, Bell's claim now stands unchallenged in popular history.[7]

But clearly, Alexander Graham Bell was not indispensable to the invention of the telephone. There's even evidence that half a decade before 1876, when Bell and Gray were virtually tied in the race to "invent" the telephone, Antonio Meucci, an Italian stage technician, had quietly crossed the finish line. Meucci had already essentially developed a telephone, which he called the "teletrofono." It appears that he had been able to establish voice transmission between his Staten Island workshop and his nearby home as early as the 1850s. By 1871, Meucci had filed a caveat for his apparatus, but in 1874, unable to afford the $10 renewal fee, he allowed it to lapse. Had he not, Bell would have raced his application to the patent office only to discover that the telephone had already been invented years earlier.[8]

It's also clear that the personal computer would have been invented with or without Bill Gates. Furthermore, it's possible that, without Gates, the revolution in personal computers would have evolved along less commercial lines. A number of the early pioneers were committed to developing personal-computer software for the public realm, free from corporate domination. Engelbart, for instance, was deeply motivated by the idea of using the computer primarily as a tool to advance human capacities to cope with the enormous problems facing the world. But despite his brilliant innovations, Engelbart was never able to realize his vision. Nor were dozens of other talented pioneers with aspirations of collectively building computer operating systems freely accessible to all. Their dreams were blocked in part because of the supremacy of Bill Gates. As Gates achieved greater and greater market dominance, he was able to use his power to relentlessly squeeze out others, prompting years of government antitrust actions that ultimately failed against Microsoft's deep pockets. In the process, Gates took control of the computer revolution, which could have been a vehicle for human empowerment or betterment, and turned it instead into a commercial Shangri-la, where virtually every computer user in the world is obliged to contribute to the enlargement of his ever-growing personal jackpot.

Whatever Bill Gates's contribution to the development of the personal computer, it was only possible because of innumerable developments starting well before Jacquard's invention of punched-card technology, including a vast range of scientific and mathematical developments that preceded them for centuries: the invention of everything from geometry and algebra to the printing press, and even the development of human writing, beginning in ancient Mesopotamia. Patent-law expert Alfred Kahn argues that no invention is the work of one individual but is rather "the aggregate of an almost infinite number of individual units of invention, each of them the contribution of a single person. It is little short of absurdity to call any one of the interrelated units the invention, and its 'creator' the inventor."[9]

It is this enormous knowledge and technological inheritance—which has grown at a particularly breathtaking rate in the last hundred years—that accounts for so much of the wealth we enjoy today. The Nobel Prize–winning economist Robert Solow clarified this in a groundbreaking study in 1957, when he identified that the key element in the phenomenal productivity growth between 1909 and 1949 was not the contribution of either capital or labor, as was commonly believed. Instead, Solow attributed the lion's share of the growth—about 88 percent—to "technical change in the broadest sense."[10] Herbert A. Simon, another Nobel Prize–winning economist, referred to the huge store of knowledge from the past as "social capital," and argued that access to it was our main source of wealth, responsible for about 90 percent of national income.[11] Still another Nobel laureate, George Akerlof, points to the economic significance of this technological inheritance in noting that "our marginal products are not ours alone . . . [but] are due almost entirely to the cumulative process of learning that has taken us from stone age poverty to twenty-first century affluence."[12]

Indeed, it's hard to figure out the rationale for the huge discrepancies in today's incomes when so much of what any of us are able to accomplish is due to all the learning and knowledge accumulated in the centuries preceding us. As Alperovitz and Daly put it: "Before anyone is a 'talented' entrepreneur or a 'menial' laborer, or anything in between, most of the economic gains that get distributed to individuals in a given year or period are derived from what is inherited from the past, not created by them in the present."[13] All this inevitably raises the question of who should benefit from the wealth made possible by this huge technological inheritance.

As things currently stand, the overwhelming beneficiary is whoever (like Bill Gates) manages to adapt some aspect of our technological inheritance into a marginally new product that gains market dominance—often through a combination of luck, opportunism, and ruthlessness. But why should Bill Gates or any other individual take such an extraordinarily large share of the jackpot? Does the technological inheritance that made his marginally new product possible really belong so exclusively to him? If it belongs more properly to all of us, and if this inheritance is the overwhelming source of all wealth today, shouldn't society as a whole enjoy a larger share of the bounty?

This group inheritance is implicitly acknowledged in the tax system, which collects a share of each person's income and deposits it in the national treasury for the general use of society. The question is: Does the tax system collect a sufficiently large share of a person's income to compensate for the enormity of the technological inheritance? In the case of low- and middle-income earners, the answer is probably yes. After all, their incomes are not so large, and they need to be left with sufficient funds to support themselves and their families. But what about the very rich?

A number of important social theorists have argued for greater acknowledgment of the role of society in generating incomes—and greater payback through the tax system. John Stuart Mill, the nineteenth-century British political philosopher best known for his writings in defense of individual liberty, also argued, particularly in his later years, for a recognition of the important role society plays in individual earnings. Mill noted that it was society, not just individual effort or labor, that determined what a person was able to do or create, and that society was morally entitled to receive due compensation for its contribution.

In 1870, for instance, Mill was involved in the founding of the Land Tenure Reform Association, considered an important step in the evolution of modern social welfare philosophy. While arguing that private ownership of land might be desirable to achieve optimal production, Mill, in his draft of the association's program, insisted that increases in land values due to the general growth and development of society properly belonged to the community at large.[14] Mill extended this approach to increases in values of all sorts of property that are caused by factors having nothing to do with the contributions of the individual property holder. In a well-known passage from his *Principles of Political Economy,* he explained: "Suppose there is a kind of income which constantly tends to increase, without any exertion or sacrifice on the part of the owners . . . it would be no violation of the principles on which private property is grounded, if the state should appropriate this increase of wealth, or part of it, as it arises."[15] Mill went on to make the case that the failure of society to appropriate its due would result in property holders receiving undue benefit—thereby bestowing on them an "unearned appendage" to their existing wealth.

Many others have developed arguments along this line. The renowned American Revolutionary War–era writer Thomas Paine noted that, if an individual is separated from society, even given a whole continent to possess, "he cannot acquire personal property. He cannot be rich." Thus, continued Paine, "all accumulation . . . of personal property, beyond what a man's own hands produce, is derived to him by living in society; and he owes on every principle of justice, of gratitude, and of civilization, a part of that accumulation back again to society from whence the whole came." British philosopher and reformer Leonard T. Hobhouse, writing in the early 1900s, developed a similar argument. As great fortunes were being amassed through the industrial revolution, Hobhouse reminded the prosperous business owner to consider "what single step he could have taken" if it hadn't been for the "sum of intelligence which civilization has placed at his disposal" and the "inventions which he uses as a matter of course and which have been built up by the collective effort of generations."[16]

Mill, Paine, Hobhouse, and others were clearly developing a case for the moral legitimacy of taxation as reimbursement for society's contribution. As Hobhouse argued, taxation should not be seen as "redistribution" but rather as "just compensation"—the restoration of the unearned, excess wealth to its proper place in the community's coffers. "The true function of taxation is to secure to society the element in wealth that is of social origin, or, more broadly, all that does not owe its origin to the efforts of living individuals." Hobhouse went on to suggest that setting taxes on large incomes too low deprives society of its just share of the rewards, and even amounts to a kind of distorted welfare system in which wealthy individuals unfairly receive the fruits of society's industry.

Certainly, if most of what we are able to create is inherited from the past, it seems reasonable that a significant part of any resulting windfall—which happens to come the way of an individual who is often simply lucky—should go back to society. Jacques Turgot, an eighteenth-century French economist, referred to the technological and cultural heritage of the past as a "common treasury."[17] This apt phrase suggests not only that this heritage is something we receive collectively, but also that it is a treasure, a store of riches that should provide benefits for all.

The case for returning a substantial share of large incomes and fortunes to the common purse is based not only on the contribution of the inheritance of the past, but also on the ongoing contribution made by the public treasury. In many cases, inventions are the direct result of substantial government funding of research. So, for instance, in addition to the technological bequest Bill Gates received from Jacquard et al., there was the fact that Gates learned computer programming largely through access to the mainframe computer at the government-funded University of Washington. For that matter, virtually all the early research leading to the development of the personal computer was paid for from the public purse—from Engelbart's Augmenting Human Intellect project, funded by the U.S. Air Force, to a whole range of pathbreaking government-sponsored computing projects in the 1940s and '50s, including those at Harvard, MIT, the University of Illinois, the Rand Corporation, the Los Alamos Laboratories, the Stanford Research Institute, and the Office of Naval Research.[18]

More broadly, of course, massive government funding of public education makes possible the advanced society we live in, in which people are literate enough to be able to use a computer. And without government funding of police and fire departments as well as roads and the whole urban infrastructure, our sophisticated economy in which citizens can afford to buy personal computers would not exist. Indeed, as noted, government creates the market itself—through laws, regulations, and institutions that govern banking, commerce, and international trade, in addition to establishing and enforcing property rights.

Without all this, no one individual could ever make much of a difference—no matter how brilliant, dedicated, motivated, or hardworking he might be. In the overall picture, one person's contribution would still inevitably be infinitesimally small. If this seems to underestimate the importance of individual greatness, consider some of the most outstanding minds in history and try to imagine how far they would have gotten without the benefit of society and all the knowledge accumulated before them. Alperovitz and Daly put it well: "If [Isaac] Newton, in his lifetime, had to learn everything humanity had learned from the time of the caveman to the late seventeenth century—if he had no knowledge inheritance whatsoever to work with—he could not have contributed much more than an insightful caveman could in his lifetime."[19]

And Bill Gates, stranded on a desert island, would have his work cut out just figuring how to keep himself warm.

# CHAPTER 6

# Why Other Billionaires Are Even Less Deserving

It was late in 2006 when an aging, little-known economic consultant named Gary Shilling arrived at a tony office in New York's Upper East Side for a meeting with hedge fund manager John Paulson and his team of high-powered analysts. Shilling, who operated out of more modest quarters in suburban New Jersey, may have seemed a little out of place with Paulson and this younger crowd of urbane money traders, but Paulson had sought him out after reading a newsletter Shilling produced. Paulson had been impressed by Shilling's analysis of the nation's economic prospects—and how sharply out of sync it was with the rosy picture painted by others. Just about every other economist and market watcher was adamant that, even after five years of record-breaking growth, housing prices would continue to surge upward. But Shilling wasn't convinced. As he told his intrigued audience at Paulson & Co., housing prices were about to come crashing down. And that, he said, would trigger a sharp increase in mortgage foreclosures. The scene would not be pretty.

In fact, Paulson and his minions had been watching the housing market intently for the past two years, tracking the explosive growth of risky debt that was obscured by the stunning rise in house prices. He had a gut instinct that Shilling, well into his seventies, was on to something, and it didn't take long for the hedge fund manager to figure out where it could lead.

"Boy, if you're right, the financial system will fall apart," said Paulson.[1]
Shilling confirmed that he fully expected that to happen.

As the pieces began to fit into place in his mind, Paulson concluded that the global economy was closer to the precipice than anyone seemed to realize.

At last, the moment he had long waited for seemed to have arrived.

Like a few other savvy Wall Street players, Paulson had been looking for an opportunity to bet that the housing bubble would burst. There was enough information around about the shoddy nature of many of the subprime mortgage deals—with clients who had little in the way of assets, income, or employment—that a number of close observers realized a lot of "homeowners" would soon be in dire straits, unable to meet their monthly payments. In the betting parlors of Wall Street, this represented a chance to make some serious money.

The best vehicle for betting against the housing market, as Paulson and a few other Wall Streeters had figured out, was to take out "insurance" on packages of mortgages that had been bundled together and sold as a stock. This was an odd concept that twisted the conventional notion of insurance. Typically, for instance, a car owner takes out insurance on his car, paying a small monthly premium to protect himself against the potentially heavy financial loss he would suffer if his car were to be in an accident. In this case, the asset was not a car but a stock. Still, that made sense, since a stock could decline in value, so an investor holding the stock might want to protect himself from the possibility of such a decline. What was unusual here was that the Wall Street types were taking out insurance on something they had no personal stake in, on something that involved other people's assets. It was like buying insurance on a car owned by a stranger, in the hopes of collecting money if the stranger's car crashed. This "insurance"—known as a credit default swap (CDS)—was simply a bet. The fate of thousands of mortgage holders and their dreams of homeownership had become an opportunity for Wall Street hotshots to roll the dice, in the hopes of winning a jackpot.

In some ways, this form of gambling wasn't very risky, because the most the bettor could lose would be the cost of his premiums. (For $1 million a year in CDS premiums, it was possible to insure some $100 million worth of these mortgage stocks.)[2] The problem was that it was impossible to know exactly when the housing market would collapse and cause the mortgage stocks to tumble in value. In the meantime, the cost of paying the premiums would add up. A few bettors had already been badly burned, spending too much on premiums and eventually pulling out of the game, frustrated and bitter that the housing market hadn't yet imploded. Paulson too had been betting on a housing collapse, but he'd assembled a big enough war chest from his wealthy hedge fund clients to keep playing, despite the continued buoyancy of the housing market. After the meeting with Shilling, he was convinced that now was the time to go really big.

One frustration for Paulson was that there just weren't enough of these stocks, known as collateral debt obligations (CDO), to bet against. So he decided to become proactive. He approached a number of investment banks with the request that they create more CDOs to sell to clients, so that he could then take out insurance betting these would fail. The arrangement Paulson had in mind was rife with potential conflicts of interest. He clearly wanted to help pick the mortgages that would make up the new CDOs. And he would obviously favor particularly risky subprime mortgages, thereby increasing the likelihood that the CDOs would become worthless and he would be able to collect on the "insurance" he had taken out.

Bear Stearns, the giant investment bank where Paulson had once served as managing director, said no to his scheme. But Goldman Sachs agreed to the arrangement, providing Paulson with his dream opportunity: a chance to bet on toxic CDOs worth about $5 billion. And all went according to plan. The housing bubble burst soon afterward, causing untold misery among homeowners and rendering the $5 billion in CDOs worthless—and allowing Paulson to collect $1 billion in "insurance." In fact, that was only a fraction of the money Paulson earned by betting on the collapse of the housing market in 2007. When the winnings from all his bets were counted, he emerged with $3.7 billion, making him the tallest man in that year's income parade.

All this turned Paulson into a mini-hero on Wall Street. The financial press celebrated him for his cunning moves in scoring the biggest one-year jackpot ever. *Wall Street Journal* reporter Gregory Zuckerman recounted in stirring detail every step that led to Paulson's winning gamble in a book whose title gives away the author's enthusiasm: *The Greatest Trade Ever.* In the book, Paulson comes across as a sympathetic character, an "underdog" who overcame obstacles and "triumphed over the hubris" of Wall Street. "Paulson was no singles hitter, afraid of risk," Zuckerman writes breathlessly. "Anticipating a housing collapse—and all that it meant—was Paulson's chance to hit the ball out of the park and win the acclaim he deserved."[3]

The acclaim he deserved? Paulson's hit helped trigger the collapse of global financial markets, leaving tens of millions suffering around the world. Certainly, the activities of Paulson, and others like him on Wall Street, could in no way be construed as socially beneficial. Their actions do nothing to improve the efficient allocation of capital—the function that financial markets are supposed to perform. Instead, they amount to little more than gambling, which has no social utility. Martin Wolf, a columnist for the UK *Financial Times*, noted that Paulson's moves served "absolutely no useful purpose."[4] By buying insurance on CDO investments in which he had no ownership stake, Paulson wasn't protecting himself from losses, but rather was placing a bet that the CDO investments would fail— like buying insurance on someone else's car, hoping it would crash. But it was worse than that. Paulson managed to get Goldman Sachs to create faulty CDOs, so that he would have excellent odds in betting against them. Paulson was effectively arranging to have a manufacturer build a car with a faulty brake pedal and then, when the brakes inevitably failed and the car crashed, collecting on the insurance he'd taken out.[5]

In April 2010, the U.S. Securities and Exchange Commission (SEC) charged Goldman Sachs with fraud for selling CDOs without telling buyers that they'd been designed with the help of Paulson, who was betting they would fail. However, no charges were laid against Paulson, since he hadn't been involved in misrepresenting the CDOs to buyers. Still, even if Paulson escapes charges, he was clearly instrumental in getting Goldman to create the toxic and destructive CDOs that lie at the heart of the SEC's fraud case.

Some observers have joked that Wall Street should be regulated, not by the SEC, but by the Nevada Gaming Commission. In that spirit, Simon Johnson, a business professor at MIT and former research director of the International Monetary Fund, says that it appears as if Paulson and Goldman Sachs were running a "crooked roulette table"— something that gets one banned for life from Las Vegas. Johnson argues that, whether or not Paulson is charged, he should be banned for life from securities markets.[6]

Certainly, the Paulson–Goldman scheme set off a series of events with extremely negative repercussions. Investors purchasing the toxic CDOs lost billions of dollars, unaware that they were buying faulty merchandise. Furthermore, the scheme exacerbated the impact of the housing collapse and the near-bankruptcy of insurance giant AIG, which had sold some $64 billion of CDS "insurance" on CDOs related to subprime mortgages. AIG was unable to pay out the money it owed to those, like Paulson, who had bought insurance on now-worthless mortgage-related CDOs. (Goldman too had bought such insurance from AIG, which put the firm in the position of both creating the highly risky CDOs and taking out insurance betting they would fail.) But it gets worse. Insisting that AIG's bankruptcy would devastate credit markets, the U.S. government stepped in to prop up the giant insurance conglomerate. In a deal overseen by then Treasury secretary Henry Paulson,[7] Washington bailed out AIG with $170 billion. Out of that huge pool of taxpayer money, AIG paid Goldman $14 billion to make good on the insurance Goldman had bought on its CDOs.[8] Similarly, it paid John Paulson $1 billion.

This means that a billion dollars of taxpayer money went to ensure that Paulson was able to collect his gambling jackpot. By the logic of the marketplace, Paulson should have been left with nothing when the massive bets he'd made, based on faulty products, helped bankrupt the gambling parlor; instead, in the protected comfort of Wall Street's sheltered casino, he walked away with vast amounts of taxpayer dollars bulging from his pockets.

So Paulson not only helped spark the financial collapse—with its ruinous repercussions for millions around the world—but he made off with $1 billion of the public's money for his role in what appears to be a crooked gambling scheme.

While some in the financial world may celebrate him as a home-run hitter, another view was captured in a handwritten sign held by protestors marching on Wall Street: "Jump, you fuckers!"

If Bill Gates is a poster boy for billionaires, Paulson might be considered the opposite: someone who accumulated great wealth in a way that actually harms society. While Gates could be credited with contributing to the development of the personal computer, Paulson helped trigger a financial meltdown and a worldwide recession.

For that matter, Paulson is hardly the only fabulously wealthy individual whose overall contribution to society might seem to veer into negative territory. There's also Joseph Cassano, former head of the financial products division at AIG. Cassano was instrumental in peddling some $500 billion worth of CDSs, including the $64 billion connected to subprime mortgages, leading to the collapse and bailout of AIG. Then there's the aforementioned Angelo Mozilo, former CEO of Countrywide Financial, who made a fortune directly peddling subprime mortgages to unsophisticated, would-be homeowners. There's also Sanford I. Weill, former head of Citigroup, whose extensive lobbying efforts helped kill the Glass–Steagall Act, thereby undermining regulatory supervision of financial markets and allowing Wall Street to turn itself into a giant casino. Indeed, much of Wall Street would fit one way or another into this non-poster-boy category of billionaires. (And we haven't even mentioned the likes of out-and-out billionaire crooks such as Bernie Madoff, who, in crossing the line into obvious criminality, have lost any claims to deserving their fortunes.)

Of course, if contribution to society were the criterion for determining an individual's compensation, the income parade would look very different. By most people's standards, the giants reaching up into the clouds would be people like nurses, doctors, teachers, and social workers, while the bankers and hedge fund managers would find themselves among the dwarves. (In reality, however, the pay of the top twenty-five hedge fund managers in 2009 was the same as that of 658,000 school teachers.)[9] While few would say that our system of rewarding people financially accurately reflects their true social contribution, our society does implicitly subscribe to the view that there is some connection between social contribution and compensation. According to neoclassical economic theory, which has dominated Western thinking for the past century, a person's compensation is a reflection of his marginal product—that is, his contribution to total economic output. So, to make a contribution to society, one doesn't have to be doing social work or directly helping others. By adding to society's economic output, the individual is deemed to have increased the well-being of the community. Under this theory, those who contribute most to economic output receive the largest rewards.

In reality, however, it is hard to make the case that those with the biggest incomes (John Paulson, for instance) have made the biggest contribution to economic output, let alone to any broader goals in society. Supporters of neoclassical theory get around this problem by arguing that a person's contribution to economic output is simply a reflection of what others are willing to pay him for his services. This has a nice simplicity about it; rather than society judging the value of an individual's output, it is left to the market to determine value.

But a problem quickly becomes obvious: under this formulation, a person's social contribution is determined by how valued her services are by those who have money and are therefore able to pay for her services. Is this really a meaningful measure of a person's social contribution? Is a tax lawyer who exploits every ambiguity in the law to benefit her wealthy clients really worth ten to twenty times more than a community clinic lawyer who figures out legal ways to prevent poor families from being evicted from their homes? Is a dentist who performs cosmetic work really worth many times more than a dentist who, responding to pressing community needs, devotes her practice to performing basic dentistry on children? Are politicians who go on to lucrative careers after serving the interests of the rich and powerful really more socially valuable than those who have minimal career prospects after political careers championing the rights of the poor and challenging the status quo? It's hard to see much of a moral principle in a system that rewards people on the basis of how much they're willing or able to pander to the rich.

The flaws in neoclassical economic theory are more evident now than ever, given today's frenzy of pay at the top. Joseph Stiglitz, the Nobel Prize–winning economist, points to the discrepancy between the huge pay of the Wall Street crowd and that of the late agronomist Norman Borlaug, who saved millions of lives by developing methods for improving agricultural productivity: "If neo-classical theory were correct, Borlaug would have been among the wealthiest men in the world, while our bankers would have been lining up at soup kitchens." Stiglitz notes that there appears to be no justification for today's top earners receiving so much more than those who performed similar functions in the recent past. He doubts that the difference is due to any superior skills or talents on the part of the current managerial class. "Does anyone really believe that America's bank officers suddenly became so much more productive, relative to everyone else in society, that they deserve the huge compensation increases they have received in recent years?"[10]


Clearly, if we just consider social contribution, it is hard to make the case that John Paulson deserves his fortune. But there's a fallback argument used to justify large wealth accumulations, often made by the rich themselves. It goes like this: I deserve my money because I earned it. According to this line of argument, as long as John Paulson made his money without breaking any laws—and he has perhaps just gotten in under the wire on this one—the money is deservedly his.

The notion that a person has "earned" his income is based then merely on staying within the laws. But an individual's income is to a large extent simply a product of the particular set of laws that happen to be in place at that time and in that jurisdiction. So, for instance, if financial markets had been more tightly regulated—as they clearly should have been—Paulson wouldn't have made nearly as much money as he did in 2007. He made his money in CDOs and CDSs, which are part of the largely unregulated derivatives market.

As noted earlier, there were serious attempts to regulate this market in the 1990s, particularly by Brooksley Born, then head of the Commodity Futures Trading Commission, the agency responsible for derivatives. While Born's commission regulated certain derivatives traded on exchanges, it had virtually no control over the kinds of custom-made derivatives that Paulson, Goldman Sachs, and AIG were concocting. Born felt there was a need to regulate these as well, but her efforts in this direction were strongly resisted, not just by Wall Street but by high-ranking government officials with close ties to Wall Street, including Federal Reserve chairman Alan Greenspan. With such powerful forces lined up against regulation, Congress even took the unusual step of actually passing a law that prohibited Born's commission from regulating custom-made derivatives. Had Congress been less beholden to Wall Street (which donates heavily to congressional campaigns) and permitted Born's commission to regulate this highly volatile field of financial speculation, things would have likely turned out very differently, and John Paulson would have probably remained a rather minor figure in the hedge fund business. He was able to collect $3.7 billion in 2007 only because powerful players were able to block badly needed laws regulating the derivates market. This reality seems to undermine the strength of any moral claim that he "earned" the money.

Similarly, Bill Gates's ability to "earn" his fortune was partly determined by the weak set of laws protecting copyrights in the newly emerging field of computer innovations in the 1980s. Had today's more rigorous legal standards been in force back then, Gary Kildall would have had strong grounds to sue Gates for copyright infringement, according to writer Harold Evans.[11] If Kildall had prevailed in such a lawsuit, Gates would almost certainly not be sitting on a fortune of $53 billion today. Rather, he might be making a comfortable—but unspectacular—living as a software entrepreneur, along with thousands of other individuals with similarly impressive computer skills.

So the notion that a billionaire deserves his fortune because he "earned" it rests on a rather weak moral foundation. The laws that made his fortune possible are the product of the biases and whims of judges who shape the common law, and of legislators who often succumb to pressure and financial rewards from wealthy interest groups. Indeed, as we see in the Paulson case, the laws that enabled him to get hugely rich were simply the product of the enormous political leverage exercised by powerful players on Wall Street.

Perhaps the more basic moral question is this: Can extreme inequality be justified? The richest 9.5 million people—0.14 percent of the world's population—control about one quarter of its assets.[12] What is the moral basis for allowing such a vast amount of the planet's bounty to be held in so few hands? By what right do a mere handful of individuals manage to horde such a large share of the earth's resources?

In much earlier times, these sorts of questions didn't really emerge, because people's circumstances in life were considered beyond human control. Medieval nobles enjoyed coddled lives while peasants struggled to survive, but there was little concern about justifying such discrepancies. A person's station in life—and the bounty (or lack of bounty) that went with it—were thought to be determined by birth, as part of God's plan. It was therefore everyone's duty, according to medieval thought, to simply submit to God's will and accept one's fate.

All that changed, however, with the transition to the Enlightenment and the modern era. Things that had simply been accepted in earlier times now had to be justified. Inequality was one of those things that seemed to cry out for justification. Why did some people have so much more than others? Since the gap between the pleasurable lives of the rich and the wretched lives of the poor could no longer just be attributed to a plan ordained by the Almighty, rational justification was now required. Enter John Locke, justifier extraordinaire.

Writing in the 1680s, the renowned English philosopher set out arguments that were to become the basis of the modern world's acceptance of inequality. It's worth reviewing them here, partly to highlight some contradictions in them, and also to show how Locke's position has been misrepresented in an attempt to expand and strengthen the case for inequality.

Locke argued that, while land and resources were originally given by God to "mankind in common," the result of this joint bequest isn't that property is held by all, but rather that it is held by none. However, Locke insists that this can be changed. If an individual applies his own labor to the property, he adds something of value to it, and in so doing develops a legitimate claim to its exclusive ownership: "It hath by this labor something annexed to it that excludes the common right."

There is something intuitively appealing about Locke's reasoning, which perhaps explains why it has resonated so deeply in Western minds for more than three centuries. He is arguing that human labor, or more broadly human effort, is what justifies property ownership. This seems fair and even empowering, since humans have control over their own labor. If they are willing to put forth effort and exert themselves with the sweat of their brows, they can obtain property. What could be fairer? What a wonderful leap forward from the medieval world, where peasants were stuck in their lowly, impoverished station, on God's orders, no matter how hard they were willing to toil!

But Locke had left out society. In focusing exclusively on the rights of the individual, he brushed aside the rights of everyone else. After suggesting that land and resources were given to "mankind in common," he simply discards the collective nature of the bequest. To observers today, this may seem reasonable, since we're so used to ignoring the broader rights of society in favor of individual rights. But in the seventeenth century, such an approach involved a deliberate omission, an intentional denial of the rights of the many. Traditionally, peasants had enjoyed "common rights" to the land, where they were legally permitted to graze their cattle and forage for wood, peat, berries, and the leftover produce of the harvest. Locke was suggesting wiping out these historic "common rights" and allowing individuals to claim exclusive rights. Political theorist C. B. Macpherson pointed out that in an earlier period there had been two kinds of property rights: the right to exclude others and the right not to be excluded by others. This second one—the right not to be excluded—established a right of access to property. But under the system proposed by Locke—which became the norm in the market economy—only the first right survived. As Macpherson put it: "The very idea of property was narrowed to cover only the right to exclude others."[13]

This was a huge change that swept away the rights of countless people—people who were poor and powerless and "of no importance to anyone but themselves," as historian E. P. Thompson memorably put it. Peasants responded with spontaneous protests and attempts in the dark of night to sabotage the planting of hedges and building of fences aimed at keeping them off the newly privatized land—protests that continued in various forms over several centuries. But since peasants don't get to record history or shape the public debate, their rights were simply eliminated, and have been largely forgotten in the mists of time. Still, the consequence of the removal of these rights is worth pausing over. Political theorist Anatole Anton argues that the "right of exclusion" that Locke championed is a right that "defies moral justification"—or at the very least requires some serious explaining, which Locke never really provides. "Taking something from a group and giving it to a single person . . . cries out to the democratic sensibility for reasons," writes Anton. "Private property, from a democratic point of view, amounts to the surrender of democratic control of social resources to private individuals. Surrender might be the right thing to do, but surely some good reasons ought to be given for so doing."[14]

Locke's justification is based on the transformative power of individual labor that, as noted, has some considerable intuitive appeal. But then Locke goes on to develop the argument in a way that seems to weaken his case considerably: "Thus, the grass my horse has bit, the turfs my servant has cut and the ore I have dug in any place where I have a right to them in common with others, become my property." Well, surely, it's one thing for Locke's prototypical man to make a claim to the ore that he has dug with his own labor, but quite another to claim ownership of the product of his servant's labor. Wouldn't that logically belong to the servant? For that matter, how did the servant end up a servant? And how did the horse come to be in this guy's possession, to form part of his property? If we're supposedly starting from basic principles, examining the legitimacy of the case for private property, how does Locke's prototypical man already happen to own a horse and be in command of the services of a servant? With this looser notion of one's labor—to include labor done by others inexplicably under one's command—Locke's invocation of the transformative power of labor loses some of its intuitive appeal.

However, Locke's words were a godsend to those favoring a more market-oriented arrangement of society. Indeed, they have become a cornerstone argument used to justify capitalism. By suggesting that human labor is the basis for private property, Locke gave private ownership an apparently compelling moral legitimacy rooted in the human realm, no longer reliant on the authority of God. And the fact that Locke deftly expanded the definition of labor to include work done by one's servant and horse meant that private property accumulations weren't limited to work that one could physically carry out oneself. Without this limitation, the possibilities seemed endless: one could hire a legion of servants (or factory workers) and use dozens of horses (or machines), and then lay claim to the product of the collective sweats of all of their brows! There was no limit to the private fortune one could accumulate—all within the umbrella of moral legitimacy set out by Locke. It was clearly no more than a hop, skip, and a jump to the world of Bill Gates.

It's not hard to see why Locke has been celebrated as a seminal thinker by those keen on capitalism and its inequalities. However, in reality, Locke didn't simply ignore the fact that allowing individuals to accumulate private property has repercussions for others and possibly compromises their rights. In fact, he included a caveat to the effect that someone could claim property as his own—only provided that there was "enough and as good" left over for others. Needless to say, this changes things significantly; it makes the acquisition of private property conditional on the availability of comparable resources and opportunities for others. What about land and nonrenewable resources? Clearly, eventually, there wouldn't be "enough and as good" of these vital commodities left over for others; certainly all the available arable land would quickly be claimed, and that eventuality would come all the quicker under the expanded definition of labor, in which an individual could employ a large workforce and modern machinery to use up a finite resource. If Locke's caveat is to be taken seriously, his justification for private ownership turns out to be rather limited in scope, and does not provide much of a moral basis for the amassing of huge private fortunes. This probably explains why pro-market theorists, citing Locke to justify the legitimacy of large property accumulations, have mostly just ignored the caveat.

Like Locke, most of the major theorists who have contemplated issues of distributive justice have insisted on caveats when it comes to the rights of individuals to accumulate large fortunes. John Stuart Mill, Thomas Paine, Leonard T. Hobhouse, and Jacques Turgot all argued that much of an individual's wealth is actually owed back to the community. John Rawls, the leading theorist of political liberalism, only condones the accumulation of great fortunes if it can be shown that this benefits the poorest members of society. Rawls and other liberal as well as progressive thinkers clearly have some serious reservations about extreme inequality, refusing to accept its moral legitimacy unless it can be shown to provide benefits throughout society, particularly to those most excluded from the bounty. In fact, virtually all the major theorists in the field of distributive justice have been unenthusiastic about large inequalities.

The only exceptions are modern conservative thinkers, sometimes loosely called neoconservatives, who began to rise to prominence in the late 1970s. Whereas other theorists from Locke through to modern liberals and progressives offer only conditional support for extreme inequality, neoconservatives treat wealth accumulation—in unlimited amounts—as a natural human right, essentially free of conditions or qualification. In their formulation, society and its entitlements all but disappear as the individual moves front and center and is endowed with huge natural entitlement to the fruits of the earth.

The leading theorist of this modern conservative school is libertarian Robert Nozick, whose influential 1974 book *Anarchy, State, and Utopia* became the intellectual underpinning of the recent conservative movement. Nozick discards the Lockean notion that an individual only becomes entitled to property by applying her labor to it. Nozick's lack of interest in the centrality of labor is striking. For most people, this is the aspect of Locke's concept of property rights that is the most appealing, since it suggests that human toil and effort should be the grounds for entitlement—a principle that seems eminently fair. Instead, Nozick assumes that an individual has some sort of natural right to claim property, as long as no one else has a prior entitlement to it. (This seems to beg the question of where the original entitlement comes from. Nozick simply insists that the property must be fairly acquired. But how so?)

But it is in his treatment of the rights of others and the broader society that Nozick and other modern conservatives really move away from traditional theories of distributive justice. Recall Locke's important caveat that an individual can only appropriate a piece of property if that leaves "enough and as good" for others. Nozick reduces this standard to insist only that others not be left worse off by someone gaining title to a piece of property. Of course, even this lesser standard would seem to impose some constraints. If an individual claims a piece of land, for instance, he is clearly leaving others worse off, since they can no longer claim that same piece of land. However, Nozick insists that, except in very unusual circumstances—such as someone owning the only water hole in a desert—an individual's appropriation of property does not leave others worse off. He reaches this odd conclusion by assuming that the property appropriated would otherwise simply remain unused and would attract no interest from others.[15] This assumption is is bizarre and seems based on a peculiar conception of human behavior. Of course, if the goal is to come up with a moral justification for unlimited personal acquisition, it is necessary to assume such acquisition is harmless to others, and that's what Nozick does, even though it obliges him to make some odd assumptions.

Nozick goes on to further justify inequality by arguing that, whatever the gap between the fortunes of those at the top and the bottom, as long as these different holdings are the result of arrangements freely entered into on both sides, without coercion, there isn't a problem. In other words, workers may earn a fraction of what their boss earns, but as long as they freely agreed to that situation—by accepting their jobs—then all is fine. But just because there is no overt coercion doesn't mean there aren't subtle but very real forms of compulsion. For instance, the workers may have had little choice but to accept the jobs offered, because they were hungry and there was no other work available. Or more broadly, they may have had little choice because of the power wielded by employers and the ability this gives employers to shape the economic rules in their favor, such as keeping minimum wages low or placing restrictions on the right to unionize. Similarly, consumers may have no choice but to pay an exorbitantly high price for a product—say, a vital prescription drug—because a company holds an exclusive patent on it. Power, discrimination, and monopoly are huge, largely hidden factors that oblige people to "freely" accept terms that may amount to coercion in all but name.

The neoconservatives' intense focus on the right to private property is, in itself, revealing. It allegedly springs from a deep respect for the rights of the individual. But why limit the notion of the individual's natural rights to that of property ownership and economic entitlements in the marketplace? Why not assume the individual also has a natural right to the fulfillment of basic social needs—such as, say, access to a decent education or adequate health services? When it comes to defining natural rights, neoconservatives seem to care fiercely—but exclusively—about the individual's entitlement to property, and his right to accumulate unlimited amounts of wealth.

Our winner-take-all reward system is based on the idea that there are uniquely gifted or talented individuals whose social contribution is so great that they deserve infinite financial rewards. But this formulation ignores the reality that wealth generation is only possible because of the massive contribution of society, stretching all the way back to the beginning of the Stone Age. Since billionaires are now deemed to have made it on their own, they are also said to owe little back to society. Indeed, the whole notion of responsibility to society has been so denigrated that billionaires are considered deserving of their fortunes when they contribute next to nothing to society—or even when they directly imperil the public interest.

# CHAPTER 7

# Hank Aaron and the Myths about Motivation

On a warm evening in April 1974, Hank Aaron thrilled a packed Atlanta baseball stadium when he slugged a massive home run deep into left field, beating Babe Ruth's long-standing lifetime record of 714 home runs. Over the next few years, Aaron would go on to hit another 40 home runs, earning him the title Home Run King, as well as setting career records for runs batted in, total bases, and extra base hits, and establishing him as one of the greatest baseball players of all time.

For his dazzling efforts, Aaron was paid $200,000 a year, making him the highest-paid baseball player of the early 1970s. Today, the king of baseball is Alex Rodriguez of the New York Yankees. Rodriguez has his own set of impressive statistics, leading the major leagues in categories for home runs, runs scored, and runs batted in, as well as total bases and extra base hits. For this, Rodriguez earned $32 million in 2011. Adjusting for inflation (but not for steroids), that makes Rodriguez's pay more than thirty-five times higher than Aaron's. Yet it would be hard to argue that his performance is more than thirty times better.

Certainly, it's clear that Hank Aaron was a thoroughly motivated player who achieved spectacular results. The fact that his salary was a mere fraction of what equivalent players earn today suggests that the extra pay may be unnecessary as a motivating factor.

In fact, there's little evidence that today's phenomenal pay packages—in sports, entertainment, business, and finance—are more effective in motivating today's players, performers, or executives than the more modest packages were a few decades ago. For that matter, there's precious little evidence that today's performances are even any better. Can anyone seriously make the case that today's top entertainment superstars—Lady Gaga, Justin Timberlake, George Clooney—are noticeably superior (or superior at all) to Judy Garland, Frank Sinatra, Gregory Peck?

And when we look at the world of business, the case for today's supersized pay at the top seems even more tenuous, if not preposterous. In 1950, for instance, General Motors paid CEO Charlie Wilson $586,000 (the highest CEO salary at the time, worth about $5 million in today's dollars) for managing what was then a thriving, highly profitable company, widely considered America's leading corporation. In 2007, General Motors paid CEO Rick Wagoner $15.7 million—even as the company he headed suffered a $39 billion loss. So GM paid roughly three times as much in 2007 to get results that were infinitely worse.

Examples like this abound in business and the financial world. Indeed, the 2008 Wall Street meltdown has brought the disconnect between executive performance and executive pay into sharp, tragicomic relief. Wall Street firms paid out a staggering $18.4 billion in executive bonuses in the early months of 2008, even as many of those firms collapsed in bankruptcy or were only saved by government bailouts. Merrill Lynch, for instance, earned no profit in the 2007 and 2008 financial years, yet paid out $30 billion in bonuses for those years.

The winner-take-all phenomenon of gigantic pay packages at the top has become the norm in a wide range of fields today, in a way that it wasn't a few decades ago. While the results may seem bizarre or even ludicrous, the skewing of income sharply toward the top has been a key factor in contributing to the rise of a new class of multimillionaires and billionaires. The rationale behind it has been central to the neoconservative case justifying today's extreme inequality. Indeed, it's the fallback position when the first part of the argument—that the rich deserve their fortunes—turns out to be riddled with holes. Okay, so even if the rich don't deserve their fortunes, these huge rewards are necessary, we're told, to create the motivation for the most talented individuals to perform at exceptional levels, so that the economy will function at optimal efficiency and we'll all gain.

It is almost an article of faith among conservative economists and commentators that anything that diminishes the size of the financial rewards for society's most talented members—such as high taxes—saps them of their motivation to work at full capacity, thereby impeding the overall growth of the economy. The proposition that high taxes are detrimental to growth and prosperity is so widely accepted that it is put forward as if it's self-evident.

This near-certainty is particularly odd since there is almost no evidence to back up such a contention, and much evidence that contradicts it. By looking at recent American history, we can compare what happened under two very different scenarios. In the postwar period (from the end of World War II until 1980), high marginal tax rates at the upper end effectively limited the amount of income that an individual could receive. After 1980, there was little restraint on large incomes. If the neoconservatives were correct about the important motivational effect that financial incentives have on performance, then the high-tax period would presumably have discouraged top performance and resulted in lower economic growth. Yet, if we look at the evidence, no such thing happened.

Tax rates on high-income earners were extremely high in the early postwar years, with the top marginal rate consistently above 80 percent (and above 90 percent most of the time) during the first two decades, from 1944 to 1964. After that, the top rate dropped to 70 percent, then down to 50 percent in 1980.[1] It plunged further in the Reagan years, falling all the way down to 28 percent in 1988. During the Clinton administration, it was pushed back up to 39 percent, but then eased back down to 35 percent under George W. Bush.

If high taxes act as a disincentive to work, then presumably the very high taxes on high-income people in those early postwar decades would have had a stifling effect on economic growth. But exactly the opposite happened. Productivity—the true measure of economic progress—grew at an annual rate of 3.1 percent in the 1950s, '60s, and early '70s. And it has grown at a significantly slower rate since then. Economists Joel Slemrod and Jon Bakija draw attention to this apparent paradox: "The strong growth periods were the periods when the top tax rates were the highest."[2]

We're not trying to make the case that high marginal tax rates encourage economic growth, but simply that the evidence doesn't support the assertion that they discourage it. Indeed, the evidence seems to contradict the widely held notion that high taxes on top earners lessen their motivation to work and therefore have a detrimental effect on the country's economic performance. (Another possibility is that the contribution of the top earners isn't as important as it's chalked up to be and really doesn't have much impact on overall economic growth—in which case there may not be any economic reason not to tax these people more heavily.)

If we look at the contemporary international evidence, we find a similar picture. It's widely believed that America's relatively low tax rates are key to its success in the global economy, and that countries with high tax rates have more trouble competing and therefore experience slower growth. But once again, the evidence doesn't bear this out.

The ability to make meaningful cross-country comparisons has improved significantly in the last decade due to the increased availability of data. And as this improved data from OECD (Organisation for Economic Co-operation and Development) countries shows, there is no clear correlation between high tax levels and economic growth. It's true that some of the world's most prosperous nations, such as the United States and Japan, have low tax levels. But other nations, most notably the Scandinavian ones, have had stellar economic performances with much higher tax ratios. As Slemrod and Bakija point out: "That Sweden could maintain a 2000 GDP per capita of $24,779—6 percent above the OECD average, in the face of a whopping 54.2 percent tax-to-income ratio—challenges the hypothesis that high taxes are a sure cause of economic decline."[3] Other leading public finance scholars reviewing the international data have come to similar conclusions.[4]

So the data doesn't support the argument that large incentives at the top are necessary to encourage economic growth. It should also be noted that, even if it could be shown that such incentives do promote growth, there is a further prong to the argument that would need to be proved: that overall economic growth benefits society as a whole, as opposed to simply rewarding those at the top. But the evidence for any broadly shared benefits is even weaker. During the most recent U.S. business cycle, from 1989 to 2006, a staggering 91 percent of all income growth went to the top-earning 10 percent of households, with a hefty 59 percent going to just the top 1 percent. The bottom 90 percent of households received a meager 9 percent of all the income growth. Indeed, from 1979 to 2006, the bottom 90 percent saw their share of the national income decline, while the share enjoyed by the top 1 percent increased by 204 percent, and that of the top .01 percent went up by a phenomenal 425 percent.[5]

The most thorough recent empirical study on this issue found little evidence to support the notion that a rising tide lifts all boats. The study, by Harvard's Dan Andrews and Christopher Jencks and Australia National University's Andrew Leigh, looked at almost a century of data for twelve industrialized countries and found that, while higher gains at the top appear to lead to a small increase in growth, "it is difficult to be sure from our estimates whether the bottom 90 percent will really be better off or not."[6] The authors concluded that the bottom 90 percent are likely to be much better off if growth is slow and equal, rather than rapid and unequal. Their findings were perhaps best summarized in the headline reporting their study in the *Wall Street Journal*: "Trickledown Economics Fails to Deliver as Promised."[7]

So rather than supporting the "trickle-down theory," the evidence leads to the commonsense conclusion that policies aimed at benefiting the rich do precisely that, and no more.

·     ·     ·

If there's little hard evidence to bolster the economic case for large incentives at the top, this isn't really surprising, once the theoretical arguments are examined. According to the neoconservatives—and indeed to most mainstream economists—high marginal tax rates have the effect of discouraging those in the top income brackets from working harder to earn more income, since this income will be taxed at higher rates. For example, if a corporate lawyer can earn $1,000 for an extra hour of work, and faces a tax rate of 30 percent, that will leave her with $700 after tax, making it worth her while to work the extra hour. If the tax rate is instead, say, 60 percent, leaving her with only $400 after tax, she might well decide to go home and watch TV instead.

It's easy to see how this argument gains traction. At face value, it seems intuitively correct. The lawyer works to earn income; the more she is paid, the more she is motivated to work. If taxes reduce her pay significantly, she is going to be less motivated to work. That's certainly logical. On that other hand, it seems just as likely that high taxes could have exactly the opposite effect. The lawyer works to earn income. If that income is reduced significantly by taxes, she will work longer to make up for the loss, because she wants to maintain an elevated standard of living. Both explanations make sense, and both fit with observations of human behavior. And yet it is the first argument—the one that justifies low taxes for high-income earners—that is generally advanced by economists.

The truth is, human motivation and behavior are infinitely more complicated, nuanced, and variable than a straightforward version presented in economic arguments. In the formulation of standard neoclassical economics, the prototypical human (*Homo economicus*) is deeply motivated to satisfy his appetite for material goods. Although he would rather avoid work, he can be enticed into doing it if he is rewarded with income, since that allows him to increase his consumption of material goods.

One can understand why economists have chosen such a one-dimensional, mechanistic character as Homo economicus as their central player. Clearly, they need to simplify human behavior into predictable and knowable patterns in order to present economics as a hard science—rather than just another social science, where findings are acknowledged to be somewhat subjective and arbitrary. But while it's understandable that economists want their findings to be treated as authoritative, it's doubtful whether human behavior really fits into the paradigm they offer. Yes, the human appetite for consumption is real, and potentially huge. But it's clearly not the only thing that motivates humans to do the things they do. Many critics have charged that such a simplistic human prototype as Homo economicus—which has become the model on which our entire economic system is based—is nothing more than a convenient but fairly meaningless cartoon character.

Evidence in the fields of psychology and other social sciences suggest that the actual motives and behavior of real-life people are quite different from those of Homo economicus. Robert E. Lane, a political scientist at Yale University, reviewed more than a thousand studies of human behavior related to the economy for his book *The Market Experience.* Lane concluded that the way people actually behave bears little resemblance to the greedy, consumption-oriented conduct assumed by standard economic theory. Indeed, a vast array of studies shows that, once people achieve a basic material standard of living, economic factors greatly decline as important sources of happiness and satisfaction and are superseded in importance by factors such as family, friendship, self-esteem, and a sense of personal and intellectual development.[8] Or as economist Robert H. Frank put it in his book *Luxury Fever:* "Behavioral scientists find that once a threshold level of affluence is reached, the average level of human well-being in a country is almost completely independent of its stock of material consumption goods."[9]

Before we move on to what really does matter to people who live comfortably above the breadline, it's worth pausing here to note briefly what goes on below the breadline. As Frank observes: "Most careful studies find a clear relationship over time between subjective well-being and absolute income at extremely low levels of absolute income."[10] In other words, while human wants and desires may become more varied and complex once basic needs are secured, until this happens, people are primarily motivated to meet their basic material needs, without which they enjoy little life comfort or satisfaction. Perhaps the crude Homo economicus model, if it has any validity, is most useful as a model of behavior for those at the bottom of the economic heap. This raises the question of whether the argument about higher pay leading to greater work effort might be most applicable to very low-income workers, who, after all, are typically stuck doing work that is dull, routine, and offers little opportunity for creativity. In such cases, the amount of pay looms particularly large. Such workers don't just badly need money to meet the most basic human needs, but also to compensate for the lack of other job-related satisfactions. For a hotel cleaner earning $10 an hour, for instance, an extra $1.75 an hour would make a significant difference.

Interestingly, however, the argument about higher pay being necessary for greater motivation is primarily used to justify lower taxes on the rich, not on the poor—even though the arguments seem to apply better to the poor. Indeed, in the case of the poor, the opposite argument is often made—that too much income will cause them to slack off. Hence the need to keep welfare and unemployment insurance benefits low, lest those at the lower end be encouraged to remain idle.

But let's get back to the rich. If we follow the logic mentioned above, we could conclude that higher pay might seem least likely to work as a motivator in the case of those with big incomes. First of all, they already have ample income—so ample, in the case of billionaires and near-billionaires, that pay increases or decreases are unlikely to have any effect on how much they consume, since they are already presumably consuming as much as they possibly can (or care to). Secondly, and more importantly, unlike the hotel cleaner, those at the top of their professions enjoy a level of work satisfaction that is, quite simply, immense. Additional pay might induce the hotel cleaner to spend that extra hour cleaning up after others, but there is no shortage of nonmonetary benefits that provide additional motivation for the business executive to work late to close a big deal, or for the rock star to do an encore in front of a stadium full of delirious fans, or for the baseball player to hit a home run with the bases loaded in the bottom of the ninth.

In fact, the world of work—particularly self-directed, challenging work that one happens to be very good at—offers a stunning array of satisfactions that deliver rewards at the most primal human level. Psychological studies have established that the most basic human psychological needs—for a sense of self, a sense of personal competence, and for self-esteem—are very often tied in closely with one's work. "People's favorable attitudes towards themselves are their most treasured property; in many ways, these are the maximand on which all their other values and motives rest," observes Lane.[11] Work is a crucial way in which people achieve favorable attitudes of themselves, since it gives them a sense of their own competence and ability to function in the world. Pay is an important part of this—but primarily as a proxy for these more basic psychological rewards. Notes Lane: "In the end, all economic behavior is energized and guided by the pursuit of a sense of personal effectiveness, self-esteem and self-consistency"—that is, a sense of an integrated personal identity.

Considering all this, Homo economicus may amount to a serious misrepresentation, if not an outright distortion, of the human personality. In the Homo economicus model, work is considered an undesirable activity—a "disutility," in economic parlance—that humans would rather avoid but perform as a means to earn income so that they can have the pleasure of consuming material goods. This may well be true when the work is cleaning toilets. However, particularly at the upper level, work is often an exceptionally desirable activity in itself—one that offers deeply satisfying rewards that are far more important than consumption.

So it seems unlikely that reducing the pay rewards of the very rich would stifle their desire to work. It's obvious that the most talented individuals in any field are motivated by far more than money. Even billionaires readily admit that money isn't their only or even their primary objective. Leo J. Hindery Jr., the sports cable TV entrepreneur, confided to the *New York Times* that he would have worked just as hard for a much smaller payoff. Wall Street banker Sanford Weill also acknowledged that "I worked because I loved what I was doing." Weill said that he didn't even really know how much he'd made until he retired and had "a chance to sit back and count up what was on the table." Similarly, Kenneth C. Griffin, who received more than $1 billion in 2006 as chairman of hedge fund Citadel Investment Group, commented that "wealth is not a particularly satisfying outcome. . . . The money is a byproduct of a passionate endeavour."[12]

For that matter, some of history's most talented individuals who have made some of the greatest contributions to society have had little trouble performing without much in the way of financial incentives. Norman Borlaug, who saved millions of lives by developing methods for improving agricultural productivity, spent most of his life living modestly in Third World villages. Vincent van Gogh somehow found the motivation to produce hundreds of works of great art, even though he managed to sell only one of them in his lifetime, receiving a pittance for it just before he died. And William Shakespeare was inspired to produce perhaps the greatest dramas of all time without even the prospect that they'd become Hollywood blockbusters.

None of this is meant to imply that financial incentives don't matter. They clearly do—particularly at the lower levels, where workers need powerful inducements to get them to perform work that is often dreary, repetitive, unpleasant, and unrewarding. And they also matter at the upper levels. While the deep psychological satisfactions of work may matter most, money does act as a proxy for these rewards. Earning an income reinforces an individual's sense of personal competency and self-esteem. Earning a large income greatly reinforces an individual's sense of personal competency and self-esteem, leaving him with very pleasantly favorable attitudes toward himself.

Financial incentives act as powerful motivators that encourage effort, diligence, creativity, and just plain hard work in people at all levels. The question is, How much is enough to provide the crucial level of motivation? If even some billionaires are willing to confess that they would have worked just as hard for less, it might be worth considering whether society could pay them less—or tax back significantly more of what they receive—without diminishing their incentive to work.

And here another important psychological factor comes into play: what seems to matter most to people, once they get above the breadline, isn't how big their compensation is, but how it compares to the compensation of others. Karl Marx observed this human characteristic when he pointed out, "A house may be large or small; as long as the surrounding houses are equally small, it satisfies all social demands for a dwelling. But if a palace rises beside the little house, the little house shrinks into a hut."[13] Robert Frank made a similar observation: "The middle-class professional who lives in Manhattan is unlikely to be burdened by dissatisfaction that her apartment has no room for a Ping-Pong table or wine cellar, and she almost certainly entertains no expectation of having a swimming pool. Yet that same woman living in a Westchester county suburb might not even consider a house that lacked these amenities." In other words, it's not the absolute size of the material reward that matters, but how that reward stacks up against the material rewards of others—where it puts the individual in the pecking order. As Frank says: "Evidence from the large scientific literature on the determinants of subjective well-being consistently suggests that we have strong concerns about relative position."[14]

This emphasis on relative positioning is backed up by centuries of philosophical thought and observation. As early as the fourth century BC, Aristotle noted that humans are, above all, social animals who naturally seek to relate to and engage with other humans. They feel the need to be part of a larger human community in which they enjoy the acceptance and good opinion of others. Receiving pay for work is a key way that people in our society can establish their place in the community, by proving their competency and worthiness.

So what matters most about a pay package is not its absolute size but how it measures up against others. This perhaps explains why, in the early postwar years, business executives, entertainers, and sports stars were motivated to perform very well—indeed just as well as, if not better than, today's much higher-paid equivalents do. Although their absolute pay levels were much smaller back then, they were still paid very, very well relative to others at the time. It was this gap between them and others in their world—which gave them an elevated status in their community—that served as the stimulant to high performance.

Of course, now that the gap between the top and the bottom is so much bigger today, isn't the stimulus for high performance all the greater? Probably. But how much stimulus can productively be harnessed? What if Hank Aaron was performing the very best he possibly could when he broke those major league records? What would have been gained by topping up his salary to thirty times its already extremely high level?

Current thinking in our winner-take-all culture would suggest that the added financial incentive would have driven Aaron all the harder, so that he might have performed even more spectacularly. Possibly. Or perhaps he'd already gone to the bottom of the well of his capabilities. Who knows? But certainly this raises some questions, such as, Is the extra bit of performance—if it could be coaxed out of him through massively higher pay—really worth the extra cost?

The stupendous paychecks of those at the very top may be creating serious distortions, not just in some people's lives but more broadly in the economy. If Hank Aaron's 1974 salary was sufficient to push him to perform stunning baseball feats, what is the effect of making that financial incentive thirty times larger? It's possible that it makes no difference, that what drives top baseball players to spectacular achievement is the thrill of being regarded as the best in the world at something they love, in which case topping up their pay so handsomely is simply a needless and foolish squandering of money. On the other hand, it's possible the increased pay does have an effect, not only in attracting many more participants to compete for a prize that only a few can win, but also in placing ever more pressure on those trying to grab Hank Aaron's crown. Could this additional pressure perhaps explain why so many professional athletes, unable to do any better on their own, turn to steroids and other performance-enhancing drugs? Is there really any other way to continually improve upon the performances of the equally talented players who went before them? Are top athletes on a treadmill where they can't possibly go any faster but are willing to try anything—including cheating—to reach new heights, goaded on by the sheer enormity of the stimulus dangled in front of them?

In the age of winner-take-all compensation, a similar propensity for cheating seems to have infected the upper levels of the business and financial worlds. It's worth considering whether the mindset that led Wall Street types to abandon all sanity and morality—mixing together toxic brews of junk mortgages, car loans, and credit card debts and then selling pieces of these sickly concoctions to unknowing "investors"—is partly the result of the overstimulation of their greed impulses.

When the broader public first became aware of collateral debt obligations and credit default swaps during the financial meltdown in the fall of 2008, the most common reaction was bewilderment. The hypercharged Wall Street world was so removed from the regular world most people inhabit—where pay bears some relationship to hours worked, effort, and results—that it seemed baffling and indecipherable. How did grown men and women make decisions that were not just over-the-top greedy but were so evidently irresponsible and threatening to the well-being of so many others, including themselves? One possibility was that the billion-dollar compensation packages on view all around them had simply stimulated their hypothalamuses to the point of mental, physical, and moral exhaustion, encouraging them to risk everything for the billion-dollar prize, without which life had become almost meaningless. The point is not to excuse their behavior, but rather to raise questions about what role excessive financial rewards may have played in encouraging it. If the effect of extreme financial stimulation is to encourage greedy-bordering-on-dysfunctional behavior, then the large financial rewards of our winner-take-all compensation system may not just be unnecessary, but actually destructive.

It's commonly argued, of course, that companies need to pay high salaries to attract the most talented individuals and keep them from going to competitors. So while it may be true that a lower-paid ballplayer would be just as motivated to hit that bases-loaded home run in the bottom of the ninth, he would probably be enticed by an offer to move to another team that would pay him more. In a competitive free market, then, high pay is necessary to ensure that companies and organizations can attract the best talent so that they can function optimally.

It should immediately be noted that this argument in no way refutes the desirability of imposing high taxes on large incomes. High taxes would not, for instance, prevent teams from attracting the best players by offering gigantic pay packages. Teams could pay as much as they wanted to—and the players could still go to the highest bidder. Only after all this is resolved, and everyone is out playing ball, would taxes kick in. The high marginal rates would not interfere at all in the selection process, since they would only apply after the fact and would apply the same to all (this is the beauty of tax rates; they are neutral, applying the same set of rules to everyone).

It should also be noted that while high pay in sports and entertainment may be the result of highly competitive markets, this is less true in the world of business and finance. Of course, businesspeople and financiers make similar arguments—that huge rewards are necessary to attract the best talent. Indeed, this has been the corporate world's main justification for continuing to lavishly reward CEOs and top executives: top talent can command top dollar; that's just the way the free market works.

But on closer examination, it turns out that CEO pay is determined less by the workings of the free market (a misleading concept at the best of times) and more by the power wielded by those at the top of the business and financial world. One of the ways this plutocracy has exercised the extraordinary power it's achieved in recent years has been to drive up its own pay to astronomical heights. This has been easy to accomplish because executive pay is determined by corporate boards of directors, which are typically made up mostly of other, similarly positioned executives—people who are often friends, colleagues, former classmates from MBA courses, or simply associates who frequent the same golf clubs or art auctions as those whose pay is being judged. As a vehicle for determining pay, these corporate boards are more like cozy clubs than bodies likely to render meaningful, arm's-length market assessments.

Ostensibly, of course, corporate boards represent shareholders. So they theoretically represent a large number of people and interests. In reality, however, shareholder elections are pretty much insider events, particularly in cases where there are large numbers of shareholders who are unlikely to be sufficiently organized to challenge the dominant management group. It's even rare to have a competing slate in a shareholder election. One notable critic of the compensation system is Richard Posner, a U.S. Court of Appeals judge and senior lecturer at the University of Chicago Law School. As Posner bluntly puts it: "Shareholder election of directors resembles the system of voting in the Soviet Union and other totalitarian nations."[15]

Even leaving aside the actual friendships and close associations between members of the board and those they are assessing, there is an additional potential conflict of interest. "A board of directors is likely to be dominated by highly paid business executives, including CEOs of other companies," writes Posner. "They have a conflict of interest, since they have a financial stake in high corporate salaries, their own salaries being determined in part by the salaries paid to persons in comparable positions in other companies." Added to that personal conflict of interest is the likelihood that these executives will regard the high level of compensation going to themselves and those they are judging as an appropriate reflection of the intrinsic worthiness of corporate executives.

The problem becomes circular, since the CEO of a company influences the selection of its directors, who then determine the CEO's compensation. If the directors authorize a large compensation package for the CEO who has put them in place, that CEO is likely to appreciate the important contribution the directors are making and support generous directors' fees. The CEO and his team also select the company's auditors, who certify the company's financial statements. If the CEO is pleased by the auditors' report, he might well retain these same auditors to provide consulting services, under which the auditors might steer underwriting contracts to investment banks, whose securities analysts give the company very positive reports. Altogether, Posner suggests that the relationship between the CEO, the members of the board of directors, and the firm's auditors typically involves a great deal of "mutual back-scratching."[16]

The problem is compounded by a tendency of corporate boards to match what other corporate boards are doing. "We pay our executives not on the basis of performance, but on the basis of peer group," notes John Bogle, former chairman of the Vanguard Group. Bogle says that this creates a "ghastly ratchet effect" as cozy corporate boards bring up the pay of their CEOs to match what's going on at other similarly cozy boards.[17]

All this suggests that the exorbitant pay CEOs and other top executives enjoy has less to do with the operation of the so-called free market and more to do with the extraordinary power they exert over their own pay. If the wages of a company's clerical or janitorial staff were set by boards controlled by clerks and janitors, would you be surprised to see the salary of a good filer or floor-mopper shoot up?

In addition to controlling corporate boards, top executives have been able to use their clout on the political front to win legislative victories that allowed them to push their own pay ever higher. This can be seen in the case of "executive stock options"—an arrangement that allows an executive to buy a certain amount of the company's stock at a point in the future, at a prearranged price—which in recent decades have become key vehicles for raising CEO compensation.

Say, for instance, the executive has an option to buy stock for $10 a share. If the stock rises in value, the executive would exercise his option, paying only $10 for shares that are now worth perhaps $20, $40, or even $100 a share, allowing him to profit enormously. On the other hand, if the stock fails to rise—or falls in value—the executive would simply not exercise his option, making the stock option a no-lose proposition for him.

Stock options were developed in the 1930s and have been used for a long time. But they became newly popular in the 1980s as a way to encourage strong executive performance on behalf of the company. The argument was that stock options aligned the interest of the executive with the company. An executive holding stock options would have a vested interest in the company doing well, because a successful company would have a higher stock price. It was a win-win situation that would encourage the executive to ever higher levels of performance, according to the theory. Higher growth for the company meant a bigger stock reward for the executive.

But, as stock options became increasingly popular, it became clear that they offered a perverse incentive for CEOs. They encouraged executives to focus on pushing up the stock price in the short term, often inducing them to take huge risks and use accounting tricks to produce enormous spikes in the stock price. But a jacked-up stock price is generally unsustainable and is typically achieved at the expense of other actions that would have served the company better in the long term. So the option provided an incentive for executives to behave in ways that were often at cross-purposes to the best interests of the company, its shareholders, and its workers. Calvin Johnson, a tax professor at University of Texas Law School, goes so far as to suggest that a "corporation that has given its top management stock options has given its management a private incentive to undertake risks that are suicidal for the company as a whole."[18]

This problem could have been avoided, had stock options been structured differently. In Europe, for instance, stock options can't simply be cashed in whenever the executive wants, but only at a fixed date in the future, thereby providing the executive with an incentive to drive up the company's long-term value. European options are also linked to other measures of corporate performance beyond simply the company's stock price—such as how well the company is doing compared to others in the same industry. These restrictions make it much harder for European executives to qualify for generous stock payouts, and they often don't.

These tougher European rules were well understood in U.S. corporate circles—and fiercely resisted. Instead, corporate boards allowed companies to structure options with no performance requirements and no control over when the executive chose to exercise the option. The problem was greatly exacerbated by accounting regulations that allowed these growing CEO pay packages to remain hidden from view, preventing shareholders from seeing the massive cash outlays going to top executives. As options became wildly popular by the early 1990s, there were attempts to correct this serious lack of transparency. In June 1993, the body that oversees corporate accounting in the United States, the Financial Accounting Standards Board (FASB), voted unanimously to change the rules governing options in ways that would make the true costs clearly visible—a move that would have almost certainly made corporate boards hesitate about doling out ever more generous options. But the corporate world fought back vigorously against the highly reasonable rules proposed by the FASB, taking its objections to a higher regulatory authority, the SEC, and to Congress. Arthur Levitt, who had just taken over as SEC chairman, recalled the intensity of the business lobbying effort against the proposed FASB rules: "In my first three months in Washington, I spent about one-third of my time being threatened and cajoled by legions of business people."[19] Levitt wasn't convinced, but the corporate lobbyists had an easier time enlisting the support of powerful members of Congress, particularly Democratic senator Joe Lieberman. Overwhelmingly, by a vote of 88–9, the Senate passed a resolution condemning the FASB proposal. With the Senate gearing up for tough legislation that would have stripped the FASB of its authority, even Levitt fell into line. Without his support, the FASB dropped its plan to insist on more transparency. Like Brooksley Born and her attempt to impose some restraint on the derivatives market, the FASB regulators were stopped in their tracks.

With a lax accounting system remaining in place, the floodgates were open. The spotlight was kept well off rising CEO pay packages, allowing them to quietly grow ever larger. In the early 1990s, options had accounted for less than a quarter of executive pay. But by 2001, some 80 percent of executive compensation was in the form of stock options, notes Levitt, who looks back with regret on his role in failing to stop their explosive growth. "I consider this my biggest mistake as SEC chairman."[20]

All this suggests that the huge run-up in pay at the top has been largely the product of deliberate moves by CEOs, both through their control of corporate boards and their influence over legislators. None of this is perhaps surprising, but it contradicts the view typically offered by economists and commentators who insist that today's huge incomes are the product of globalization and technological change. While globalization and technological advances—such as a television—may account for the higher incomes of sports and entertainment stars by greatly increasing their audiences and celebrity status, they don't explain the spectacular rise in the pay of CEOs. Even if we assume that globalization and technology have made corporations more profitable, this still doesn't explain why such a large share of the profits has drifted to the executive office suites.

The technology factor is often cited to explain why so many workers today are earning such low incomes. We're told that skills have become more important than ever in this technological age, leaving unskilled workers highly disadvantaged. This is true. Even so, many highly skilled workers have also experienced minimal income growth. There's been almost no real income growth for the bottom 90 percent of income earners—a group that includes millions of highly skilled workers and well-educated professionals, including, for instance, teachers and nurses. It is hard to explain this clear pattern of income gravitating higher and higher up the income ladder exclusively by reference to skill or education levels.

It is also worth noting that the increased concentration of income at the very top is a phenomenon that's really only occurred in the Anglo-American countries—the United States, Britain, Canada, and Australia. But if globalization is a key factor in explaining increasing inequality, why isn't the same trend visible around the globe, or at least in other countries that are competing successfully in the global economy, such as Germany, France, or Japan?

The reason is that technology and globalization are only partly responsible for the huge increase in incomes at the top. Those who are pleased with the current trend toward increased inequality have seized upon these two factors to explain it, perhaps because they appear to be neutral forces beyond human control. If technology and globalization are responsible, then there's no point in trying to do anything about this strange new inequality. The emergence of a new class of billionaires is just the natural outcome of modernity, and attempting to limit it would only hold back the tides of progress, ultimately hurting us all.

But the evidence suggests that the increase in inequality has not been an inevitable development caused by neutral forces beyond our control, but rather the product of a concerted campaign by a powerful elite determined to enrich itself.

It seems that there are serious flaws in both the economic and moral case for large income concentrations at the top. And yet there's a simple fallback position for those seeking to justify these income concentrations and keep tax authorities at bay. It goes like this: "If you raise our taxes, we'll move our money offshore."

With this threat, they take control of the chessboard.

Or do they?

CHAPTER 8

# Taking the Fun out
# of Tax Havens

The wealthy Wyly brothers of Texas have always wanted to be known
for their generosity, which has been considerable. In addition to
Republican causes—including the "Swiftboat" advertising campaign
that brought a swift end to the presidential bid of decorated war veteran John Kerry—Charles and Sam Wyly have contributed amply to
the cultural scene in Dallas. The Dallas Center for the Performing Arts
Foundation, the Dallas Museum of Art, the Dallas Symphony, and the
Dallas Theater Center have all been recipients of the Wylys' largesse.
Descriptions of their generosity and community spirit proliferate on
the official Wyly website, where the brothers are heralded as "civic
leaders" committed to "supporting community causes." An article on
the site notes that Charles, from his early days as a Boy Scout, required
himself to do a good turn every day. "I've always considered myself a
giver," the article quotes Charles as saying, "a cheerful giver."

One community cause the Wylys haven't been cheerful about contributing to however is the public treasury.

Exhaustive investigations by the SEC and a Senate subcommittee[1]
found that the brothers have long stashed a large part of their massive
fortune in an elaborate web of offshore trusts based in the Cayman
Islands and the Isle of Man, well hidden from U.S. tax authorities.
The trusts, which are believed to have sheltered some $750 million in
assets, held a huge array of assets, including ranches in Colorado, a

million-dollar painting of Benjamin Franklin, antique furniture, and a necklace valued at $750,000—all assets enjoyed by the Wyly brothers and their families. After a six-year investigation, the SEC brought a lawsuit in 2010 accusing the brothers of setting up "an elaborate sham" of fifty-eight trusts and shell corporations based in tax havens designed to fraudulently sell more than $500 million in offshore assets. (The brothers have consistently denied any wrongdoing.)

The Senate subcommittee staff poured through 1.5 million pages of documents to piece together the complex set of financial arrangements constructed by the brothers and their financial advisors.

Although the Wyly story has some rags-to-riches elements, the boys were in fact born during the Depression into a Louisiana family that had owned a cotton plantation for several generations. When a cotton crop failed, the family did face hard times, even living for a while in a shack without plumbing or electricity. Both parents went to work for the state prison. But the family bounced back and ended up owning and running a small local newspaper in Delhi, Louisiana. Charles and Sam went to Louisiana Tech University; Sam went on to do an MBA at the University of Michigan. The brothers moved to Texas and developed businesses together, initially in the computer software field, later branching out into retail, the restaurant business, mining, and oil refining. Eventually the Wylys started up two hedge funds and a private equity fund. And along the way, the brothers became prominent Republican donors, contributing more than $20 million to Republican candidates over the years.

It was in the early 1990s that the Wylys became interested in moving money offshore, after one of their close advisors attended a seminar given by California lawyer David Tedder, who specialized in complex offshore tax-avoidance schemes. Tedder's approach was aggressive; he insisted that no one—no matter how rich—should pay inheritance taxes. He recommended that clients arrange their affairs so that when they died, they'd have no more than $100 of property in their names (having hidden the rest offshore). Intrigued by what their advisor reported, the Wyly brothers themselves attended a subsequent seminar by Tedder, and went on to retain his California firm for financial advice between 1991 and 1993. (In an unrelated case ten years later, Tedder was fined $1 million and jailed after he was convicted of money laundering and attempted fraud for helping conceal the movement of money between U.S. gamblers and an offshore betting operation.)[2]

The offshore arrangements used by the Wylys are interesting, partly because they involve stock options. Unlike other forms of pay, stock options are only taxable when the option is exercised—that is, when it is cashed in to take advantage of a rising stock price.

But, as is so often the case, a concession like this only whets the appetite of the rich and their financial advisors to devise ways to reduce taxes further. Starting in the early 1990s, a number of U.S. accounting firms began promoting a tax shelter that allowed even more favorable tax treatment of stock options.

The shelter involved transferring stock options to a third party. Before we go any farther, we should note that there is no valid reason why stock options should be transferable to a third party. The ostensible point of paying an executive with stock options is to give him an added incentive to increase the profitability of the company that employs him by giving him a vested interest in the rise of the value of its stock. But if his stock options are transferred to someone else, that incentive is effectively gone. Nevertheless, U.S. tax law permits stock options to be transferred to a third party—which opens up the possibility that the transfer will become an opportunity for tax avoidance.

Ostensibly, the tax laws prevent such tax avoidance by imposing rules to govern stock option transfers. For instance, if the options are transferred to an independent entity—say, a company with an arm's-length relationship to the individual—then the executive is considered to have sold the options and will have to pay tax on them, just as if he had cashed them in himself. On the other hand, if the options are transferred to a related company—one that is, say, controlled by the executive or a member of his family—then no tax is triggered by the transfer. However, as soon as the related company exercises the options on the stock, the executive will be required to pay tax on the gain.

In other words, the tax laws are designed to prevent the executive from using the transfer as a way to avoid paying tax on the stock options. He is required to pay tax—either when the options are sold to an arm's-length company or when the options are exercised by a company he controls. Still, the fact that stock options are allowed to be transferred to a third party creates a level of complexity in the laws and therefore an opening for creative lawyers seeking to devise ways to spare their clients from paying the taxes.

So, for instance, under the tax shelter that was promoted in the 1990s—which the Wylys employed—stock options were transferred to a related company located in a tax haven. The related company made a promise to the executive to pay for the stock options—but not until some date far off in the future, perhaps twenty or thirty years later. The accounting firms insisted that, since no payment was made to the executive for many years (and perhaps never), the executive hadn't received any benefit, so he owed no tax. In the meantime, the related company was deemed to be free to exercise the stock option, to buy and sell company stock, and to accumulate the profits in the related company tax-free.

CEOs didn't need much coaxing to give this tax shelter a try. By 2003, the Internal Revenue Service calculated that U.S. corporate executives had used the shelter to hide nearly $1 billion in taxable income from stock options.[3] When the IRS moved to clamp down, more than a hundred executives agreed to cooperate in exchange for reduced penalties and payment of back taxes.[4]

The Wylys however insisted there was nothing wrong with their arrangement. The Senate investigation concluded otherwise. According to the Senate report, the Wylys "engaged in increasingly sophisticated efforts to hide assets, shift income offshore and dodge U.S. taxes."[5] They did this by transferring stock options and warrants worth $190 million in compensation to offshore trusts and shell companies. In return, these offshore companies promised to make annuity payments to the brothers—many years later. Meanwhile, the companies cashed in the stock options without paying any tax, allowing huge amounts of money to accumulate in the companies, where the money was then invested or loaned in ways that benefited the brothers.

Rejecting the Wylys' argument that the offshore companies were independent operations,[6] the Senate investigation concluded that the brothers and their advisors were in fact masterminding the whole complex offshore operation. It found that the Wylys had "directed the exercise of those stock options and warrants, used the shares to generate investment gains, and used at least $600 million in untaxed offshore dollars to provide substantial loans to Wyly interests, finance business ventures, acquire U.S. real estate, and purchase furnishings, art, and jewelry for the personal use of Wyly family members."[7]

In all this, the brothers were advised by an extensive team of lawyers and financial professionals; their offshore companies and trusts used the services of leading financial institutions, including Credit Suisse First Boston, Lehman Brothers, and Bank of America. (Lehman Brothers opened 125 accounts for Wyly offshore entities, while Bank of America opened 65 accounts for them.)[8]

Yet, after some six years of investigations, the Wyly empire—estimated to be worth more than a billion dollars—has survived intact. Attempts by the SEC to recover $550 million from the brothers are still pending, but an army of lawyers continues to keep the authorities at bay.

In August 2011, Charles Wyly, seventy-seven, was killed in a car accident while driving his Porsche near one of his homes in Aspen, Colorado. For the most part, Charles was remembered in the media as he would have wanted to be—for the successful business ventures he built with his brother, the impressive fortune they had amassed, and their extensive charitable giving.

The Wyly offshore empire was just one of six cases probed as part of a massive investigation into tax haven abuse conducted by the Senate Permanent Subcommittee on Investigations. Headed by Republican Norm Coleman and Democrat Carl Levin, the committee concluded, in 2006, that there was a "sophisticated offshore industry, composed of a cadre of international professionals including tax attorneys, accountants, bankers, brokers, corporate service providers, and trust administrators" that enabled American citizens to store $1 trillion in assets offshore, evading between $40 to $70 billion in taxes each year.[9]

In addition to identifying this substantial loss of revenue, the Senate subcommittee findings suggest that the highest-income Americans are actually even richer than the numbers in this book suggest. That's because the studies we've relied on—chiefly those by economists Emmanuel Saez and Thomas Piketty—calculate income statistics based on U.S. tax data. Yet an estimated $1 trillion of American assets are being deliberately hidden from tax authorities, leaving little doubt that there are serious omissions in the tax data. It's probably safe to assume that the vast majority of those hiding assets in offshore bank accounts or sham companies are high-income individuals.

The Senate report also gives us a glimpse into how the world of tax-haven treachery works. It sheds light on the thriving, recession-proof industry of lawyers and financial professionals who meticulously scrutinize every aspect of corporate and tax law looking for ways to hide the assets of wealthy clients from the reach of tax and regulatory authorities. As noted earlier, lawyers make up some 6.2 percent of the very top 0.1 percent of U.S. earners. A good many of these extremely high-earning lawyers are no doubt to be found working in this secretive world of "wealth management."

On the eve of the financial meltdown in April 2008, an exclusive luncheon was held in midtown Manhattan, where roughly six dozen wealthy Americans sipped very rare wines and mingled with special Parisian guest Henri Loyrette, the director of the Louvre. One could say that the room was full of HNWIs, which sounds like a polite word for swine flu but is actually the acronym the financial community uses for High Net Worth Individuals—people with investable assets worth more than $1 million, the point at which an individual becomes of serious interest to a banker.

The elegant gathering was hosted by the giant Swiss bank UBS, the world's largest manager of private wealth. It was just one of many such events organized by the bank as part of its strategy of reaching out to America's multimillionaires and billionaires. In recent years, UBS has stepped up its efforts to become the banker of choice of HNWIs by opening posh offices in New York, Chicago, Houston, and other U.S. cities with pockets of significant wealth. Its bankers also court the wealthy with lavish private events at the America's Cup, Art Basel, Boston Symphony Orchestra concerts, and other sporting and cultural events frequented by the very rich.

This is the exclusive and discreet world of wealth management, that is, the arranging of personal or corporate financial affairs to maximize investment returns and minimize (or avoid altogether) tax payments. Managing one's wealth is a task that looms large in the lives of a select few, while being utterly beyond the experience of the vast majority of the population. Like everything else that caters to the rich, the offices and reception halls where "wealth managers" conduct their business are elegant and opulent. The fine trappings distract attention from the fact that a significant part of what goes on here amounts to criminal activity.

Tax avoidance by the rich is a massive industry that includes both legal and illegal aspects. The legal part is made up of a huge array of think tanks, lobbyists, and public relations firms pitching the case for low taxes on the rich to government officials, lawmakers, and the public. In addition, an army of tax lawyers and accountants serve wealthy clients by handling their financial affairs in ways that minimize their tax burdens. All this, which undoubtedly saves the rich—and thus deprives governments of—billions of dollars a year, is done within the limits of the law.

But there's another massive part of the business that veers into the illegal. It focuses on hiding money from tax authorities by moving it into offshore bank accounts. While there's nothing illegal about having a foreign bank account, it is illegal to fail to report income to tax authorities, including by hiding it offshore to avoid detection. Estimates suggest that more than one-third of the global wealth of HNWIs, or somewhere between $8 and $10 trillion, is stored offshore in countries—including well-known tax havens like the Cayman Islands, the Channel Islands, Switzerland, and Liechtenstein—where lax banking laws have allowed the internationally wealthy to keep their fortunes secret.[10] Banks in tax haven countries don't offer anything—besides complete secrecy—that isn't offered by domestic banks. So there's no conceivable reason to go to the trouble of putting one's money in an offshore account other than to hide it, presumably from tax authorities—a federal offence in the United States. If the size of the tax haven banking industry and the money stored in it is any indication, there are a great many crooks among the wealthy, almost none of whom have ever been charged.

It is striking how slow moving authorities in many countries have traditionally been in clamping down on this huge area of criminal activity. This sluggishness is curious, since more vigorous prosecution would inevitably lead to substantial inflow into government coffers—much more so than in the case of other property-related crimes. But while governments vigorously go after low-income individuals who defraud social assistance programs, they have been notoriously lax in pursuing high rollers who commit tax fraud.

This has recently changed somewhat in the United States, partly because of the revelations produced by the Senate subcommittee report that looked into the offshore deals of the Wylys and others. The spotlight was turned even more dramatically on the furtive world of offshore banking the following year when something extraordinary happened: Bradley Birkenfeld, a high-level, Geneva-based banker came forward, providing startling insider information about the methods and operations of his former employer, UBS.

The forty-two-year-old Birkenfeld, a U.S. citizen, seemed at first an unlikely whistleblower. Born and raised in privileged circles in Boston, Birkenfeld had enjoyed a high-flying life as a private banker for UBS, living in a posh apartment in Geneva with a chalet in the Swiss Alps and traveling around the world on an expense account courting wealthy clients at lavish events and private dinners. But his growing concerns about his own involvement in possible illegalities in the bank's tax shelter operations led him to raise questions with senior UBS officials. When the officials proved unresponsive, Birkenfeld quit. In accepting his resignation, UBS demanded that he keep bank records strictly confidential, threatening him with both criminal and civil prosecution in Switzerland if he divulged information.

But Birkenfeld got a lawyer and paid a visit to U.S. government officials in May 2007. Strangely, although Birkenfeld provided extensive evidence to officials from the Department of Justice, the IRS, and the SEC, they were slow to act. Frustrated and concerned that the bank would soon cover its tracks, Birkenfeld decided to approach the Senate subcommittee that had demonstrated such a strong interest in exposing offshore banking practices. "I don't mean to sound alarmist," Birkenfeld's lawyer wrote in an e-mail to the subcommittee, "but my client has risked his livelihood and even his life to expose massive tax fraud on an international scale and yet no one in two branches of government seems to be concerned. . . . We have limited opportunity to change an entire industry designed to evade US taxes. Let's not fiddle while Rome burns."

Birkenfeld quickly got the attention he wanted from the subcommittee, and he provided it with detailed testimony about how UBS helped American citizens evade U.S taxes. But Birkenfeld also ended up getting some attention he didn't want. Several months later, as he returned to the United States from Switzerland, he was arrested and charged with conspiring to help California-based real estate billionaire Igor Olenicoff hide $200 million in assets from U.S. tax authorities.

In his testimony before the subcommittee and also at his own trial in the summer of 2008, Birkenfeld lifted the curtain on the dark inner sanctum of private banking. He confessed how he had participated in elaborate schemes to help wealthy U.S. clients evade taxes by creating fictitious trusts and corporations to conceal offshore ownership and helping clients file false tax returns. "I was employed by UBS," he said when asked why he had done these things. "I was incentivized to do this business." He presented a UBS manual that instructed bank employees how to hide client information from police and immigration authorities while passing through customs. He described how he himself had smuggled diamonds into the United States in a toothpaste tube for a wealthy client, and how Swiss bankers communicated with their clients with encrypted messages to avoid detection by authorities.

Birkenfeld explained that he and other UBS bankers trolled for wealthy clients at art shows, golf and tennis tournaments, yachting regattas, musical performances, and any other events "where rich people hang out." He provided a UBS PowerPoint presentation that showed the bank's "key clients" were UHNWI (*Ultra* High Net Worth Individuals)— those worth more than $30 million. Another UBS slide highlighted the fact that there were 222 billionaires in the United States and Canada, with a combined net worth of $706 billion. Yet another slide identified where to find this crowd hanging out: Aspen; Palm Beach; Sea Island, Georgia; and Montecito and Los Altos Hills, California.

With detailed evidence that the bank conspired with U.S. citizens to hide their incomes, UBS was obliged to pay a fine of $780 million and also to hand over the names of some 4,500 U.S.-based clients with undeclared accounts in the bank.

Birkenfeld had helped unearth a treasure trove of tax evasion cases, some of which have been prosecuted. Many of the UBS clients avoided prosecution however by cooperating with an IRS amnesty program initiated after they were identified. Oddly, the harshest penalty in the UBS case so far has been meted out to Birkenfeld himself, who is currently serving a forty-month prison sentence, despite the fact that he came forward voluntarily. Prosecutors accused him of advising Olenicoff, the California billionaire who was his biggest client, to move assets from Switzerland to Liechtenstein before Birkenfeld started blowing the whistle. Certainly Olenicoff fared much better than his banker did. The billionaire plead guilty to filing a false tax return, paid $52 million in penalties and back taxes, and received two years' probation.

In a separate case that happened almost simultaneously with Birkenfeld's, an insider blew the whistle on LGT, a bank owned by the royal family of Liechtenstein. Heinrich Kieber, a computer technician working for LGT, sparked an international scandal when he sold confidential data on more than 1,400 LGT clients to authorities in Germany, which passed them on to officials in Italy, Britain, the United States, and other countries. Kieber, a native of Liechtenstein, then went underground, adopting an assumed identity in a witness protection program.

The Kieber revelations, like those of Birkenfeld, were a striking breach of the usually impenetrable world of tax haven banking. Kieber's data caused an uproar in Germany and led to the conviction of one of the nation's leading businessmen, as well as to 450 other tax-evasion investigations and the resignation of some high-ranking officials. In Italy, the tax evaders were publicly humiliated when their names were released in the media. In the United States, the Senate subcommittee eagerly seized an opportunity to flesh out the picture already provided by Birkenfeld. Appearing on videotape with his face in darkness, Kieber told a subcommittee hearing that the bank records showed not just tax evasion, but corruption and links to global dictators.

Together, the revelations of Birkenfeld and Kieber dealt a considerable blow to the world of tax haven banking and led to another scathing report by the Senate subcommittee, now headed by Senator Levin.[11] Secrecy—which the Swiss had elevated to a national principle—no longer appeared to be something that the banks could ensure. All this coincided with the international financial meltdown in the summer and fall of 2008, bringing additional attention to tax haven banks for their role in augmenting the volume of footloose funds available for financial speculation. One of the few international reforms that the Group of Twenty (G20) had little difficulty agreeing on at its London summit in April 2009 was a ramping up of pressure on countries that failed to comply with international tax-compliance standards. A united stand by the world's most powerful economies prompted a number of long-resistant tax haven countries—including a considerably chastised Switzerland—to agree to fall into line.

·    ·    ·

All that was encouraging. The Western nations, led by the United States, seemed to have acquired new energy for clamping down on tax havens in cases involving out-and-out tax evasion. None of this however would do anything to restrict the use of tax havens for practices like "transfer pricing," which are less overtly illegal but still drain billions each year from the U.S. Treasury and from the treasuries of other countries around the world. Typically, corporations set up dummy companies in tax haven countries, then juggle their books so that their profits are transferred to these dummy companies, which are subject to the extremely low tax rates of the tax haven jurisdictions. In the spring of 2009, the Obama administration promised to go after this longtime and highly lucrative tax avoidance scheme in an effort to collect an extra $200 billion a year in taxes from U.S. corporations. But after a deluge of corporate lobbyists descended on Capitol Hill, the White House backed off a few months later, saying that the promised reform would have to wait. As the *Wall Street Journal* explained: "The Obama administration has shelved a plan to raise more than $200 billion in new taxes on multinational companies following a blitz of complaints from businesses."[12]

Meanwhile, the Senate subcommittee has kept up pressure for tougher action. In July 2011, Senator Levin brought forward a bill—the Stop Tax Haven Abuse Act—which would, among other things, tackle the problem of transfer pricing. It would require corporations to make detailed annual reports that break down country-by-country exactly where their production, staff, and sales are located. This would make it much more difficult for them to claim profits in tax haven jurisdictions, where their only operations usually consist of dummy companies with no staff and no production facilities, and often just a mailbox.

In addition, Levin's bill would stop the kind of gimmick that the Wylys used. Under the proposed law, U.S. citizens transferring property (including stock options) to a foreign trust would have to continue to pay tax on any income earned from that property, regardless of whether or not they controlled the trust. The bill would also increase penalties substantially for those caught violating U.S. tax laws.

Interestingly, an earlier version of this bill was cosponsored by then Senator Barack Obama.

For that matter, while Obama backed off on his promise to collect an extra $200 billion from multinationals engaging in transfer pricing, his administration did push through a change that could have far-reaching implications for tax evasion. In the spring of 2010, it won Congressional approval for the Foreign Account Tax Compliance Act (FATCA), which forces all foreign financial institutions—banks, stockbrokers, hedge funds, pension funds, trusts, and insurance companies—to make extensive reports about their U.S. clients to the IRS. The reporting must include detailed information about financial activities in all bank accounts held by U.S. clients.

FATCA, which is scheduled to come into effect in 2014, attracted relatively little attention when it passed through Congress, but it has generated a storm of opposition since then from foreign financial institutions. Led by Canadian banks, the financial institutions have complained that the compliance costs will run into the billions, since they'll have to scour their records to find evidence of clients holding U.S. citizenship. And they've won the support of U.S. banks in fighting the new measure. Even though the U.S. banks aren't affected by FATCA, they fear it will lead other countries to enact similar measures requiring U.S. banks to report on bank accounts held by their citizens—a hugely lucrative business for U.S. banks.

The reporting requirements in FATCA, assuming that they survive the lobbying onslaught, could go a long way toward preventing U.S. citizens from hiding money offshore. But there would be a simpler way to do this—and one that would virtually eliminate the costs of compliance, and make the monitoring apply to financial institutions and citizens of all countries. The idea, pioneered by U.S. tax scholar Michael J. McIntyre, has been promoted internationally by the UK-based Tax Justice Network.[13]

Here's how it would work: All financial institutions, whenever they make any sort of payment to a client, would be required to report that payment to the tax authorities of the country where the client resides. The report would be automatic, in electronic form, and would include a unique number to identify the client. That way, all governments around the world would be notified of all payments made to their wealthy citizens and be able to tax them accordingly—in the same way that governments receive notification from their domestic banks about payments to citizens within the country and use that information to verify the tax returns of those citizens. Indeed, our proposal here is simply to extend to the international arena a system that has long worked well domestically within the United States and in other countries. The international system could be enforced by an existing body like the World Trade Organization, the Bank of International Settlements, or the United Nations.

This would be particularly beneficial to Third World nations, which desperately need the tax revenue that could be raised on the investment income earned by their rich citizens in tax havens and other secrecy jurisdictions. Global Financial Integrity, a Washington-based public policy organization, has estimated that illicit financial flows out of Third World countries was $1.26 trillion in 2008 alone, and ranged from $850 billion to $1.06 trillion per year in each of the five preceding years. These illicit capital outflows exceed the combined aid budgets of the entire rich world (U.S. $103.7 billion in 2007) by a ratio of about 10 to 1. Thus, our proposal for an automatic exchange of financial information not only would assist the United States in collecting taxes from tax-evading rich Americans, but would also greatly assist Third World countries in attaining sufficient revenue to tackle the wide range of problems caused by extreme poverty.

Perhaps this scheme sounds too ambitious, but in fact it is no more complicated than the international system of passports, which works well and with few compliance problems. Each passport has a unique identification number. Every time a person crosses a border, her number is swiped into a computer, which instantly discloses information about her. Transmitting an electronic record of all payments made by all banks would be no more complicated than that.[14]

It turns out that among the benefits of the computer age are not only video games, but also the easy tracking and taxation of the gigantic hidden fortunes of the world's billionaires.

The rich clearly believe that they have a powerful weapon for fending off higher taxes: the threat that they'll move their money offshore. And governments often acquiesce in the face of this threat, lowering the wealthy's taxes on the grounds that they'll be less likely to engage in tax avoidance and evasion schemes.

This is an odd way to deal with the problem.

When people of modest means break the law by stealing—perhaps because they don't have enough income—the government's response isn't to make sure they have more income. Instead, the response is to punish the offenders, even to strengthen the penalties so that others will be discouraged from considering such activity.

But when the rich break the law by hiding income offshore, the treatment tends to be much gentler. As mentioned, the IRS offered generous amnesty programs in cases where wealthy U.S. taxpayers were caught hiding money offshore, even though jail time would have more likely discouraged other wealthy people from similar behavior. So, while the poor breaking the law causes governments to get tough, the rich breaking the law seems to lead governments to offer them amnesty, even to consider lowering their taxes.

Another threat, used either explicitly or implicitly by the rich, is that if taxes aren't kept low, they will leave the United States entirely. In other words, they won't simply stash some of their fortune in a secret offshore account; rather they will pack up all their assets and move to more tax-friendly territory.

This threat has a powerful effect, leaving the public fearful of a huge withdrawal of money from the economy, of communities bereft of vital capital. In fact, the threat is dramatically overblown. Contrary to the mythology, it's not actually all that easy for the rich to simply pack up and leave. As long as they remain U.S. citizens, they are taxed on their worldwide incomes. They are required to file U.S. tax returns, no matter where they live, even in the remotest corner of the world. What if they renounce their U.S. citizenship? Actually, just as it's not very easy to *acquire* U.S. citizenship, it's also not very easy to *renounce* it; there are obstacles that make renunciation difficult, particularly if it appears that the purpose is to avoid taxes. And if wealthy individuals succeed in renouncing their citizenship and leaving, there are exit taxes—that is, taxes on their accrued gains. These exit taxes can be substantial, and they're enforced. In fact, packing up and leaving—with one's fortune intact—isn't nearly as easy as it sounds.

Besides, if the rich do go, it's not clear how great the loss is. They can't take the country's natural resources with them nor its skilled workforce or advanced infrastructure. Besides, as we'll see in the next chapter, there's growing evidence that more equal countries—ones that aren't top-heavy with billionaires—have much better social, health, *and economic* outcomes.

The real solution to threats from the rich isn't to give them ever lower tax rates out of fear they'll move their money out of the country. The real solution is to democratically decide how best to distribute the tax burden, and to get tough with individuals who avoid taxes by breaking the law.

As noted, this would be very simple to do by using basic computer technology to put in place an international system for reporting all bank payments. People wanting to conceal income from authorities would then find it no easier to move money undetected around the world than to travel without a passport.

Checkmate.

# CHAPTER 9

# Why Billionaires Are Bad for Your Health

Many adjectives come to mind when thinking of how to describe Americans, but "short" probably isn't one of them.

We're used to the notion of the United States as the world's dominant power—a land of untold resources, wealth, and consumption. And one reflection of this abundance is the fact that for most of the past two and a half centuries Americans have been literally the tallest people on earth. Feeding off the abundant wild game and rich agriculture of their vast new land, colonial Americans measured a full three inches taller than Europeans.

The mythological American is the towering figure of John Wayne. He's the tall, muscular sheriff in the Wild West or the strapping Marine rushing in to win the day in World War II. Potent and appealing as these images may be, they're more nostalgia than reality today. The truth is—compared to Europeans—Americans have effectively shrunk. In the movie remakes, John Wayne should be Dutch.

The truth is that the inhabitants of the Netherlands are now the tallest people in the world. They're almost three inches taller on average than Americans, and they continue to grow. Dutch males average six foot one—seven inches taller than they were just over a century ago. And crowded around the towering Dutch at the top end of the height scale are other northern Europeans—Norwegians, Swedes, Danes, Belgians, and Germans.

Among advanced industrial nations, Americans are now at the very bottom end of the height scale. And no, it's not the influx of short Hispanics that's brought down the average. The height pattern is the same even when the sample is limited to non-Hispanic, native-born Americans.

Height is a potent symbol. But it also appears to be a useful measure of the well-being of a nation's citizens. Economic historians John Kormos and Benjamin Lauderdale, who have conducted an extensive investigation of the changing height patterns among nations, conclude that it is a telling indicator of something very basic about a society: "Height is indicative of how well the human organism thrives in its socioeconomic environment."[1] It is a particularly good indicator of how well societies care for their young, since height is set early in life, notes Thorvaldur Gylfason, a professor of economics at the University of Iceland. Unlike body weight, which can fluctuate significantly over a lifetime, tallness is determined during certain growth spurts in infancy and adolescence. It is heavily influenced by nutrition, which generally reflects the broader social and economic conditions of a child's life.[2] Height, then, is a good indicator of how well a society is creating conditions that allow its citizens to develop and thrive.

Height may be most useful for its simple, provocative quality. It is a concept we can all relate to, and one we instinctively, at a gut level, associate with a certain primitive superiority. It captures our attention better than other, more familiar measuring sticks, like life expectancy or infant mortality. The "shrinking American" is a powerful way to highlight how dramatically the United States has failed in the last few decades to keep pace with other advanced nations in creating conditions that allow its own citizens to develop and flourish. This American decline has been profound and relentless, so much so that the United States is now the outlier among industrial nations, having fallen significantly behind the rest of the pack—particularly the northern Europeans—in a wide range of areas of social well-being.

And the reason, it turns out, is integrally tied up with the rise of billionaires.

• • •

The notion that poverty is bad for human well-being is easily grasped. We can all readily appreciate how people with inadequate access to food, shelter, and the basic amenities of life end up suffering from a wide range of problems, with detrimental effects on their health and welfare. We can also easily understand how such material deprivation leads to personal distress that manifests itself in dysfunctional behavior, such as higher crime rates and more violence, teen pregnancy, and drug addiction. The link between poverty and many forms of personal suffering and social breakdown is not only thoroughly documented, but intuitively obvious.

What is not so obvious is that extreme levels of inequality in society have an effect similar to poverty. This has become clear in a growing body of research. As epidemiologists Richard Wilkinson and Kate Pickett put it in *The Spirit Level:* "All problems which are more common at the bottom end of the social ladder are more common in more unequal societies."[3] This explains why even rich countries with high material living standards often have significant social problems. And it is not just the poor in these countries who suffer from them. Countries with higher levels of inequality have higher levels of social problems— at all levels of income. Typically, the incidence of such problems is highest at the bottom end, but it continues through all income levels, becoming gradually weaker with each step up the financial ladder. Simply living in an unequal society puts one at greater risk of experiencing a wide range of health problems and social dysfunctions.

This may sound unlikely, but the evidence is powerful. Wilkinson and Pickett have assembled data on all the advanced industrial nations in an attempt to determine the relationship between their level of income inequality and their performance in a number of key health and social areas, including life expectancy, infant mortality, obesity, mental illness, children's educational attainment, teenage births, and rates of homicide and imprisonment. In chart after chart, the same picture emerges: the greater the level of inequality in a country, the higher the rate of the particular health or social problem being measured. To provide a good overview in one chart, Wilkinson and Pickett have created an Index of Health and Social Problems, which captures each country's overall social performance and then correlates the index with the country's level of inequality. The picture is striking. The countries with the least inequality—Japan and the Scandinavian nations—are at the bottom left-hand corner, while the ones with the most inequality—the United States, Portugal, and the United Kingdom—are in the top right. In between, the other countries fall around a straight line between the two extremes, their level of inequality correlating almost exactly with the size of their social problems. The chart reveals a relationship between inequality and social problems that is so pronounced it cannot be accidental.

It's also clear that it isn't the overall "richness" of the country that determines its level of social problems. The United States and Norway are both very rich countries; they have almost identically high per capita national incomes. But the distribution of income within the two countries is very different—highly equitable in Norway, highly inequitable in the United States. (The U.S. national income level is very high, despite the large number of poor Americans, because a small number of fabulously rich citizens hauls up the average.) But the striking thing is that the two countries experience vastly different levels of social dysfunction. Norway has extremely low levels of health and social problems, while the United States has a record that is way worse than every other Western nation, almost off the chart.

This whole area of research was launched in the late 1960s with the Whitehall study, a massive investigation into the health of British civil servants. The highly stratified civil service, located mostly in buildings on a road called Whitehall in central London, provided an almost laboratory test case for British epidemiologist Michael Marmot to examine the impact of status levels on health. At the time, it was widely believed that those at the top of an organization experienced tremendous stress because of their demanding jobs and that this explained why they dropped dead of heart attacks at an alarmingly high rate. But as Marmot assembled the data on some eighteen thousand civil servants, it quickly became clear that this popular notion wasn't just wrong, it was actually upside down. Those at the top were not actually dying of heart attacks at a faster rate than those in lower-ranking jobs. Just the opposite was happening. A subsequent follow-up study, Whitehall II, confirmed the same clear trend: the lower down the status scale within the hierarchy, the higher the rate of heart attacks—as well as a host of other diseases. Notes Marmot, who now teaches at University College in London and the Harvard School of Public Health: "The men at the bottom of the office hierarchy have, at ages forty to sixty-four, four times the risk of death of the administrators at the top of the hierarchy."[4]

Marmot's remarkable findings have since been reinforced in dozens of other studies. There is now a large body of evidence showing that, as one moves lower down the hierarchy, one has a greater risk of poor outcomes in a number of areas, including life expectancy; infant mortality; stroke; diseases related to the heart, lung, kidney, and digestive tract; tuberculosis; HIV-related disease; suicide; and violent death. One intriguing study, for instance, compared the longevity of Oscar–winning film stars to another group of film stars with slightly lower status—those who had costarred in winning films and those who were nominated but didn't end up winning the ultimate prize. The researchers, Donald Redelmeier and Sheldon Singh, postulated that actors who actually win an Oscar experience a huge boost in status and prestige as they move to the very top of the Hollywood hierarchy, well above even otherwise successful actors who have not won the coveted prize. Strikingly, the researchers found that the actual Oscar winners lived four years longer than the slightly lower-status Hollywood stars.[5] Indeed, the findings of a wide range of studies looking at the impact of status have been so consistent that, as Marmot notes, one's status can be considered an excellent indicator of one's likely health outcome: "Where you stand in the social hierarchy—on the social ladder—is intimately related to your chances of getting ill, and your length of life. . . . The higher the status in the pecking order the healthier [people] are likely to be."[6]

Of course, this doesn't mean that high-status people don't some-times die young or that low-status people don't ever live long lives. But when the broad picture is surveyed, strong patterns emerge, and these patterns consistently show higher death levels at lower status levels. Does this simply reflect the likelihood of people in lower status positions to smoke more, exercise less, and have bad diets? Perhaps—but even when these known behavioral health risks are taken into account, there is still a clear gradient showing better health related to one's status in the social hierarchy. Dennis Raphael, a professor of health policy at Toronto's York University, maintains that, contrary to popular perception, the primary factors shaping health aren't medical treatment or lifestyle choices (smoking, exercise, or high-fat diets) but rather factors like one's income level, employment and housing situation, and degree of acceptance in the community.[7]

This may seem puzzling. It's easy to understand how social status or a person's position in the pecking order would affect something subjective like her mood, level of happiness, or sense of well-being. But it's harder to understand how it would affect something as tangible as actual bodily disease. Yet this is precisely what the evidence suggests. The connector that explains the link between status considerations and actual physical health outcomes is stress, and the body's response to it.

We can see how this works by looking at animals. In the wild, animals respond to stressful situations—being cornered by a large, hungry predator, for instance—by immediately mobilizing energy in the bloodstream and directing it to the muscles. At the same time, bodily functions that aren't immediately necessary (digestion, waste disposal, grooming, ovulation, storing energy for the future) are shut down by the inhibition of insulin secretions and of parasympathetic tone, as well as by the activation of the nervous system, glucocorticoids, and glucagon. All these responses mobilize the animal's resources to maximize its performance in escaping or perhaps taking on the predator. In the process, they alter the body in a number of ways, including increasing the animal's heart rate and blood pressure.[8]

Humans respond to stress in much the same way, when we, for instance, find ourselves suddenly confronted with an assailant or the car we are driving hits an ice patch and swerves out of control. We may also respond to more subtle threats to our well-being when we are, say, obliged to speak in public, appear at a job interview, or report to a demanding boss. Then there are other sorts of personally threatening situations that may be long-term or chronic—fear of becoming unemployed or being unable to meet a mortgage or credit card payment, worrying about being considered inadequate—that can trigger sustained activation of the body's stress mechanisms.

Stress levels can actually be measured, since humans under stress release the hormone cortisol (also called hydrocortisone), which shows up in saliva and blood. Two psychologists at the University of California, Sally Dickerson and Margaret Kemeny, examined the results of more than two hundred published reports of experiments measuring cortisol levels in human volunteers exposed to various stressful situations. Dickerson and Kemeny found that stress levels were particularly pronounced when individuals felt they were being negatively assessed or looked down upon, "tasks that included a social evaluative threat (such as threats to self-esteem or social status) in which others could negatively judge their performance, particularly when the outcome of the performance was uncontrollable, provided larger and more reliable cortisol changes than stressors without these particular threats." Highly stressful, for instance, were experiments in which volunteers had to perform tasks in front of an audience that would score them. The stress proved most acute when the tasks were impossible, leaving the individual feeling helpless to spare herself the embarrassment or humiliation of performing poorly in front of others. Dickerson and Kemeny concluded: "Human beings are driven to preserve the social self and are vigilant to threats that may jeopardize their social esteem or status."[9]

Of course, stress can take many different forms, and not all of it involves threats to our social status. Getting up to give an Oscar-accepting speech no doubt gives the actor a wildly thumping heart.

Similarly, corporate CEOs and high-ranking political figures are under a great deal of pressure to perform. But with that stress comes prestige, power, and control over their situations. Wall Street players undoubtedly feel the pressure of handling billions of dollars, but they also get the thrill of being able to manipulate markets and juggle—and earn—huge fortunes. All this makes them feel important and in control, as if they've got the world by the tail. No wonder dowdy, middle-aged, male bankers wake up in the morning and (as Matt Taibbi put it) see Brad Pitt in the mirror.

It seems to be far more stressful to wake up and see the Hunchback of Notre Dame in the mirror. Indeed, the worst stress seems to come from situations in which the individual feels humiliated or low in status compared to others. Marmot identifies feelings of a lack of control or autonomy as the key to triggering an unhealthy stressful situation. In extensive interviews with the civil servants in his Whitehall studies, Marmot found that lower status was inevitably tied up with less control and autonomy in the workplace. Clerical jobs were not only boring and poorly paid but gave workers no control over their situation. Typists were even subject to rules restricting them from talking to each other on the job, sending a clear signal to them that they weren't trusted or valued by the organization.

It's not hard to see how income levels are associated with social status. The income we receive is an important indicator of where we stand in the social hierarchy—particularly in our highly materialistic society. Neoclassical economic theory assumes that capitalism correctly rewards the individual for her contribution to society, suggesting that one's income properly reflects one's worth and therefore one's status in the community. Whether this is true or not—and, as we argue in this book, it isn't—these are the values and ideas that dominate modern North American thought. Furthermore, income levels are closely tied up with levels of autonomy and control in the workplace. In general, the high-paying jobs are also the ones with the most freedom and power.

The toilet cleaner cannot decide to reward himself with an extra-long lunch hour or choose to delegate the scrubbing part of his job to others so that he can concentrate on developing big-picture strategies for redesigning washrooms. As one descends the pay scale, the desirable features associated with work—status, control, autonomy, opportunity for creativity, pride in one's product—recede a little further on each downward rung.

There are sometimes offsetting factors that reduce the stress of a low income. A struggling artist, for instance, might accept minimal pay as a deliberate trade-off that allows her to do work she loves. She may even enjoy considerable social status among her peers, who admire her talent and her willingness to starve for her craft, and who may consciously reject income as a meaningful measure of value. But for the most part, our incomes are the single most important indicator positioning us in the broad social hierarchy, regardless of what field we are in. Indeed, in our society, income is the closest thing we have to a universally recognized measure of what we are deemed to be "worth."

In relatively equal societies, there is less of a gap between the incomes of individuals at different levels in the social hierarchy, and therefore less emotional and psychological stress about being positioned lower down. Equal societies also tend to have higher taxes, with tax revenues directed toward the population's broad social needs—health care, education, family support, unemployment insurance. This not only helps provide a level of basic support for all; it also promotes a more cooperative, less individualistic approach, with an emphasis on goals like equal opportunity and fairness rather than ever-greater material accumulation. The result is less focus on income status and fewer social divisions. When everyone uses the public health-care system and sends their children to public schools, status distinctions tend to be less acute, and the stress accompanying them diminishes.

In unequal societies, just the opposite happens. The very rich tend to withdraw into their own rarified world, traveling by limousines and private planes, entertaining themselves at exclusive clubs and resorts, and living physically apart from the rest of the population, often behind

gates or even walls. They come to see themselves as essentially independent of society, purchasing their own health care and education
and relying on their own security systems. This leads to resentment
that their tax dollars are paying for costly public services that they don't
much use, leaving them determined to reduce these costs to keep their
taxes from rising. Given their political clout, they're able to maintain
enormous pressure on politicians to keep taxes low, thereby starving
the public system of the funds needed to maintain shared services and
programs that are basic to the well-being of the broader community.
The deterioration of key public services and programs increases the
vulnerability of most members of society, as well as exacerbating social
divisions and stress levels.

All this appears to lead to a deterioration in social relations and a
breakdown in trust. As society becomes more stratified, with more no-
ticeable differentiation between income levels, people tend to identify
and associate more closely with the people at their own level, making it
more difficult to relate to or empathize with those at other levels. The
resulting breakdown in trust can be seen in the results of the European
and World Values Survey, in which random people in different countries were asked whether they agreed with the statement "Most people
can be trusted." Those in more equal countries were much more likely
to agree; in egalitarian Sweden, 66 percent agreed, while in the United
States, only 38 percent did.[10] This lack of trust in others can be seen in
the large number of gated communities in the United States and the
popularity of SUVs. That these bulky, high-off-the-ground, fortresslike
vehicles have replaced snappy little convertibles as the car of choice
suggests that Americans have come to value looking sporty and sexy below meeting their perceived needs for a high level of physical security.

Not surprisingly, perhaps, there also appear to be higher levels of
mental illness in highly unequal societies. Some mental illnesses are
considered genetic, but recent decades have seen a dramatic rise in
the rates of other, stress-related illnesses, notably anxiety and depression, particularly in highly unequal countries like the United States,
Britain, and Australia (closely followed by New Zealand and Canada).

Meanwhile, rates for these syndromes remain relatively low in more equal societies like the Netherlands, Belgium, and Japan. Wilkinson and Pickett note that, to a large extent, mental health is rooted in self-worth. "People who don't value themselves become frightened of rejection; they keep others at a distance, and get trapped in a vicious circle of loneliness."[11] Conditions of extreme inequality feed such feelings, reinforcing anxiety about status.

In some, these feelings lead to violent actions. Feeling socially threatened and humiliated is the key cause of violence, according to James Gilligan, a psychiatrist at Harvard Medical School and director of the Center for the Study of Violence. Gilligan notes that violent behavior is a response to threats or perceived threats to an individual's pride, threats that leave him feeling ashamed, put down, or humiliated. This is particularly potent in young men who lack other sources of pride in their lives—typically, men with no jobs, income, or education who come from socially broken families in which they were inculcated with little in the way of self-esteem or a sense of their own worthiness. When such individuals are insulted or humiliated, they have nothing to fall back on, no other part of their lives to escape into. The challenge to their pride is all there is, and it must be met. Gilligan insists that, in more than thirty years of working with violent offenders, he has "yet to see a serious act of violence that was not provoked by the experience of feeling shamed and humiliated . . . and that did not represent the attempt to . . . undo this 'loss of face.'"[12]

Once again, such threats seem to be enhanced in countries with extreme income inequality. Documentation of international homicide rates by the United Nations shows the United States at the far extreme, almost off the chart, with a murder rate dramatically higher than any other industrialized nation. The U.S. rate, for instance, is 64 murders per million people, more than four times higher than Britain's (15 murders per million) and more than twelve times above that of highly egalitarian Japan (just 5.2 per million).[13] Health analyst Danny Dorling notes that growing income inequality in Britain in the 1980s was reflected in the rising homicide rate: "There is no natural rate for murder. . . . For murder rates to rise in particular places . . . people have to be made to feel more worthless. Then there are more fights, more brawls, more scuffles, more bottles and more knifes and more young men die."[14]

Even for people who don't resort to violence or end up with health problems, extreme income inequality appears to have other negative consequences. Among the "healthy" responses to the rise of billionaires in our midst is a greater focus on keeping up with the very high material standards they set. Economist Robert Frank has dubbed this "luxury fever," a disease he insists infects the whole society.[15] He notes that the proliferation of luxury goods for the wealthy has the effect of making the regular goods consumed by the rest of us seem inadequate in comparison. This leads to a general inflation of expectations. Gas barbecues or wristwatches that seemed perfectly satisfactory a couple of decades ago have now been replaced with much more exotic versions—barbecues that can cook ten breasts of chicken while keeping warm an additional twelve steaks and thirty ears of corn, and wristwatches that glow in the dark fifty meters underwater. After a while, it starts to seem normal to have these more exotic items; it's all just part of keeping up with the flow of modern life.

Advertising and the media constantly remind us of the high material standard enjoyed by those at the top of the hierarchy. TV sitcoms and advertisements typically depict very wealthy suburban families as the norm in society, leaving viewers quietly aware of how shabby their own houses, cars, and clothing are in comparison. These messages are absorbed by children and teenagers, putting additional pressure on parents by having their own children reinforce the idea that they must emulate these impossibly rich lifestyles.

With billionaires constantly pushing up the public's notion of what's materially possible, the standard just keeps rising, subtly and not so subtly imprinting itself on our brains. These greater expectations creep into every corner of our lives. Take children's birthday parties. They used to be modest affairs revolving around pin-the-tail-on-the-donkey games and the presentation of a homemade cake. Today they're more likely to involve a real donkey—or perhaps a more upscale pony—or a live clown or pottery instructor, as well as the presentation of a professionally made cake elaborately decorated with models of the child's favorite cartoon characters. If nothing else, the simple addition of "loot bags"—purchased at specialty stores and presented to every child exiting the party—can add hundreds of dollars to the cost of the event. Parents under financial strain may strongly wish to revert to the old type of party, but they fear looking inadequate by failing to live up to their child's expectations of what is now considered normal in many middle-class circles.

Needless to say, the proliferation of useless trinkets inside the loot bag doesn't seem to make children today happier than children were back in the 1950s, '60s, or '70s. Indeed, studies have shown that all the extra gadgetry and bells-and-whistles now available haven't improved the overall happiness level of North Americans. What they have done is create an enormous pressure to keep up, simply to maintain one's position in the social hierarchy. This requires us to work more. So, rather than taking more time off as our society gets richer, we're working longer hours, increasing our consumption levels in tandem with the material standards set by those higher up the food chain. Instead of spending more time with family or pursuing satisfying activities and interests (as the more egalitarian Europeans have tended to do), we've opted for longer hours on the job (Americans work an average of 274 more hours—about six more weeks—per year than Scandinavians),[16] enabling Americans to buy more of the generally useless things that are the markers of status and position in a highly stratified society.

Of all the negative social consequences of extreme inequality, perhaps the most striking is its impact on social mobility. Central to the modern democratic ideal is the notion of equal opportunity. Even those who don't seem to care about income inequality tend to support the idea that everyone should have an equal chance to better herself in life. The hugely different realities in the lives of the poor and the rich and the resources they have available to them might seem to make this impossible, but it nonetheless remains an ideal almost universally subscribed to in Western societies, particularly the United States.

In reality, however, social mobility is significantly lower in countries with high levels of income inequality, such as the United States. A group of researchers at the London School of Economics demonstrated this by accumulating data from eight countries, recording the incomes of fathers at the time of the birth of their sons and the incomes of those sons at the age of thirty. The results clearly showed that the sons were far more likely to advance beyond the income levels of their fathers in more egalitarian countries. The most equal countries in the survey— Norway, Sweden, Denmark, and Finland—all showed high rates of social mobility. Canada was high as well, and Germany fairly high. At the other end, with much lower social mobility, was Britain, and then even farther back was the United States, with the least social mobility of the eight countries studied.[17] So Americans aren't just shrinking—they are also increasingly immobile, trapped in the circumstances of their birth. Those wanting to give their children a real chance to live the American Dream would be well advised to move to Sweden.

It's interesting to note that America's poor performance in social mobility is a relatively new phenomenon. The United States used to come much closer to its own ideal of offering economic opportunity and a chance to climb the social ladder. Another set of data, for instance, shows that social mobility actually improved in the United States from 1950 to 1980—the early postwar years, when high tax rates and more equal pay resulted in a more equal distribution of income. But after 1980, when the Reagan revolution brought about a sharp increase in income inequality, social mobility dropped off suddenly and dramatically. The pattern is similar for Britain.[18]

The explanation for this may be fairly simple. The key to social mobility seems to lie in public education. The more educated people are, the more opportunities they have for advancement and earning. In the eight countries in the study mentioned above, the ones with higher levels of equality also all had higher levels of public spending on education. (This is not surprising, since public education is one of the key priorities of government, so countries that collect a lot of taxes tend to spend a lot on education.) In Norway, the most equal of the eight countries in the study, fully 97 percent of all education spending was devoted to public education, compared to only 68 percent in the United States.

This brings us back to the important role played by public spending. High levels of public spending can be found in almost all the positive health and social outcomes that we've been discussing in this chapter. If we look, for instance, at the incidence of child poverty—a clear indicator of social distress—we see that it is almost ten times higher in the United States than in the Scandinavian countries. A staggering 21.7 percent of U.S. children live in poverty, compared to a mere 2.4 percent in Denmark, 3.4 percent in Finland, and 3.6 percent in Sweden (the Scandinavian average is 3.3 percent). Similarly, there are striking differences in levels of support for other vulnerable groups. In the United States, the elderly live on incomes that are 51 percent of their preretirement incomes, compared to 66.5 percent for the elderly in Scandinavian countries. People with disabilities are even more disadvantaged in unequal countries. In the United States, their incomes are 58.7 percent relative to the general population; in Scandinavian countries, their incomes are closer at 86 percent of the national average. Equal countries have also been far more effective at closing the gender gap. In a gender-gap index developed by the World Economic Forum, the Scandinavian countries score consistently higher.[19]

The impressive social results in the Scandinavian countries have long been noted by those arguing for a stronger government role in correcting the inequality generated by the marketplace in North America. At the same time, there's been a tendency to see the superior social benefits in Scandinavia—or even broadly in Europe—as some sort of trade-off for economic prosperity. It's been widely believed that high taxes and social spending may help lots of people, but they destroy the work incentive and thereby reduce everyone's material well-being. However, there's actually little evidence to support this contention, and a lot of evidence to refute it. Indeed, it's becoming increasingly clear that it's not necessary to choose between social benefits and prosperity—it's possible to have both.

In the wake of the 2008 financial collapse, the economic results for the United States (and Britain, another highly unequal country) have of course been very poor. But in case that's just a weird aberration, let's look at what was going on before the Wall Street meltdown. The data show that, on a number of important economic measures, countries with more equal distributions of income were doing just as well or better than more unequal ones. Let's take two extremes—the highly unequal United States and the highly equal nations of Scandinavia (which we'll lump together and consider as one entity).

If we look at GDP per capita in 2004, the United States was out in front, with $39,700 compared to $32,825 for the Scandinavian countries. But GDP per capita doesn't really tell us much about how ordinary Americans are doing economically, since, as noted before, that statistic is simply an average of all incomes and is therefore greatly elevated in the United States by the presence of a small number of extremely rich people. Moreover, the U.S. GDP per capita is high partly because so many Americans have to work long hours simply to make ends meet. Besides, income alone hardly tells a complete story of the economic situation of a nation's citizens. Another important measure is the degree of economic security those citizens enjoy—what economic supports are available in unemployment and retirement. In an economic security index developed by the International Labor Office—in which a low score indicates that a country is providing less economic security to workers—the United States scores a poor 0.61, compared to 0.94 for Scandinavia.

Defenders of the U.S. economic model often point to economic growth rates, noting that the United States experienced higher growth from the late 1990s until the 2008 financial collapse. This is true; the average growth in GDP per capita was 3.1 percent in the United States, compared to 2.3 percent in Scandinavia (and 2.0 percent in continental Europe). But when it came to other important economic measures, the

Scandinavian countries did as well or slightly better than the United States. Despite their extensive social programs, the Scandinavian countries managed to avoid deficits. While the U.S. deficit in 2004 was 4.7 percent of its GDP, the Scandinavians were running a surplus of 4.1 percent. Furthermore, on an "Innovation" index developed by the UN Conference on Trade and Development, the United States scored 0.927, while the Scandinavian countries scored a more impressive 0.951, on average. And when it came to competitiveness, as measured by the business-financed World Economic Forum in Geneva, the United States and Scandinavian countries were typically in a tight race for the laurels. Indeed, Finland hogged the top spot for a number of years in the 2000s, and all the Scandinavian nations always hover around the top of the chart. On an index of growth in competitiveness, based on the World Economic Forum measurements, and on a Global Creativity Index, the Scandinavians slightly outstripped the United States. And when it came to spending on research and development as a percentage of GDP, the Scandinavians were again ahead, spending 3.4 percent, while the United States spent 2.7 percent.

All in all, there's little to support the case that the United States was the stronger economic performer. If it was, its superiority was fairly marginal. And that was then. The 2008 financial crisis and subsequent economic downturn have played havoc with America's economy, leaving it with persistently high unemployment and a massive, trillion-dollar deficit. Then there's the fact that the causes of the financial collapse were directly connected to the U.S. economic model with its free-market ideology and essentially unregulated banking sector. That lack of regulation was (and continues to be) the product of intense lobbying by Wall Street bankers and the dominance of this overly rich and powerful group. So, however the U.S. economic model may have stacked up against the more egalitarian Scandinavian model in recent years, any possible superiority has been more than wiped out by the devastating impact of the Wall Street–generated financial collapse.

More broadly, there's some intriguing evidence that suggests inequality may discourage innovation. Three German economists recently made the case that egalitarian societies create strong incentives for manufacturers to invest in the kinds of technological innovations that enable products to be more widely dispersed among the population, contributing to overall improvements in the standard of living. Economists Reto Foellmi, Tobias Wuergler, and Josef Zweimuller have argued that though new products are often first developed as luxury items for the wealthy, the subsequent innovations that enable these items to be produced on a larger scale only happen when there is a larger market of people able to afford a more efficiently produced (and therefore cheaper) version.[20] The automobile, for instance, was originally produced for sale to the very rich, but the kind of innovation that led to the mass production of the Model T Ford at cheaper prices was encouraged by the presence of an American middle class. This suggests that a more equal income distribution may actually lead to higher levels of investment in technological innovation and therefore greater economic prosperity

So extreme inequality not only is directly linked to a wide range of health and social problems, but also appears to be bad for the economy—ultimately, extremely bad for the economy, as the 2008 financial crash shows.

Indeed, the role of a wealthy super-class in bringing about the collapse points to what is perhaps the most basic trouble with extreme inequality: the concentration of money in so few hands inevitably affects how power is exercised. When a tiny faction controls such a large proportion of the nation's wealth, it will also likely control the nation.

# CHAPTER 10

# Why Billionaires Are Bad
# for Democracy

There are many words that could be used to describe Barack Obama, but one adjective decidedly doesn't fit: aggressive. So it was more than passing strange when a prominent member of Wall Street—Stephen Schwarzman, chairman of the private equity giant Blackstone Group—compared actions by President Obama to one of the most notoriously aggressive acts by one of history's most aggressive villains. Speaking to the board of a nonprofit group, Schwarzman fiercely denounced initiatives by the Obama administration: "It's war. It's like when Hitler invaded Poland in 1939."[1]

In the arena of political commentary, few things are considered more clearly below-the-belt than comparing an opponent to Hitler. So there was a small stir in August 2010 when it was reported that Schwarzman—whom *Time* magazine had included on its one hundred most influential people list only three years earlier—had likened Obama to the Nazi strongman. When asked by the media, Schwarzman acknowledged making the remark and then apologized for it, while reaffirming the sentiment behind it. But what was striking about the Hitler comment—besides its sheer viciousness and absurdity—was what had provoked it. Schwarzman wasn't complaining about undue military force, torture, or ethnic cleansing. He was likening the president to the most reviled man in history on the grounds that Obama was trying to close a tax loophole that allowed hedge fund and private equity managers (like Schwarzman) to pay tax at a rate that Warren Buffett famously noted was lower than that paid by their secretaries.

In an era marked by gluttony and hubris, Steve Schwarzman has still managed to stand out.

His sixtieth birthday party in Manhattan in 2007 was so lavish—with live performances by Rod Stewart and Martin Short—it became Wall Street legend. Then there's Schwarzman's thirty-five-room Park Avenue residence (once owned by John D. Rockefeller), his sprawling estate in Saint-Tropez, a spectacular spread in Jamaica, and his massive Palm Beach estate, where the executive chef says it typically costs about $3,000 a weekend to feed just Schwarzman and his wife. (Among other things, they like to eat stone crabs that cost $400 each.)

Schwarzman is a major figure in private equity, part of the surging field of "alternative asset" financial institutions that, along with hedge and real estate funds, appeared on the horizon two decades ago and now control trillions of dollars in assets. While hedge funds are well-known for contributing to the subprime mortgage crash, private equity funds are notorious for taking over established firms with borrowed money and essentially pillaging them. The bought-out companies are typically saddled with increased debt from the takeover and forced to make massive dividend and fee payouts to the private equity managers and their investors, while employees are shed and union contracts gutted. The companies are usually chopped up into smaller pieces and sold soon afterwards at inflated prices, creating another windfall for the private equity managers, some of whom have become billionaires. By 2007, the Blackstone Group had taken control of more than 112 companies worth nearly $200 billion, had just completed the largest private-equity buyout ever for $39 billion, and was poised to take over Hilton Hotels. By 2011, Schwarzman ranked #169 on *Forbes's* worldwide billionaire list, worth an estimated $5.9 billion.

But the Blackstone boss has never been particularly good about figuring out the right thing to say at the right time. Even before he likened Obama to Hitler, he showed a singular insensitivity to his fellow New Yorkers during the grim Christmas season of 2009. When the *New York*

*Times* invited prominent New Yorkers to propose New Year's resolutions for the city, most contributors came up with worthy ideas for aiding the city's destitute, improving its public transit, or funding education. Schwarzman's suggestion was that New York follow in the footsteps of London in offering enormous tax benefits to wealthy foreigners.[2]

Schwarzman may be rougher at the edges than most of the hedge fund and private equity crowd. But his outburst against Obama reminds us of the "war" he and others—by themselves or by proxies—have been engaged in to minimize their contribution to the public treasury. It's an all-too-familiar tale of how effective the rich are at getting their way, even when the battle is being played out in a very public arena where a small group of billionaires advancing their own self-interests would seem a very tough sell.

Victor Fleischer didn't set out to be a twenty-first-century Robin Hood. His real aim was just to get tenure.

After graduating from Columbia Law School, Fleischer joined the New York law firm Polk Davis in the late 1990s, working on the formations of private equity and venture capital funds. He was struck by the very low rates of tax paid by fund managers, even compared to the already low tax rates being paid by executives receiving corporate stock options. Fleischer wasn't discovering something new; the rules had been in place since 1954. Nor was he outraged or even particularly interested in the question of tax fairness and the implications for the public treasury of having some exceptionally rich people pay exceptionally low tax rates. At the time, he was simply interested in the impact that the tax rules governing so-called "carried interest" might have on the law firm's clients; for instance, how the rules might affect the deal between the fund managers and investors in the fund.

The question stayed in Fleischer's mind after he left Polk Davis in 2001 and became a law professor specializing in taxation. Hoping to get a paper published to improve his chances of securing tenure at the University of Illinois Law School, Fleischer put together his thoughts on the taxation of private equity funds. Now that he was no longer constrained by working for people in the private equity field, he started to pay attention to what seemed to him to be a "quirk" in the law that distorted tax principles while undermining distributive justice. "This quirk in the tax law allows some of the richest workers in the country to pay tax on their labor income at a low rate," he wrote in the abstract of his paper, published by the *New York University Law Review* in March 2006. "[T]he status quo is an untenable position as a matter of tax policy." In the arcane world of tax policy, Fleischer had thrown down the gauntlet.

He was pointing to the fact that managers of private equity, venture capital, and hedge funds were claiming a significant part of their incomes as capital gains (taxed at 15 percent), rather than treating them as regular income (taxed at 35 percent). That substantial difference in rates was magnified by the enormity of the incomes in question. A private equity manager receiving, say, $600 million as a capital gain would pay $90 million in tax. If the same income were treated as income from salary, it would be taxed at 35 percent (and also be subject to 2.9 percent in payroll taxes), bringing the private equity manager's tax bill to $227.4 million—almost $140 million more.

The ostensible purpose of the lower capital gains rate is to compensate investors for the risk they take in investing their capital. But private equity and fund managers aren't investing their own capital. They're investing other people's capital. They're simply money managers, being paid for the service of handling other people's money. If their fund loses money, they don't suffer losses, as investors do. By claiming capital gains treatment, they are passing off regular income as capital gains, simply to save themselves taxes.

The fund managers insist that their compensation is still very risky; while some deals may lead to huge profits, others prove disastrous. True. But risk is hardly confined to fund managers. Politicians can find themselves out of work after an election; a TV anchor can get fired if ratings plunge; a Hollywood star can find work dries up as he ages. At lower income levels, the risks are far larger. Indeed, in the last thirty years, vast swaths of the economy could be designated as risky for those needing to earn a living. The sort of stable, lifelong jobs that were common a generation ago have been largely replaced by contract or part-time work, with little or no security. A layoff can mean the loss of the family home or health benefits, or even destitution—far more serious plights than anything likely to befall a hedge fund manager. (For that matter, no one ever seems to argue for special low tax rates for the real risk-takers among us—miners, oil-rig workers, acrobats, fire fighters, window washers working on tall buildings.)

The so-called "carried interest" loophole enjoyed by hedge fund and private equity managers raises the larger question of whether capital gains—even real ones—should ever be taxed at lower rates. On the face of things, the lower rate seems patently unfair. Why should some-one earning income by investing his fortune be taxed at a substantially lower rate than those earning income from the sweat of their brows or from using skills they've spent years acquiring? The unfairness is illustrated by the fact that capital gains are almost exclusively enjoyed by those at the top. So, for instance, if capital gains were taxed at the same rate as regular income, the poorest 20 percent of taxpayers would experience almost no difference. In fact, their annual tax bills would only go up by an average of $1 a year! Similarly, there would be almost no impact on those in the middle-income range, who would experience an average tax increase of just $6 a year. But for those at the top, the impact would be substantial—the top 1 percent would experience an annual tax hike, on average, of $27,039.[3]

The fairness argument has essentially been set aside, however, as business has relentlessly promoted the notion that such preferential treatment is necessary to coax those with capital to invest it. But do investors really need coaxing? Warren Buffett, one of the world's savviest investors, doesn't think so. "I have worked with investors for 60 years and I have yet to see anyone—not even when capital gains rates were 39.9 percent in 1976–77—shy away from a sensible investment because of the tax rate on the potential gain," Buffet argues. "People invest to make money, and potential taxes have never scared them off."[4]

Of course, a higher tax rate might discourage investors from making foolish investments in unpromising enterprises. But that could be a good thing. Alan S. Blinder, economics professor at Princeton University and former vice chair of the Federal Reserve, points out that the lower capital-gains rate actually encourages people to make investments that they might not otherwise make without tax incentives. "The government thus induces people to make bad investments, which is a good way to run an economy into the ground," says Blinder. "Come to think of it, that's just what the old Soviet Union did. It invested copiously, but badly."[5]

For that matter, our business culture tends to portray investors as modern-day heroes who put their hard-earned capital into worthy high-risk ventures that lead to path-breaking discoveries that enrich the lives of all of us. Sadly, the vast majority of investments don't fit into this category (and those that do qualify for additional tax incentives). Rather, as former mutual fund manager John C. Bogle notes, "most capital gains are made from gambling in the stock market."[6] So the ultimate function of the special low rate on capital gains is to save our wealthiest citizens billions of dollars a year on their winnings in the Wall Street casino.

Not many people read the *New York University Law Review*. But Fleischer's paper found its way a few months later into the hands of congressional Democrats at a time when they were looking for fresh sources of revenue to pay for the expansion of the State Children's Health Insurance Program and the Earned Income Tax Credit. The juxtaposition of high-flying hedge fund managers and children without health care seemed like a public relations nightmare for the Wall Street crowd.

Schwarzman himself helped put an unsavory face on the fund manager set—not with his Hitler comment, which came later—but with his plan to turn Blackstone into a publicly traded company in the spring of 2007. The plan would not only allow Schwarzman and other top

Blackstone executives to continue to qualify for the low capital-gains rate as fund managers, but would also allow their new multibillion-dollar publicly traded company to largely avoid paying corporate taxes. If Schwarzman won the approval of SEC regulators, he and Blackstone cofounder Peter Peterson would receive billions of dollars worth of stock, plus hundreds of millions in cash. And this would surely set a precedent, enticing other private equity funds, as well as investment banks—including giants like Goldman Sachs and Morgan Stanley—to reorganize themselves along similar lines, making the paying of corporate taxes almost optional for Wall Street institutions.

Schwarzman's move had pushed the issue of sweetheart taxation for private equity kings from law school reviews to the front pages of newspapers. A bill to stop Schwarzman—dubbed the Blackstone bill—quickly appeared in Congress. As controversy raged about low taxation of the rich, Warren Buffett weighed in with a call for the rich to pay more tax. In 2007, speaking to four hundred guests who had paid $4,600 a ticket to attend a fund-raiser for Hillary Clinton, Buffett attacked Congress for allowing the U.S. tax system to tax rich investors like himself so lightly: "The 400 of us [here] pay a lower part of our income in taxes than our receptionists do, or our cleaning ladies, for that matter."[7]

Momentum seemed to be building against the Blackstone deal and more broadly for a bill, sponsored by Democratic congressman Sander Levin, that would shut down the fund manager loophole completely. But Wall Street quickly organized a counterattack. Some of the largest private equity firms formed the Private Equity Council, and, within six months, the Council had retained four top lobbying firms to handle the case. Labor and public interest groups lobbied from the other side, presenting a letter to Congress signed by more than a hundred organizations across the country urging that the loophole be closed. But private equity had resources that were probably a thousand times greater, according to Steve Wamhoff, legislative director of the Washington-based group Citizens for Tax Justice.

No argument seemed too extreme or silly to advance in defense of maintaining the loophole. Lobbyists insisted, for instance, that the tax break was crucial in the fight against cancer, pointing to the fact that the loophole also applied to those running venture capital funds, which sometimes invest in high-risk start-up firms—including those developing products to fight cancer. Lobbyists managed to enlist the support of twenty-eight researchers and academics who supported the notion that the tax break might help cancer research. Private equity was trying to make the case that showering tax breaks on all fund managers, some of whom might be investing their funds in firms involved in fighting cancer, was an effective way to subsidize the fight against cancer—rather than simply increasing direct subsidies to cancer researchers or start-up firms.

In the end, the weakness of the case for maintaining the loophole didn't matter. In three years of Congressional battles over the issue—with the Democrats mostly voting to shut down the loophole, and Republicans voting to keep it alive—the House passed a bill to shut it down three times. But Democrats finally abandoned attempts to overcome Republican obstacles in the Senate in June 2010. So, even with the Democrats holding the White House, the House, and the Senate (including sixty seats for a while), "they were still incapable of closing the most indefensible loophole in existence," notes Wamhoff. "I would not have believed this story if I didn't see it with my own eyes."[8]

In the run-up to the debt-ceiling crisis in the summer of 2011, the most indefensible loophole in existence was once again in the spotlight. Figures from the Congressional Budget Office showed that closing the loophole could save $21 billion over ten years. That wouldn't eliminate the debt, of course, but given the scope of the debt problem, it seemed a lot of money to simply ignore. *New York Times* columnist Nicholas Kristof devoted a column to the tax break, awarding it the grand prize for the "Most Unconscionable Tax Loophole."[9] The president himself zeroed in on it again. "How can we ask a student to pay more for college before we ask hedge fund managers to stop paying taxes at a lower rate than their secretaries?" Obama said in an address to Congress in July. "It's not fair. It's not right." Given the apparently desperate search for ways to reduce the debt, the tax loophole for hedge fund managers   probably among the nation's least loved characters—seemed like low-hanging fruit.

But the Tea Party crowd now becoming power players in the Republican Party was as resistant to compromise as Obama was prone to it. They blamed the mounting deficit entirely on Obama (even though George W. Bush had added $5.07 trillion to the debt, primarily due to his tax cuts and military spending, while Obama had added just $1.44 trillion, mostly fighting the recession).[10] Spotting an opportunity to use the deficit to achieve deep spending cuts, the hard-line Republicans refused to raise the debt ceiling without a long-term strategy for debt reduction, which they insisted be entirely achieved through spending cuts. In the final deal, signed into law just hours before the deadline for a Latin American–style default, the hijackers appeared to win, with $917 billion in deficit-reduction measures all to come from spending cuts (and another $1.5 trillion to be worked out by a bipartisan committee). The radical Republicans had turned the fairly routine business of raising the debt ceiling—something Republicans had agreed to eighty-seven times since World War II—into a bloodbath of spending cuts.

An observer could easily conclude that all this simply shows how resistant Americans have become to tax increases. But in fact it shows no such thing. In the years leading up to the debt-ceiling showdown, Americans have repeatedly told pollsters that they support higher taxes *on the rich* as a way to reduce the deficit. A *Washington Post*–ABC News poll reported in July 2011, as the crisis reached a crescendo, found that 72 percent supported raising taxes on those earning more than $250,000 a year.

What the debt-ceiling fiasco really showed was how a band of Republican extremists had effectively taken the U.S. political system hostage and were moving to enact the Right's longtime fantasy of dismantling popular New Deal programs—particularly Social Security— which had been politically untouchable since the 1930s. Americans were told that these programs were simply no longer affordable—even though the country had grown considerably richer over the decades. In fact, what had changed was not the affordability of the programs but the intransigence of the nation's elite to paying taxes.

So while programs helping students, the elderly, and the poor were to be picked over by deficit-cutting politicians with surgical precision, private equity and hedge fund mangers were to be spared any increase in taxes. They could get back to work pillaging companies and destabilizing financial markets with full peace of mind, knowing they'd continue to enjoy a tax rate lower than the mechanics who service their private jets.

Indeed, only a month after the debt-ceiling crisis, Stephen Schwarzman was back on the offensive, no longer just defending the special tax break that saved him millions of dollars a year, but now insisting on the need for broad tax reform—*so that low-income people would pay more.* Schwarzman's concern was that many Americans manage to avoid paying income tax at all because their incomes are so low. His solution was a flat tax, so that everyone would pay some income tax. "If some people are left out and some people have special deals, it doesn't feel like the kind of situation where everyone's going to get on board," Schwarzman told CNBC.[11] For Schwarzman, "special deals" aren't loopholes for billionaires but exemptions for those with low incomes—mostly the elderly, people with children, and the poor—who've been dubbed "lucky duckies" by the *Wall Street Journal* for their apparent tax-free status.

It was a sentiment that was increasingly heard from conservatives in the wake of their debt-ceiling triumph. When Warren Buffett renewed his call for higher taxes on the rich with a controversial op-ed that month in the *New York Times,* he unleashed a torrent of angry responses from the wealthy. Harvey Golub, former CEO of American Express, responded by noting that almost half of all U.S. tax filers paid no income tax at all. They should start paying tax, argued Golub, a member of the executive committee of the American Enterprise Institute: "[T]hey should pay something and have a stake in our government spending their money too."[12] (In fact, when all taxes are considered—state and local, as well as federal—low-income Americans are heavily taxed.)

Having rebuffed Obama's invasion, the Wall Street crowd was now itching to launch a counterinvasion. No longer was the goal just to protect their own loopholes. They now sought to solve the deficit crisis, which they had greatly contributed to with their reckless financial speculation, by digging into the empty pockets of low-income Americans. It wasn't that the rich weren't paying enough tax; it was that others weren't paying enough. It was time to go after the lucky duckies. A new rallying cry could be heard rumbling from the boardrooms of Wall Street: *Make the Poor Pay!*

It is perhaps self-evident that wealthy interests exert disproportionate influence over the political agenda and, in the process, undermine democracy. As Aristotle noted some three hundred years before the birth of Christ, "Where the possession of political power is due to the possession of economic power or wealth . . . that is oligarchy, and when the unpropertied class has power, that is democracy." A few hundred years later, the Greek historian Plutarch already considered the subversive role of money in politics as one of those self-evident truths that one grows weary of observing: "An imbalance between rich and poor is the oldest and most fatal ailment of all republics." In the early twentieth century, U.S. Supreme Court justice Louis Brandeis put it bluntly: "We can have democracy in this country or we can have great wealth concentrated in the hands of a few. We cannot have both."

Brandeis would have clearly been horrified by the Supreme Court's *Citizens United v. Federal Election Commission* decision a century later, in January 2010, to allow unlimited corporate spending on election campaigns. President Obama denounced the decision in his State of the Union address that month, insisting that "the Supreme Court reversed a century of law to open the floodgates for special interests—including foreign corporations—to spend without limit in our elections." But perhaps the most eloquent denunciation came from Justice John Paul Stevens, one of the four judges dissenting in the *Citizens United* decision:

> At bottom, the Court's opinion is thus a rejection of the common sense of the American people, who have recognized a need to prevent corporations from undermining self government since the founding, and who have fought against the distinctive corrupting potential of corporate electioneering since the days of Theodore Roosevelt. It is a strange time to repudiate that common sense. While American democracy is imperfect, few outside the majority of this Court would have thought its flaws included a dearth of corporate money in politics.

Yet despite the dominance of corporations and wealthy interests today—a dominance that clearly stands to grow with the *Citizens United* decision—the notion persists that our modern Western nations are democratic, that they are controlled by the will of the majority. While most people would probably agree that the rich have more weight in politics, elections are nevertheless taken seriously in our mainstream culture and public discourse. People talk about the importance of citizens voting and see voter turnout as an indication of the health of the democracy. Presumably this reflects the widespread belief that our democracies work, that the will of ordinary citizens will prevail, that any party that strays too far from popular sentiment will be tossed out by the voters and replaced by another party that better responds to the public's needs and desires. According to this view, despite the importance of money in politics and the dominance of the backroom boys, the interests of ordinary citizens are broadly protected because fear of alienating the majority will keep the most cynical politician in line.

This analysis is bolstered by the presence in our democracies of large numbers of organizations promoting all sorts of different interests and viewpoints. With varying degrees of effectiveness, these groups manage to insert their voices into the public debate, even if only at the margin. All this helps contribute to a general sense that power is widely distributed, that multiple voices are heard, that competing groups balance each other out, and that social policy councils, associations of migrant workers, and environmental activists somehow counter the power of billionaires and business associations.

Although many on the left have always dismissed this comforting view of a functioning democracy as naive, it was accepted by mainstream political scientists throughout the 1950s and '60s. But as business became increasingly assertive and successful in achieving its goals, political scientists began questioning their own confidence in "pluralism"—the notion that power is widely distributed, that no one group exercises dominance. By the mid-1970s, two of the world's most preeminent political scientists, Robert Dahl and Charles Lindblom, began to reassess the pluralist views they themselves had long subscribed to.

In 1976, in a jointly authored new introduction to their classic text *Politics, Economics and Welfare,* Dahl and Lindblom distanced themselves from their pluralist views: "Interpretations that depict the American or any other market-oriented system as a competition among interest groups are seriously in error for their failure to take account of the distinctive privileged position of businessmen in politics. . . . In the United States, more money, energy, and organizational strength is thrown into obstructing equality than achieving it." The two political scientists concluded that "to democratize the American polyarchy further will require a redistribution of wealth and income."[13] By 1982—as the Reagan revolution moved into full gear—Dahl recanted any previous pluralist tendencies: "It is perfectly obvious that one of the most influential structures in any society is the distribution of income and wealth. Disparities of income and wealth confer extraordinary advantages and disadvantages. The distribution of advantages and disadvantages is often arbitrary, capricious, unmerited, and unjust, and in virtually all advanced countries no longer tolerable."[14]

With the arrival of George W. Bush in the White House in 2001, the political dominance of the wealthy became so pronounced that the fourteen-thousand-member American Political Science Association

(APSA) took the unusual step of setting up a task force to study the impact of rising inequality on the nation's democracy. The fifteen members were carefully chosen so that the group not only included leading political scientists but also represented a diverse array of ideological viewpoints as well as varying methodological approaches and specialties. The task force then spent two years reviewing the best available scholarship, as well as conducting new empirical studies and submitting its work to rigorous peer review. In its report, released in 2004, the APSA delivered a forceful indictment of the current state of American democracy: "Citizens with lower or moderate incomes speak with a whisper that is lost on the ears of inattentive government officials, while the advantaged roar with a clarity and consistency that policy-makers readily hear and routinely follow. The scourge of overt discrimination against African-Americans and women has been replaced by a more subtle but potent threat—the growing concentration of the country's wealth and income in the hands of the few."[15]

As the task force report suggests, the threat posed by the concentration of wealth is becoming graver. In the past thirty years, as the rich have become vastly richer, they've devoted far more resources and become much more adept at influencing all aspects of the political process in their favor. Political scientists Jacob S. Hacker and Paul Pierson have identified the mechanics of how this influence is exercised in examining the case of the Republican tax cuts of 2001 and 2003.[16] Those cuts represented dramatic changes that fundamentally altered the nation's fiscal landscape and its distribution of income. They were passed into law even though they provided average citizens with only very modest benefits and considerable long-term risks, while giving the wealthy a truly massive windfall. Some commentators have suggested that the tax cuts became law because ordinary voters ultimately support favorable treatment of the rich, possibly in the hopes of someday joining their ranks themselves. But Hacker and Pierson, in carefully analyzing the extensive polling data on the issue, show that Americans clearly did not favor the substance of the Bush cuts.

Although some polls suggested that there was broad support for the cuts, Hacker and Pierson note that such polls simply asked whether or not voters favored "Bush's tax cut proposal," without offering any alternative or pointing out the trade-offs involved. Asking if a voter wants a tax cut is a bit like asking if he wants some chocolate. Of course he does! But when the question became, "Do you want a tax cut, or would you like to spend surplus national revenues on something else?" respondents consistently ranked tax cuts below other priorities. As opposed to Social Security, tax cuts lost by a margin of 74 to 21; versus Medicare, they lost 65 to 25; versus a grab bag of "education, the environment, health care, crime-fighting and military defense," the margin was 69 to 22 percent. Voters showed a clear preference for an agenda sharply at odds with the one being offered by the Bush administration.

The rejection of the substance of the Bush tax cuts became even more pronounced on the question of where the benefits should go. In other words, if there was going to be a tax cut, the public consistently and strongly opposed the idea that the benefits should go almost solely to the well-to-do. For instance, a March 2001 survey asked respondents whether federal taxes should be cut across the board, which, the survey noted, would give the largest share of the cut to the wealthiest Americans, or whether cuts should be aimed more at middle-income Americans. When presented with these two options, 73 percent of respondents favored the plan that skewed benefits toward the middle class. Who would have guessed?

Moreover, it appears that the Bush administration was well aware of the public's preferences. In a now-released internal memo from 2001, a top Treasury official named Michele Davis advised her boss, Treasury Secretary Paul O'Neill, to push the president's tax-cut plan at an upcoming event, while cautioning him to keep in mind that "the public prefers spending on things like health care and education over cutting taxes." Davis, who served as O'Neill's press secretary, clearly understood that her government's plan was at odds with what the public wanted. But rather than feeling reined in by public opinion, the

Bush administration and its officials appeared to see the popular preference as merely a problem that had to be carefully handled. "It's crucial that you make clear that there are no trade-offs here," Davis wrote
matter-of-factly to the Treasury secretary, even though there clearly
were trade-offs. "Roll-out events like this are the clearest examples of
when staying on message is absolutely crucial. Any deviation . . . will
change the way coverage plays out from tomorrow forward."[17]

Davis obviously never intended the public to see her note, which
was directed solely at those who presumably shared the administration's determination to put the tax cut in place despite the public's
strong reservations. And the administration had gone to great lengths
to make sure that the public had little sense of what was actually going on. This included the Treasury Department releasing some highly
misleading statistical information, and President Bush himself stating
barefaced lies, like insisting in 2000 that "by far the vast majority of my
tax cuts go to the bottom end of the spectrum." The public was further
confused by the actual design of the tax cuts, in which the meager
benefits going to the middle class were provided quickly upfront while
the really massive benefits directed toward the upper end kicked in
a few years later, when public and media attention would inevitably
have moved on.

The result was a stupendously large redistribution of resources to
the very affluent. The richest 0.1 percent of Americans saved 284 times
more from the Bush tax cuts between 2001 and 2010 than people in the
middle 20 percent of the U.S. income distribution[18]—a result that, as
the polling data show, the American public did not want.

More generally, there's a growing body of research that shows that—
on a wide range of issues—U.S. elected officials are unresponsive to
the policy choices of ordinary citizens. Martin Gilens, a professor of
politics at Princeton University, reviewed almost two thousand survey
questions put to the public in the last three decades, correlating them
against what policy changes were actually made. Strikingly, Gilens
found that the chances of a policy change being enacted depended on
the income level of those supporting it, and that "influence over actual

policy outcomes appears to be reserved almost exclusively for those at the top of the income distribution."[19]

A similar study by Larry Bartels, a political scientist at Vanderbilt University, compared the results of public opinion surveys with the votes of U.S. senators on issues including abortion, civil rights, the minimum wage, and government spending. Once again, the chances of senators paying attention to the preferences of citizens depended on how well-heeled the citizens were. The voting patterns of senators were closely in line with the preferences of those in the top third of income distribution, and considerably less so with those in the middle third. The views of people in the bottom third appeared to have had no impact on senators.[20] What these studies suggest is that, as in the tax area, the preferences of the majority don't really matter in the political process. The notion that the majority will ultimately get its way—a belief that lies at the very foundation of the popular notion of democracy—seems to be largely a myth.

In fact, the majority has rarely gotten its way in recent years. The commonly held assumption is that ordinary Americans have drifted to the right politically in the last few decades, pushing American politics with them or at least allowing the right to take advantage of their more conservative sympathies to bring in a right-wing agenda. But Hacker and Pierson reviewed thousands of polls and opinion surveys conducted in the last two decades and found no evidence to corroborate this popular impression of a general shift to the right. (Even evangelical voters—although strongly conservative on social issues—haven't moved to the right on economic issues; indeed, they've only voted Republican because the party has vigorously promoted their social causes.)[21] Hacker and Pierson conclude that, contrary to the popular perception, there's been no rightward drift in American public opinion on key issues about the economy and the role of government. "[S]urvey questions regarding the role of government and key areas of public policy show little or no rightward shift—and perhaps even a leftward shift," they write. "[T]hey offer not a whiff of support for the common presumption that a major right turn in American public opinion has driven the dramatic transformation of American public policy over the last generation."[22]

But the shift to the right in the voting patterns of elected U.S. congressmen and senators has been real and profound. This may seem puzzling. It wouldn't, however, have puzzled Mark Hanna, the nineteenth-century Republican senator and infamous backroom strategist who memorably noted: "There are two things that are important in politics. The first is money and I can't remember what the second is."

Barely a month after Barack Obama had been sworn in as the forty-fourth U.S. president, riding a wave of immense popular support with his "Yes, we can" rallying cry echoing around the country and the world, a voice seemed to appear from nowhere saying, "No, actually you can't." Ostensibly, it came first from Rick Santelli, a relatively obscure investment manager-turned-commentator on CNBC, who denounced Obama's plans to help struggling American homeowners as "promoting bad behavior." In a wide-ranging rant from the floor of the Chicago Mercantile Exchange on February 19, 2009, Santelli said, "We're thinking of having a Chicago Tea Party in July. All you capitalists that want to show up to Lake Michigan, I'm gonna start organizing." Within hours, a protest movement had swung into action on the Internet, talk radio, and cable TV, and rallies were scheduled across the country for the following week.

To Mark Ames and Yasha Levine, journalists who had written for an expatriate newspaper based in Moscow, there was something fishy about the whole affair. "As veteran Russia reporters, both of us spent years watching the Kremlin use fake grassroots movements to influence and control the political landscape. To us, the uncanny speed and direction the movement took and the players involved in promoting it had a strangely forced quality to it."[23] Ames and Levine noted that, only hours after Santelli's rant, a previously inactive website called ChicagoTeaParty.com, which had been registered six months earlier by a right-wing activist, sprung to life, declaring itself the official home of the Chicago Tea Party. Whether or not Santelli was part of deliberate plan to launch the Tea Party—he denies that he was—Ames and Levine quickly pointed out what other journalists have later confirmed: that the apparently spontaneous outburst of disaffected Americans was greatly helped along by an organized and sophisticated campaign ultimately funded by two of America's richest men, Charles and David Koch.

In many ways, the emergence of the Tea Party as a potent force in American politics can be seen as the culmination of almost four decades of behind-the-scenes effort on the part of the billionaire brothers. The political views of the Koch brothers have always been on the extreme right, nurtured by their father, Fred Koch, a cofounder of the ultra-right-wing John Birch Society. Since inheriting his massive privately held oil fortune in the late 1960s, the brothers have been pouring untold millions of dollars into promoting libertarian causes. The probing of Ames and Levine, as well as a comprehensive, investigative piece by Jane Mayer in the *New Yorker* in August 2010, has shown that the brothers established a vast network of ultra-conservative political organizations, advocacy groups, publications, and think tanks. Included in this network is the high-profile Cato Institute, which has aggressively pushed for an end to Social Security, and the Mercatus Center, located at George Washington University, which has been a leading advocate of environmental deregulation and inaction on climate change. (Its scholars have reassured the public that "if a slight warming does occur, historical evidence suggests it is likely to be beneficial, occurring at night, in the winter and at the poles.")[24]

The brothers have mostly stayed out of politics directly (apart from David Koch's stint as the vice presidential candidate for the Libertarian Party in 1980, positioned to the right of Ronald Reagan). Perhaps the Kochs sensed how politically toxic a couple of billionaires could be to a movement whose central aim has been slashing taxes on the rich and dismantling programs, like Social Security, that keep millions of Americans out of poverty.

Hence they've masked their involvement. But their fingerprints are all over groups that have played an essential role in fostering the Tea Party's rise, particularly Americans for Prosperity, which David Koch started in 2004. In a rare speech to a celebratory AFP gathering in the Washington area in 2009, Koch confirmed his involvement: "Days like today bring to reality the vision of our board of directors when we started this organization five years ago."[25] Still, with Koch and his kingly lifestyle remaining mostly out of sight, AFP has been able to present Koch-funded political events as populist gatherings of ordinary citizens trying to fight vested interests. Advertisements for a 2010 summit called Texas Defending the American Dream, for instance, proclaimed, "Today, the voices of average Americans are being drowned out by lobbyists and special interests"—without mentioning that the event was being sponsored by two of America's wealthiest men, whose lobbying and special interest pleading had become so extensive it was dubbed the Kochtopus decades earlier.[26]

In fact, the Kochs were really just one—although a leading one—of the ultra-rich U.S. families that in the 1970s turned their attention and directed their wealth to the task of pushing American politics sharply to the right and putting in place policies that more clearly favored their own interests.

The business elite is and always has been the most powerful force in U.S. politics, by virtue of its dominant role in the economy. But what is striking—and perhaps inspiring to revisit—is the extent to which the power of business was somewhat curtailed in the 1930–1970 period, and the extent to which this allowed policies favoring other members of society to flourish. It's interesting to note that this decline in the political power of business and the wealthy elite coincided with the decline in their share of the nation's income. The share of national income going to the richest 1 percent declined dramatically after the 1929 crash, falling from a high of almost 24 percent in the late 1920s to just 10 percent in the early postwar period. This drop represented a dramatic shift, indicating that money was much more widely distributed in society. That wider distribution of financial resources breathed new life into American democracy, making possible a set of policies favoring the broader public that almost certainly would never have made it onto the U.S. political agenda had the rich remained so economically dominant.

Much of the financial wealth of the elite had been wiped out in the 1929 crash, leaving them stunned and confused at a time when a badly suffering public was not inclined to forgive them for their role in bringing on the crash and its disastrous aftermath. With their prestige and clout greatly reduced, they were unable to resist Franklin Roosevelt's New Deal, a wide range of programs that drew on ideas from the Progressive Era of the earlier part of the century (another period when income had been more widely distributed following the introduction of the progressive income tax in 1913). "Many of these [New Deal] programs were measures that America's business class had resisted for a generation," notes historian Kim Phillips-Fein, "and the government enacted them at a moment when the power and prestige of business was at its nadir."[27]

The labor movement was quick to capitalize on its newfound friend in the White House. In fact, labor had played an important role in getting Roosevelt elected, with the United Mine Workers contributing half a million dollars as well as providing thousands of volunteers who went door-to-door in working-class neighborhoods to get out the vote. The strengthening of labor laws during the Roosevelt administration led to a significant increase in unionization and a feeling of empowerment in labor ranks. Inspired to confront the notoriously anti-union car manufacturers, the United Auto Workers staged an illegal sit-down strike in December 1936, bringing production to a halt at a General Motors plant in Flint, Michigan. Such bold tactics would have typically been beaten back in the days before the New Deal, when Republican presidents (and even Democrats like Grover Cleveland) had sent in federal troops to defend corporate interests from labor disruptions. But Roosevelt refused to intervene, and six weeks later GM accepted the UAW as the bargaining agent for its employees. A spokesman for the company expressed the new business passivity: "Let us have peace and make automobiles."

Business attempts to organize a counterattack in the form of the American Liberty League—orchestrated and funded largely by the wealthy du Pont brothers in the 1930s—quickly fizzled, especially after it became clear that the league had no popular base and was just a "Millionaires Union," as the Democrats dubbed it. Indeed, Roosevelt loudly denounced any attempts by business or Wall Street forces to reassert themselves. He publicly dubbed them "the agents of organized greed," accusing them of seeking "the restoration of their selfish power."[28] The public eagerly absorbed the president's populist message. When the Liberty League threw its support behind Republican Alf Landon in the 1936 presidential election, Roosevelt scored one of the biggest landslides in U.S. history, and the league and its business supporters retreated to the sidelines.

And, to an extent that is hard to imagine today, that's where they stayed politically for the next few decades. The Liberty League, funded by some of the wealthiest interests in the country, quietly disbanded in 1938. Overwhelmed by the forces that seemed aligned against them, the wealthy largely backed off from challenging many of the popular reforms.

It was in this climate that Roosevelt was able to bring in a far-reaching Social Security system, modeled on social insurance programs that had long existed in Europe but been sharply resisted by dominant business interests in the United States. Roosevelt called for a bold program covering every American. "I see no reason why every child, from the day he is born, shouldn't be a member of the social security system," the president told his secretary of labor, Frances Perkins. "When he grows up, he should know he will have old-age benefits direct from the insurance system to which he will belong all his life. If he is out of work, he gets a benefit. If he is sick or crippled, he gets a benefit." And health insurance might be added to the program "later on." As for paying for it, Roosevelt told one critic that it was important the program be paid for out of payroll taxes "to give the contributors a legal, moral and political right to collect their pensions and their unemployment benefits. With those taxes in there, no damn politician can ever scrap my social security program."[29]

Business did object, with the National Association of Manufacturers denouncing the scheme as the first step toward "the ultimate socialistic control of life and industry." But there was also pressure on Roosevelt from the Left, which seemed to have wider support, posing more of a potential threat to his political success. In addition to labor unions, Father Charles Coughlin reached millions of listeners with his radio broadcasts that combined Catholic theology and social justice themes in ways that resonated with American workers stung by the industrial collapse throughout the Midwest. Dr. Francis Townsend also rose to national prominence with an old-age pension scheme under which the federal government would pay $200 a month to every American over sixty. Tens of millions of Americans joined Townsend Clubs across the country, signing petitions to urge Congress to enact the plan. Even more radical and nationally prominent was Huey Long, Louisiana's firebrand governor and later U.S. senator. The charismatic Long, who was known to harbor presidential ambitions, advocated a "Share Our Wealth" program that promised to heavily tax corporations and the rich in order to fund public pensions and a guaranteed income for American families. Like the Townsend Clubs, Share Our Wealth Clubs sprouted up all over the country.[30]

With pressure from the Left and a fairly subdued business community, Roosevelt had little trouble getting a far-reaching Social Security bill passed into law in August 1935, by an overwhelming margin of 371 to 33 votes in the House and equally stunning margin of 76 to 6 in the Senate. (In many ways, the Social Security system envisioned the still more radical economic "bill of rights" that Roosevelt later called for in his 1944 State of the Union address. Linking freedom to economic security, FDR outlined a set of economic rights for Americans that he called "self-evident" for the postwar world, including the right to a job, adequate food and clothing, a decent home, adequate medical care, and freedom from domination by monopolies. As he told the nation in January 1944: "We have come to a clear realization of the fact that true individual freedom cannot exist without economic security and independence.")

The reticence of the business elite in fighting the profound changes ushered in by the New Deal was rebuked by Barry Goldwater (later the Republican presidential nominee) when he complained of "scared-e-cat" businessmen in a 1939 editorial in the *Phoenix Gazette:* "There isn't a businessman in this country today that does not fear the future status of our rising tax figure, yet he confines his suggestions for correcting the situation to his intimates who will agree with him."[31] Rather than confront the New Deal agenda directly, many business owners resigned themselves to working within its framework, turning their attention to winning specific tax concessions for their industries or lucrative government contracts. In time, as the economy recovered and prospered after the war, and corporate profits boomed, business opposition diminished further. Resistance to the popular New Deal agenda seemed pointless as well as hopeless.

The extent of business acquiescence—so striking in comparison to today's demanding corporate elite—can be seen in the relative acceptance by business of the extremely high income tax rates of the early postwar decades. The "scared-e-cat" businessmen didn't particularly like top marginal income tax rates that reached above 80 percent (sometimes above 90 percent), but such high rates seemed to enjoy broad social support, reflecting an egalitarian ethos that regarded excessive greed negatively. With the very high rates effectively imposing a cap on what executives could earn, since almost everything above that would be taken in taxes, there was little incentive for corporate boards to push salaries through the roof. So they didn't. (Of course, executives were still well rewarded, typically earning twenty-five times what the average worker earned.) But there was little push-back from business. Even the Republican Party largely went along. Republican president

Dwight Eisenhower, in a personal letter to his brother in 1954, revealed his own acceptance of the broad terms of the New Deal:

> Should any political party attempt to abolish social security, un-employment insurance, and eliminate labor laws and farm pro-grams, you would not hear from that party again in our political history. There is a tiny splinter group, of course, that believes you can do these things. Among them are H. L. Hunt (you possibly know his background), a few other Texas millionaires, and an occasional politician or businessman from other areas. Their number is negligible and they are stupid.[32]

But a group that Eisenhower regarded as negligible and stupid was soon to start reasserting itself. The Great Society reforms brought in by Lyndon Johnson in the 1960s—particularly the expansion of Social Security to include Medicare for the elderly—convinced a growing number of business leaders that the state was becoming far too involved in ensuring the well-being of the citizenry. The march toward greater equality had to be stopped in its tracks. By the early 1970s, with postwar growth starting to stall, business had an opening. It also had a growing sense that it was losing ground to a broader antibusiness movement that came out of the mass student protests over U.S. involvement in Vietnam. The movement's ostensible leader, Ralph Nader, was attracting widespread support and sympathetic media coverage for this freewheeling campaign against "corporate power." The threat felt by business leaders was captured well in an eight-page memorandum written in 1971 for the U.S. Chamber of Commerce by Lewis Powell, a prominent Richmond, Virginia, attorney who served on a number of corporate boards (and later on the Supreme Court). The memo, which was to become highly influential in business circles, expressed a feeling of being under siege. It amounted to a manifesto warning business that "the American economic system is under broad attack" and the assault was gaining influence "from the college campus, the pulpit, the media, the intellectual community . . . and from politicians." Powell echoed Goldwater's earlier condemnation of "scared-e-cat" businessmen, urging them to "stop suffering in impotent silence, and launch a counter-attack."

Powell laid out a comprehensive plan for a counterattack that bears an almost uncanny resemblance to what actually happened. He argued that business largely owned, funded, or had influence over the key media, religious, and academic institutions in society, and should use its leverage to counter what he perceived as the liberal, antibusiness bias of these institutions. He advocated explicit business intervention in the political sphere, where he said the American businessman had become "truly the forgotten man." This had to be countered with concrete steps—expanding the "role of lobbyist for the business point of view"—in order to regain political clout with governments. It was time, wrote Powell, for business to learn that "political power is necessary; it must be used aggressively and with determination—without embarrassment and without reluctance which has been so characteristic of American business."[33]

Powell's manifesto reverberated powerfully within business circles, especially after it received national attention when it was leaked to syndicated liberal columnist Jack Anderson. The memo clearly touched a nerve, stirring some of the wealthiest interests in the county to re-engage politically. As Kim Phillips-Fein notes, "Not all businessmen shared Powell's passions. But those who did began to act as a vanguard, organizing the giants of American industry."[34] Along with the Koch brothers, a number of America's biggest corporate dynasties came forward to inject massive funds into the cause of pushing the country sharply to the right. The Olin family, owner of a giant chemical and munitions business, provided tens of millions of dollars to think tanks, organizations, and programs at major universities aimed at inculcating right-wing ideas and policy solutions. Huge financial support for libertarian and conservative causes (and later the attempt to impeach Bill Clinton) also came from Richard Mellon Scaife, heir to the massive Mellon banking, aluminum, and oil fortune. Joseph Coors, who had inherited the brewery fortune, described how he was "stirred up" by reading the Powell memo and wondered why businessmen were "ignoring a crisis."[35] (In fact, Coors had already been stirred up. As a regent of the University of Colorado, Coors had personally engaged in an aggressive battle with campus radicals, financing a campus newspaper to counteract them, and had contributed funds to a campaign to defeat liberal members of Congress.) Freshly stirred by Powell's call to arms, Coors became a key figure in establishing the Heritage Foundation, which was to become an influential promoter of radical pro-capitalist ideas as well as "the Judaeo-Christian moral order." The foundation quickly attracted major corporate funding from Dow Chemical, General Motors, Pfizer, Mobil, Chase, and the Manhattan Bank.[36] The du Ponts, who had failed so notably with the Liberty League in the 1930s, were back in the game. Du Pont CEO Charles McCoy became one of the instigators of the Business Roundtable, an exclusive group of CEOs of leading U.S. companies, who planned to use their economic clout to gain access to top government and congressional leaders.

The war chest of funds from wealthy families and corporations provided the seed money for a huge new infrastructure of organizations, think tanks, publications, and "astro-turf" campaigns funded by the wealthy but designed to appear as grass-roots movements. With this massive effort to reshape the debate and politics of America, the wealthy elite was investing in a deliberate long-term strategy—exactly what Powell had called for—realizing that institutions shaped by liberal values wouldn't change overnight, but could be completely overhauled over time through determined push-back from business. The media, owned by business interests, quickly became a helpful collaborator, and the buzzwords of free-market ideology were soon dominating the airwaves. The rightward media drift accelerated after media mogul Rupert Murdoch hired former Republican strategist Roger Ailes to launch Fox News in 1996 with an aggressive conservative message that pushed the media concept of balanced coverage ever farther to the right.

What is striking is how effective the massive, well-funded conservative organizing effort has been in moving American politics to the right—even while apparently having little impact on the basic views of ordinary Americans, whose political wishes are now all but ignored by their elected representatives.

The impact on the Republican Party has been the most profound, with conservative money ensuring that moderates in the style of Dwight Eisenhower—or even George H. W. Bush—are increasingly blocked from winning their party's nominations. Two well-financed conservative pressure groups have been instrumental in this. The Club for Growth has proved highly effective in weeding out, early on, any Republicans who dare to deviate from a tax-cuts-for-the-rich agenda. Founding president Stephen Moore (who worked at both the Heritage Foundation and Cato Institute) noted that when he approached wealthy donors for money to use against such candidates in primary contests "they start wetting their pants."[37] Similarly, Americans for Tax Reform, headed by the immensely influential lobbyist Grover Norquist, has helped impose a rigid antitax agenda on Washington by coercing Republicans into signing the organization's pledge to oppose all efforts to increase tax rates on business and the high-income crowd. Although some moderate Republicans originally resisted, increasingly they've succumbed. By September 2011, 236 congressmen and 41 senators had signed the pledge, giving antitax automatons a majority in the House and sufficient votes to prevent legislation from coming up for a vote in the Senate.

The impact of conservative money on the Democratic Party has also been immense. With increasingly expensive political campaigns in the TV age, business gained a huge advantage with cash-hungry Democratic candidates, particularly after labor's economic clout and financial contributions diminished. As labor faded, the well-financed voices of business grew louder and more persistent, aggressive, and ubiquitous. Democrats became the new scared-e-cats, retreating in lockstep as the conservative juggernaut advanced, putting up scant resistance as the goalposts were moved ever farther to the right. The Democrats largely abandoned support for important labor policies, allowing the minimum wage to languish, supporting trade deals that encouraged privatization and favored corporate interests, and even emerging as the leading proponents of financial deregulation in the 1990s. This brought in huge campaign support from the financial industry, realigning the party with Wall Street, particularly under the influence of powerful Democratic senators Charles Schumer and Joseph Lieberman.

The Democrats have held out somewhat on the tax issue. They've mostly resisted signing the tax pledge, and have recently supported Obama's calls for higher taxes on the rich, including his "Buffett rule" plan to make those earning more than a million dollars a year pay tax rates as high as the middle class. But these measures—while sharply resisted by the Right—still represent a huge retreat from the meaningfully progressive tax policies championed by the Democratic Party all the way back to the end of the nineteenth century, during the Depression and the early postwar years. The enormous decline in the taxation of the rich over the past thirty years could not have happened without the almost complete capitulation of the Democratic Party.

This broad retreat from progressive causes was painfully evident as early as 1978. Despite Democratic control of Congress and the White House, a highly organized and well-financed campaign by business, led by the Business Roundtable, helped orchestrate the defeat of an important piece of labor legislation in the Senate after a nineteen-day filibuster—a devastating defeat that seemed to confirm labor's waning influence, even with its Democratic allies. This was followed by an even more surprising Democratic retreat on the tax front. While President Jimmy Carter had campaigned on promises to make the tax system more progressive, a Democratic tax bill that started out with provisions for higher capital gains taxes was quickly gutted after a major lobbying effort by business. In the end, the Democratic-controlled Congress passed a bill that did exactly the opposite—cut the capital gains tax almost in half, slicing the rate from 48 percent to 28 percent. The Democrats had shown a willingness to play ball with the new moneyed interests in town, presiding over the first major victories of the conservative political revolution before Ronald Reagan even set foot in the White House.

.    .    .

Franklin Roosevelt had reason to believe his social security system would remain untouchable. After all, it removed the haunting fear of poverty in old age for every American, and it was paid for by payroll taxes on those who would benefit (as well as on corporate employers). But when FDR claimed "no damn politician can ever scrap my social security program," he clearly hadn't thought through the possibility of a decades-long strategic campaign funded by some of the wealthiest members of society.

If Social Security is ever dismantled, two individuals who will be able to take the lion's share of the credit will surely be Charles Koch and the late Austrian free-market economist Friedrich Hayek, a giant of the antigovernment movement and author of the libertarian bible *The Road to Serfdom*. So it's fascinating to look at an exchange of letters between these two individuals dealing with the subject of the U.S. Social Security system. We might expect this bit of 1973 correspondence between the two men—dug up by the intrepid investigative reporter Yasha Levine from the Hayek archive at Stanford University—to give us insight into the vehemence or nature of their objection to Social Security. Instead, we find them blandly discussing how the system could be used to enable Hayek to gain access to U.S. medical care so that he could accept an academic post at a Koch-funded institute in California.[38]

Nowhere do the men reveal any embarrassment, awkwardness, or even a slight sense of irony at the thought that they are trying to take advantage of a system that they have gone to great lengths to depict as the very antithesis of freedom. In his 1960 book *The Constitution of Liberty*, Hayek devotes a whole chapter, titled "Social Security," to denouncing the moral and economic effects of this centerpiece of the modern welfare state. But, as we learn in his exchange with Charles Koch, Hayek had in fact opted to pay into the U.S. Social Security system while he was teaching at the University of Chicago in the 1950s. Upon discovering this, Koch—rather than being crestfallen at the moral failings of this guiding figure of the libertarian movement—is cheered by the thought

that this will allow Hayek to cash in on the benefits of the modern welfare state: "You may be interested in the information that we uncovered
on the insurance and other benefits that would be available to you in
this country," writes Koch. "Since you paid into the United States Social
Security Program for a full forty quarters, you are entitled to Social
Security payments while living anywhere in the Free World. Also, at any
time you are in the United States, you are automatically entitled to hospital coverage." Koch even helpfully enclosed a government pamphlet
on how to apply for Social Security benefits.

On one level, the letters could be read as a summary of the many
excellent features of a social security system, and what a sensible and
beneficial addition it is to the Free World. But since we know the identity of the correspondents, the question inevitably rises: Why are they
so keen to destroy a system that they clearly understand works well,
helping millions of Americans with far fewer resources than they have?

So, while it's a bit of a digression from our exploration of the relationship between economic concentration and political power, it's
worth pondering this question by considering the careful analysis of
Harry Frankfurt, the distinguished chair of the Yale University philosophy department. In a thoughtful essay in *Harper's Magazine* entitled
"Reflections on Bullshit," Frankfurt sought to develop a philosophical
theory to distinguish between truth-tellers, liars, and bullshitters.[39] In
a nutshell, his argument, as it might apply here, is that those who as-
sert that Social Security is a threat to freedom while enthusiastically
taking advantage of its benefits, are not necessarily lying, they're simply
disregarding the truth in order to advance their agenda.

Liars are people who deliberately tell untruths. Bullshitters, on the
other hand, don't really care about the truthfulness of their assertions.
When Koch discovered Hayek could qualify for Social Security, he
wasn't horrified by what that would mean to Hayek's personal liberty
or worried that this godfather of laissez-faire capitalism would end up
on some private road to serfdom. This suggests that the Right's claims
about the freedom-depriving nature of Social Security is nothing more
than an empty statement meant to advance a larger agenda. When

business interests insist that the path to freedom is through the elimination of Social Security—or that low tax rates on investors and hedge fund managers will lead to economic growth for all—they don't take these positions because they are misguided, uninformed, or even because they believe them to be true. They take them because, to put it in philosophical terms, they are bullshitters concerned about maximizing their own wealth and power, or those whose interests they serve.

The difference between the swaggering dominance of the wealthy today and the "scared-e-cat" businessmen prior to the 1970s reflects the vast difference in the economic power wielded by the business elite in the two eras. In the earlier era, the rich never fully recovered from the financial losses they suffered in the 1929 crash. Although they prospered nicely in the postwar expansion, high taxes kept them from achieving the kind of sweeping economic—and political—domination that they'd enjoyed in the Gilded Age and the 1920s. Throughout the postwar era, business was always a powerful force that largely shaped the political agenda, but other interests—notably organized labor, and the working people whose interests it championed—sometimes got their way. To business advocates like Lewis Powell, this was a travesty. Others might describe this as more closely approximating pluralistic democracy.

The campaign to roll back the postwar egalitarian advances, starting in the 1970s, gained momentum in the following decades as the rich got vastly richer and invested heavily in a sophisticated political infrastructure to advance their cause. Their political victories not only enriched themselves further but weakened other segments of society, creating economic insecurity for millions of Americans. That insecurity left ordinary Americans frightened, short of resources, and no longer inclined to trust and rely on unions, which seemed increasingly impotent in the face of rising business wealth.

The 2008 financial crash and its brutal aftermath has raised the possibility that the pendulum might swing back, once again diminishing the wealth and power of the elite. This hasn't happened yet—although the Occupy Wall Street demonstrations in the fall of 2011 point to a building storm.

So far, however, the privileged elite have mostly managed to protect and even enhance their financial position, with the Wall Street crowd using its clout to win a massive $4.7 trillion bailout.[40] The elite have also managed to derail attempts to raise their taxes. As of the fall of 2011, the very rich seem poised to dismantle programs that are vital to the well-being of millions of ordinary Americans and that for decades seemed politically untouchable.

Mark Hanna may well have identified a crude truth about American politics when he said, "There are two things that are important in politics. The first is money and I can't remember what the second is." Perhaps the second thing, which the Republican strategist so casually forgot, is that it matters how widely money is distributed. We therefore offer up a corollary to Hanna's rule: When money is distributed more equally in society, ordinary citizens speak with louder voices, making meaningful democracy possible.

The most serious problem with extreme inequality is that the control exerted by the rich over society's resources not only compromises the nation's economy, health, and social well-being, but ultimately shuts down its democracy.

This points to a bottom-line conclusion: any strategy aimed at bringing about change must begin with a serious plan to limit the concentration of economic resources in the hands of the few. Fortunately, as we'll now see, there's a simple way to do this.

# CHAPTER II

# The True Badge of Citizenship

Vernon Hunter, an employee of the U.S. Internal Revenue Service, was at work in his office in Austin, Texas, one afternoon in February 2010 when his life was abruptly brought to a bloody and horrific end. An airplane driven by a man enraged by the U.S. tax system had just slammed into the side of Hunter's building, killing himself and Hunter and injuring a number of other IRS employees. With memories of 9/11 still haunting the nation, the fiery killing of Vernon Hunter by a suicide bomber seemed certain to stir anger and outrage. Yet oddly, it passed almost without notice.

It wasn't that fears of terrorism no longer stirred passions in America. Six weeks earlier, a foiled attempt by a Nigerian student to blow up an airliner approaching Detroit with a bomb hidden in his underwear had sparked mountains of outrage over the breakdown in security. Both the Nigerian would-be attacker and the Texas pilot bomber were motivated by political rage, so their actions were clearly acts of political terrorism—the subject that had consumed America since 9/11.

The Nigerian was said to be a Muslim extremist who was protesting America's military interventions in Islamic countries. The Texan, Joe Stack, left behind a long manifesto expressing anger and frustration, primarily against government and the tax system, and concluding "violence is the only answer." Yet while the Nigerian student was quickly branded a terrorist, with commentators complaining that U.S.

authorities had respected his legal rights in the process of detaining him, there was hardly any criticism—let alone full-blown outrage—directed toward the Texas killer.

Indeed, Stack's grotesque act of violence was treated almost with kid gloves, with politicians and public figures holding back condemnation. Both the local Texas prosecutor and a White House spokesman went out of their way to deny that Stack was a terrorist. Media anchors and commentators were surprisingly restrained, with ABC's *Good Morning America* asking the adult daughter of the Texas bomber whether she considered her father a hero. A hero? What an odd question. "Yes, because now maybe people will listen," replied Samantha Dawn Bell, adding merely that she acknowledged that her father's action had been "inappropriate." (In a later interview, she retracted her suggestion that her father was a hero, but continued to defend his views.)

Republican congressman Steve King of Iowa tried to shift the blame for the Texas attack onto the IRS. "I think if we'd abolished the IRS back when I first advocated it, [Joe Stack] wouldn't have a target for his plane. . . . It's sad the incident in Texas happened, but by the same token, it's an agency that is unnecessary and when the day comes when that is over and we abolish the IRS, it's going to be a happy day for America."[1] In the context of almost a decade of near-hysteria over terrorism in America, these comments about "the incident" by an elected member of Congress were stunning in their mildness, and in their apparent tolerance for terrorism and murder. Yet there were no calls for Congressman King's resignation, nor even any condemnation from the Republican caucus.

The IRS reported that there were 1,014 threats made against its employees in 2009 (up from 834 in 2005), suggesting that while the Texas bomber may be unusual in actually resorting to violence against tax officials, he is not the only one out there thinking about it. Given this climate of extreme antitax hostility, it would seem all the more important for public figures to firmly condemn the attack on the IRS building. But while condemning acts of terrorism is the bread and butter of U.S. politics, there were few voices lambasting Joe Stack, or even lamenting the tragic and horrific passing of Vernon Hunter, who, in addition to being a father of six, was a military veteran who had served his country in Vietnam. Politicians and media figures seemed reluctant to wade in, no doubt fearful of ending up on the wrong side of a faction that has grown extraordinarily powerful. The antitax movement is now so established, its message so deeply embedded in U.S. political culture that an act of terrorism committed in its name is largely given a free pass.

On the surface, it seems simply obvious that people would hate taxes. After all, taxes require people to hand over money. But then, there doesn't appear to be similar antipathy toward other things that require people to hand over money—like grocery bills or the check that arrives at the end of a restaurant meal. Of course, in these situations people are paying for goods and services that they receive. But taxes also pay for goods and services that people receive, and that are at least as essential to their well-being: an education, pensions, police and fire protection, national security, roads, highways, bridges, canals, libraries, museums, parks, sewer systems, garbage pickup, snow removal, water purification, food inspection, disease control, and so on. The success of the antitax lobby lies in its ability to separate taxes in the public's mind from these many services and necessities that taxes pay for, and which the public truly values.

These efforts, exemplified by the invention of Tax Freedom Day, simply omit the reality that citizens get things in return for taxes, and instead focus exclusively on the amount of taxes citizens pay. Tax Freedom Day—developed in the United States by the business-funded Tax Foundation and popularized with the active help of the media—is designated as the day of the year when the average family has earned enough to pay off its annual tax bill. Only then is the family considered to have stopped "working for the government." (Does it follow then that, for the rest of the year, Americans will be working for Walmart, Safeway, Costco, and other places they'll spend money?)

Of course, it should be acknowledged that there is an important difference—people choose to shop at Walmart, Safeway, and Costco, while taxes are not optional. But the attempt by antitax lobbyists to present taxes as coercive obscures their essentially democratic nature. Taxes result from decisions made through our democratic system, which we all have an opportunity to participate in. Through the democratic process, we have decided to pay collectively for certain goods and services because we consider them important, and because if we paid for them individually on the open market, they'd cost a lot more and be much more difficult to provide. Rather than seeing taxes as a denial of freedom, we should regard them as an essential part of citizenship in a free and democratic society. Indeed, raising money collectively through taxation and then making collective decisions about spending it constitute the very basis of democracy. These are functions that are central to popular self-government.

It could be added here that the growing reliance of our public institutions on philanthropy—rather than on funding through the tax system—has had the effect of undermining popular self-government and democracy. Philanthropy has become increasingly important as tax revenues from the rich have declined, leaving hospitals, universities, museums, libraries, and other vital public institutions strapped for cash and reliant on charitable donations from the rich. But collecting money from the rich through philanthropy is very different than collecting it from them in taxes. When money is collected through the tax system, it is the public that decides collectively how to spend it. When the rich donate money, it is they who make the crucial decisions about how and where the money will be spent, which causes and institutions will be helped and which will be neglected. Among other things, this has meant that causes primarily aimed at helping the poor and destitute have been neglected. Wealthy patrons have shown far less interest in building community centers, swimming pools, or drug rehabilitation clinics in poor parts of town than in contributing to their alma maters or to hospitals or concert halls, where their names are often prominently emblazoned on buildings that are likely to be seen by their peers.

Philanthropy also gives the wealthy considerable influence over the actual institutions they fund, further diminishing democratic control in society. This is particularly a problem with academic institutions, which have a central role to play in democracies as centers of critical thought, where prevailing orthodoxies and power structures can be scrutinized and challenged.

There are some disturbing examples of attempts by philanthropists to limit this sort of critical academic inquiry. For example, John Allison, former chairman of the bank holding company BB&T Corp., operating through a charitable foundation, established a program that provides grants of up to $2 million to academic institutions that set up courses on capitalism with Ayn Rand's libertarian novel *Atlas Shrugged* as required reading. Some sixty schools, including four campuses of the University of North Carolina, have signed up.[2] Similarly, Florida State University has agreed to a deal with the Charles G. Koch Charitable Foundation that allows Koch representatives to screen and eliminate potential candidates for teaching positions in the university's economics department as part of a program promoting "political economy and free enterprise." The arrangement, for which the university received a mere $1.5 million, also allows the Koch foundation to annually evaluate the professors chosen, and to withdraw its funding if it is not satisfied with their performance. Koch has managed to arrange similar deals at two other state universities—Clemson University in South Carolina and West Virginia University.[3]

This serious compromise of academic freedom—as tax revenues decline and public universities become more dependent on philanthropy—underlines the important role that taxes play in a democracy. This important role, so little acknowledged today, was widely understood in earlier times, when taxes were traditionally regarded as a cornerstone of U.S. democracy. The slogan "no taxation without representation" became the rallying cry of the Revolutionary War, reflecting the connection the colonial rebels made between taxation and democracy. That connection also figured prominently in the late nineteenth-century political battle over the introduction of an income tax in the

United States. One congressman who opposed the income tax argued that, since the poor would be exempt, it would undermine democracy, because the poor would have no legitimate claim to control a government to whose treasury they had not contributed. In a passionate counterattack in Congress, the famed orator William Jennings Bryan pointed to the enormous tax burden the poor shouldered due to the tariff: "If taxation is a badge of free men, let me assure my friend that the poor people of this country are covered all over with the insignia of free men." While there was debate about which class was shouldering the bulk of the tax burden, there was a general recognition that taxes and democracy were integrally connected.

It's striking to see how far we've moved from these early notions of taxation as central to democracy. This momentous change in public attitudes can be traced back to the aggressive neoconservatism that appeared in the Anglo-American countries in the late 1970s and really took hold in the 1980s. Key to the development and promotion of this conservatism and its fierce antitax ideology was the emergence of a new school of thought in the U.S. known as "public choice theory."

In essence, public choice theorists, borrowing from modern economic thought, take as their central premise that humans are motivated exclusively by personal self-interest, greed, and material acquisitiveness. These theorists basically extend the assumptions of modern economic theory to the political sphere, insisting that all participants in the political process (voters, politicians, civil servants) are only interested in and capable of acting on their own self-interest. As critics Hugh Stretton and Lionel Orchard note, the public choice theorists have attempted "to persuade people that material greed is, and will inescapably remain the single, natural dominant motive of their political, economic and social behavior."[4] So the notion that a government could represent some sort of broad "public interest" is deemed to be naive, even fraudulent. According to the public choice theorists, there is no overarching public interest, just a collection of individual desires and preferences.

With any notion of a broader public interest set aside like this, public choice theorists turn to simply maximizing the rights of the individual and limiting the power of government to interfere with the individual, particularly through taxation. They argue that government shouldn't be allowed to use the tax system for redistribution, since this enables the majority to unfairly pursue its own self-interest at the expense of the wealthy few. To prevent this, some public choice theorists have argued for actual constitutional protections against majority rule in the field of taxation. Needless to say, many in the elite see much merit in this idea of effectively outlawing the masses from exercising their democratic power in this crucial area.

The impact of the public choice theorists has been huge. Although their writings are largely technical and remain obscure outside the academic world, they have provided apparent intellectual backing to bolster the conservative case for smaller government and lower taxes.

However, human needs are more complex and varied than public choice theory implies. Specifically, the theory fails to take into account our intensely social nature—an aspect of human behavior that has been identified in decades of research in the social sciences, particularly psychology, anthropology, and sociology. This highly social nature explains the tendency of humans to measure their success against others, to be acutely conscious of their status and rank in the social hierarchy. It also suggests that humans have a deep need for community. They naturally seek to relate to and be accepted by other people. They desire to belong to a larger community—whether family, clan, gang, club, social network, or society at large—and as part of the group, will generally participate and contribute willingly.

The late economic historian and anthropologist Karl Polanyi argued that this social aspect is the most consistent feature of human behavior and is clearly visible across continents and through time. By emphasizing the social aspect, Polanyi did not mean that people are unselfish. Humans are primarily concerned with their own welfare, just not exclusively so. But this focus on their own welfare doesn't mean that their motivation is mainly materialistic. On the contrary, Polanyi argued that the welfare of individual humans depends largely on their social relationships, and on the preservation and viability of their communities. This suggests that sustaining and strengthening those communities—by improving their social cohesion, maintaining their physical infrastructures, and protecting them against threats that can only be addressed collectively, like global warming and other environmental disasters—is ultimately as important to humans as their individual material accumulations.

Under the neoconservative dogma that has dominated American society for several decades, these social and collective needs have been given short shrift, forced to take a backseat to the supposed dictates of the marketplace and the facilitation of individual wealth accumulation. But if social needs and the desire for viable communities are as deeply ingrained in humans as Polanyi and others suggest, this intense focus on personal material acquisitiveness may not be the great liberator it's purported to be. On the contrary, it may well be depriving humans of something very basic to their hard wiring as social beings.

While focusing on material acquisition seems utterly natural and normal to us, Polanyi noted that earlier societies throughout history typically gave top priority to other goals, like worshipping religious figures, celebrating cultural icons, or honoring bravery on the battlefield. Until the emergence of capitalism in parts of the Western world in the early sixteenth century, the so-called "economic motive" of material acquisition was simply one of many aspects of community life, and not one singled out for special attention. Indeed, until the eighteenth century, there wasn't even a separate word for "the economy"; the material well-being of the community was treated simply as part of its overall well-being.

In traditional societies, the bonds of the community involved some sense of responsibility to others, a willingness to share to prevent members of the group from going hungry. While there were frequent periods of scarcity—caused by external threats like war, pestilence, or drought—the principle that everyone in the community should be free from hunger prevailed in traditional societies, according to Polanyi, "under almost every and any type of social organization."[5] Even in feudal societies, where peasants toiled on vast estates controlled by wealthy nobles, the peasants were entitled to certain "common rights" that gave them access to sufficient land and resources to cover their basic needs (albeit at a very modest level).

This suggests that cooperation and sharing of resources—something that can be accomplished efficiently through a tax system—may be a natural tendency in humans, connected to our nature as social animals. Polanyi argues that, with the emergence of capitalism, there was a deliberate attempt to eliminate the long-established practices of sharing and replace them with behavior based on personal acquisitiveness. Whereas traditional and feudal societies had discouraged greed and materialism on the grounds that they posed a threat to the common good, capitalism actively encouraged these traits, massaging them and cheering them on, indeed elevating them to the centerpiece and guiding principle of society. At the same time, the new capitalist system abandoned the traditional imperative of the social bond, to the point of actually allowing members of the community to go hungry. In fact, the threat of hunger became a deliberate strategy under capitalism, a means to prod peasants to work, even under the horrific conditions in the new mines and factories (today we might call it a "work incentive"). Breaking with centuries of history, capitalism introduced the concept of using scarcity and deprivation as a deliberate tool of social engineering and control.

Of course, capitalism is generally regarded in the West today as key in our evolution as a species toward a more advanced way of life. But Polanyi reminds us that capitalism, which was put in place by the rising merchant class in seventeenth-century England, was especially brutal in its early stages and was not appreciated nor widely accepted for a long time. On the contrary, it was so devastating and disruptive to the lives of the vast majority of people that they attempted to resist it with whatever means they could, often tearing down hedges around the newly enclosed fields with pitchforks and hoes. Among the early resisters was a group known as the Diggers, who fought for the right of the common people to regain the right to dig and forage on lands that were now being claimed as private property. Digger leader Gerrard Winstanley accused the members of the new elite of a kind of theft that permitted them to "lock up the treasures of the earth from the poor."[6]

Resistance to unbridled capitalism went on in various forms for centuries, and still continues. Without this resistance, in which members of the public seek "the protection of society," there would have been nothing to stop the most appalling abuses of the early days of capitalism, when young children were obliged to work all night in factories and mines or were stuffed up blackened chimneys to serve as human cleaning utensils. Polanyi describes the process that's taken place over the last few centuries as a "double movement" in which each step implementing capitalism was met by a determined effort by large numbers of people to protect themselves from the potential damage of these changes.

While it didn't stop the entrenchment of capitalism, the resistance did lead to the development of the modern welfare state, with its labor and social protections. This has certainly helped mitigate capitalism's worst excesses, with some countries allowing more mitigation than others. The progressive tax system has been a central feature of this welfare state, funding its programs and distributing income in a more equitable manner than the market systems installed under capitalism typically allow. The welfare state and progressive taxation have gone a long way toward restoring the social dimension that raw capitalism shunts aside.

It is this bulwark of progressive taxation and welfare state protections that the neoconservatives have moved aggressively to tear down. But their case rests on a flimsy premise—that human behavior boils down to individual greed and acquisitiveness. Such a formulation flies in the face of overwhelming evidence that humans are intensely social animals. As such, their desire to protect themselves and their communities from the full force of unleashed greed is at least as natural—and historically evident in the resistance to unbridled capitalism—as their desire to endlessly accumulate material possessions. Rather than elevating greed to a hallowed, iconic stature, as the neoconservative movement does, it would seem more in keeping with human needs to treat the impulse toward material acquisitiveness as simply one aspect of human behavior—one that can release useful energy but that, unchecked, can cause great damage to the social fabric upon which so much human well-being relies. As the late British historian R. H. Tawney eloquently put it: "So merciless is the tyranny of economic appetites, so prone to self-aggrandizement the empire of economic interest, that a doctrine which confines them to their proper sphere, as the servant, not the master of civilization may reasonably be regarded as . . . a permanent element in any sane philosophy."[7]

Perhaps the most potent argument put forward by the antitax movement in recent years has been the notion that taxes are unduly coercive, that they amount to an assault on freedom.

Yet it was the lack of coercion involved in taxation that led the late Henry Simons, a founder of the Chicago School of Economics, to endorse the progressive income tax system. Simons's arguments on the subject have largely been ignored in recent years, but they are worth considering briefly here. Simons, who considered himself a libertarian and is still revered by many conservatives, defended progressive taxation as part of his strong belief in the merits of capitalism. He recognized that capitalism could only survive in a democracy if the general public benefited from it, and this involved redistributing its bounty, which otherwise ends up concentrated in the hands of the few.

Simons argued that progressive taxation was the best way to achieve the necessary redistribution—since it involved the least amount of government intrusion in the market. Taxes, after all, don't interfere in the market's ability to determine prices and to allocate resources through the price mechanism—key features of the market economy. They don't involve a government bureaucrat imposing measures that interfere with the basic elements of supply and demand. "No fundamental disturbance of the whole system is involved," noted Simons in his classic 1938 text *Personal Income Taxation*.[8] He elaborated on this theme later, in *Economic Policy for a Free Society*, emphasizing how progressive taxation achieves redistribution without impinging on freedom: "What is important for libertarians is that we preserve the basic processes of free exchange and that egalitarian measures be superimposed on those processes, effecting redistribution afterward and not in the immediate course of production and commercial transactions."[9]

It could be added here that taxation—and even heavy taxation of the rich—was supported by no less a conservative heavyweight than Adam Smith, the eighteenth-century founder of the classical school of economics. This might come as a surprise since Smith's legacy has been largely appropriated in recent years by neoconservatives. While they've managed to tear snippets out of context to present his *Wealth of Nations* as a manifesto for unbridled capitalism, in fact Smith was wary of the social consequences of the emerging industrial capitalist system, and in particular the dangers of inequality. Throughout *The Wealth of Nations,* Smith consistently championed the rights of workers against the rights of merchants and industrialists. And he showed his cynicism toward business interests when he famously noted that "people in the same trade seldom meet together, even for merriment and diversion, but that conversation ends in a conspiracy against the public."

Far from rejecting the legitimacy of taxing earnings, Smith devoted much of *The Wealth of Nations* to a discussion of the best means of collecting taxes, and he repeatedly indicated a preference for shifting the burden off the poor and onto the rich. He strenuously objected, for instance, to a particular tax—common in his day—that was based on the number of windows in a house. "The principal objection to all such taxes is their inequality, and inequality of the worst kind, as they must frequently fall much heavier upon the poor than upon the rich. A house of ten pounds rent in a country town may sometimes have more windows than a house of five hundred pounds rent in London; and though the inhabitant of the former is likely to be a much poorer man than that of the latter."[10] Smith called for heavier highway tolls on luxury carriages than on freight wagons so that "the indolence and vanity of the rich [can be] made to contribute in a very easy manner to the relief of the poor." Indeed, although he wrote before the introduction of income taxes, Smith clearly anticipated and supported the idea of progressive taxation: "It is not very unreasonable that the rich should contribute to the publick expence, not only in proportion to their revenues, but something more than in proportion."[11]

Smith rejected suggestions put forward in his day that taxes were "badges of slavery." As he wrote in *The Wealth of Nations:* "Every tax . . . is to the person who pays it a badge, not of slavery, but of liberty. It denotes that he is subject to government, indeed, but that, as he has some property, he cannot himself be the property of a master."[12]


Even as the incomes of those at the top have risen higher and higher, their tax load has gotten lighter and lighter. The tax cuts introduced by the Bush administration in 2001 and in 2003 consolidated those of the Reagan era. But while the result has been a cornucopia of money at the top, there's also been an attempt on the part of the rich and their advocates to deny the charge of favoritism. So, for instance, the *Wall Street Journal* has vigorously opposed Obama's proposed tax hikes on high-income earners, insisting that "it's going to be hard for the rich to pay any more than they already do."[13]

The notion that the rich are shouldering an unduly large share of the tax burden echoes throughout the conservative and business press. Indeed, business commentators frequently argue that the rich pay a disproportionately large share of all tax revenue, suggesting that they are contributing, if anything, more than their fair share to the cost of operating public services. And on first glance, there seems to be some truth in these assertions. As the *Wall Street Journal* correctly notes, the share of income taxes paid by the rich has been rising; the top 1 percent now contribute a hefty 40 percent of all U.S. income tax revenue.

But this simply reflects the fact that income is now so heavily concentrated at the top. In other words, yes, the rich are paying an increasingly large share of all income taxes, but only because they receive an increasingly large share of all income. The *Journal* concedes this fact, but goes on to insist that, even so, the tax burden on the top 1 percent is onerous. After all, while they receive more than 20 percent of all income, they pay fully 40 percent of all income taxes, making their share of taxes almost double their share of income. "The tax code is already steeply progressive," the *Journal* concludes.

However, if we look at taxes actually paid, we see that the U.S. tax system is only mildly progressive.

By itself, the income tax is progressive—that is, it takes a proportionately bigger bite out of higher incomes. In 2009, the lowest 40 percent of U.S. households actually received a net benefit through the income tax, due to various tax credits. (These are the "lucky duckies" scorned by the *Journal* and right-wing pundits.) The middle 20 percent of households paid 2.3 percent of their income in income tax, while the top 20 percent paid 13.4 percent and the top 1 percent, 17.9 percent.[14]

However, in addition to the income tax, the federal government also levies a payroll tax, a few excise taxes, a corporate income tax, and an estate tax. And there are also state and local taxes, which are generally flat or often regressive. When all these taxes are taken together, the overall progressivity of the American tax system declines considerably; indeed, the burden on the rich is not much heavier than the burden on those far lower down the income ladder. For instance, with state and local taxes included, those in the bottom-earning group—the lucky duckies—pay fully 18.7 percent of their paltry incomes in total taxes. Those in the middle group pay 27 percent. Those in the top 1 percent pay 30.9 percent.

In fact, if we look closely at the numbers, we notice something bizarre—the effective tax rates paid by those at the very top are actually lower than the rates paid by those who are simply near the top. (This reflects the fact that much of the income received by the top 1 percent is in the form of capital gains, which are taxed at lower rates.) While the top 1 percent has a 30.9 percent effective tax rate, those just below them in the 90 to 99 percent level actually pay slightly higher effective tax rates—between 31 and 33 percent. If the system were truly progressive, effective tax rates would rise as income rises. But that's not what happens. Instead, effective tax rates rise only very gradually as income rises, and then they actually drop off at the very top. So rates at the summit are actually regressive. Most citizens would probably be offended by this fact if they knew about it, argues tax analyst Martin A. Sullivan: "My casual impression is that some people favor progressive rates and about an equal number favor flat rates. Very few endorse regressive rates."[15]

But let's go back to the *Wall Street Journal's* assertion that "it's going to be hard for the rich to pay any more than they already do." The *Journal* is suggesting that the rich are already so heavily burdened by taxes that any more tax would simply be unreasonable, if not unbearable. As we've seen, the newspaper reaches this conclusion by looking at the total amount of tax revenue collected from the top 1 percent and then measuring how large a share of the overall tax revenue collected this is. But as noted, this gross number is very misleading; it simply reflects the degree to which income has become highly concentrated in the hands of those at the top. It tells us nothing about the individual tax burdens of these rich individuals and, therefore, about how heavily their taxes weigh on them. And surely this is the more meaningful measure. If we are trying to assess the fairness or appropriateness of an individual's tax burden, it hardly matters how much overall tax is collected from all the people in that individual's income group—what matters is how heavy the burden is on the individual. And as we've seen, the total personal tax burden of those in the top 1 percent is not much heavier than it is for most of the rest of the population.

Furthermore, as we've seen, the rich paid much higher taxes in the past without suffering any damaging consequences. The extent of the drop in taxes on the richest Americans has been powerfully documented—ironically, by a group of wealthy Americans who favor a more progressive tax system. This group, Wealth for the Common Good, notes that the share of total federal taxes paid by the top 0.1 percent fell from 60 percent to only 33.6 percent from 1960 to 2004. If these individuals—Americans with annual incomes that averaged more than $7 million—had paid taxes at the 1960 rate, the treasury would have collected an additional $281 billion in revenue in 2007.[16]

If there's any lingering doubt about the validity to the *Wall Street Journal*'s characterization of the situation, perhaps we can dispel it by holding another national income parade.

But this time the size of the marchers will reflect their after-tax incomes. If the rich are truly paying the heavy rates of tax that the *Wall Street Journal* would have us believe, then this parade should look very different from the one we saw in chapter 1, which was based on pretax incomes. If the tax system is truly progressive—indeed "steeply progressive"—then it would act as an equalizer, producing a more egalitarian distribution of income throughout the country. In terms of the parade, we would expect a leveling of heights, with considerably taller people at the beginning and the middle, and less immense giants at the end.

But once the marchers are all lined up again, the parade looks pretty much the same as its pretax version. Both consist of a vast sea of very short workers, with people of average height only appearing around about the forty-minute mark. Significantly tall people only appear toward the end, with a tiny gaggle of enormous giants in the last few seconds. And John Paulson's face is still only visible from a spaceship. Although everyone is smaller, the proportions are roughly the same. Rather than being the great equalizer, the overall tax system is actually neutral. Its redistribution is effectively nil.

CHAPTER 12

# Revamping the Ovarian Lottery

For many on the Right and even a surprising number on the Left, inequality has become a nonissue, even as it's grown by leaps and bounds. Of course, conservatives have always had a high degree of tolerance for inequality. But in recent years, many progressives seem to have joined them, abandoning the Left's traditional demand for equality. Today, many influential progressives insist that poverty, not inequality, should be the focus, and that how well the rich are faring is irrelevant. "Let's worry about making sure the circuitry of the American dream isn't shorted, rather than whether some folks draw more current from the grid," wrote sociologist Dalton Conley in the liberal magazine the *American Prospect*. "It's the fate of the middle and lower classes that should concern progressives, not how many private jets the super-rich can afford."[1]

Conley, who heads the sociology department at New York University and has written extensively on the problems of poverty, acknowledges the resurgence of the rich and the extraordinary political power that comes with such economic power. He even notes that this concentrated economic power undermines democracy. But he argues that the way to fix it isn't to go after the rich, but rather to make adjustments to the political system. He advocates, for instance, amplifying the power of small donors on political campaigns by having the government match their donations (such as in New York City, where this is done, at a rate of six to one) or restricting the size of congressional districts, so that political campaigns would be less costly, giving smaller donors more importance. Conley also recognizes the problem that extreme inequality creates in the financial realm: "Nowhere is the linkage between inequality and political power starker than in the realm of finance—now one-fifth of the nation's gross domestic product. The so-called regulators have been totally captured by the regulated."

But while Conley acknowledges some of these key problems of extreme inequality, he is strongly opposed to making an issue out of it, calling that a "losing proposition" and an unwise political strategy. He is perhaps more emphatic on this point than others, but he is urging a strategy that many progressives have already been following in recent years. Conley's emphasis on attacking poverty rather than inequality has been largely adopted by the North American political parties that argue for any sort of progressive change. Indeed, attacks on the concentration of wealth—the wellspring of populist politics in earlier times—have largely been shunted to the margins of political debate. They've been discredited as divisive and nasty, as a "politics of envy" that unfairly targets the rich and foments feelings of class warfare. This has amounted to a profound political change. Attacks on concentrated wealth were well within the mainstream when President Franklin Roosevelt railed against the special interests of "financial monopoly, speculation and reckless banking" back in 1936. "Government by organized money is just as dangerous as government by organized mob," FDR told a wildly cheering crowd at Madison Square Garden in a speech fiercely attacking private economic power—a speech it is hard to imagine a political leader delivering today.

President Obama has reopened this front a bit, with his proposal for a new minimum income tax that would ensure millionaires pay a tax rate at least as high as the rates faced by the middle class. Although the Right has ferociously denounced this as "class warfare," it would do little to move the United States back to the sort of progressive tax system that the country had in the early postwar years. Indeed, it almost amounts to a repudiation of the principle of progressivity. Taxing millionaires at the same rate as mechanics and secretaries is hardly progressive. (A progressive tax imposes a higher rate on higher levels of income.) By indicating that it is all right for the millionaire to pay the same low rate as people with vastly lower incomes, the Obama administration is implicitly indicating that progressivity is not really a goal to be taken seriously.

Obama's reluctance to go further, to try to restore the kind of progressive taxation that existed before the Reagan revolution of the 1980s, reveals much about the self-imposed limits of progressive politics today. Conventional wisdom has it that anything beyond a return to the Clinton-era level of taxation at the top would be out of sync with American public opinion. But is that even true? When Obama made an offhand comment during the 2008 election campaign that it's good to "spread the wealth around," the Republicans reacted with glee, believing they finally had a line from Obama that they could use against him. But their relentless campaign to use the quote to portray Obama as an anti-American socialist failed to generate much outrage. Because, among ordinary people, there wasn't much outrage.

This isn't surprising, considering that polls have shown a substantial majority of Americans actually believe their country has become too unequal. As Benjamin Page and Lawrence Jacobs note in *Class War? What Americans Really Think about Inequality,* a solid majority of Americans (and even a majority of Republicans) agree that differences in incomes in America are too large.[2] Polls also showed strong support in the fall of 2009 for a surtax on high-earning families (with incomes above $1 million) to help pay for expanded health-insurance coverage. And in January 2010, a statewide plebiscite in Oregon gave voters a choice between reducing the state deficit through spending cuts or through higher taxes on corporations and high-income earners. The people of Oregon chose the tax increases.[3]

These polls are backed up by an intriguing study conducted by Michael Norton of Harvard Business School and Dan Ariely of Duke

University. Norton and Ariely created a survey to determine what a representative sample of Americans considered the desirable level of inequality in society. Respondents in the survey were asked to choose between three unlabeled pie charts—the first representing a completely equal division of wealth throughout society; the second representing the division of wealth that exists in the United States and the third representing the division of wealth that exists in Sweden. Strikingly, fully 92 percent of the respondents selected the pie chart representing Swedish wealth distribution over that of U.S. wealth distribution—without realizing which two countries were involved. This strong preference prevailed across genders, income-class level, and voting practices; even 90.2 percent of voters who had cast their ballots for George W. Bush in 2004 selected the Swedish pie chart.

What this seems to suggest, among other things, is that Americans have little idea how unequal the division of wealth in their country actually is, assuming it to be more akin to inequality levels in Sweden. In a separate part of the survey, the respondents—a nationally representative sample drawn from more than a million Americans—were asked to estimate how unequally wealth was divided in America. Their estimates were wildly off; they generally estimated that the top quintile held 59 percent of the wealth, whereas it actually holds 84 percent. But, even more surprising, when the respondents were asked to indicate what they considered an ideal wealth distribution, they veered sharply toward equality—indicating a desire for the top quintile to own just 32 percent of the wealth, which would involve a substantial redistribution of wealth away from the richest Americans. The respondents were given a chance to indicate where the wealth should go, and they mostly moved the money from the top quintile to the bottom three.[4]

All this indicates that a serious campaign for a much more egalitarian distribution of income and wealth might well resonate with the American public. The decision by left-leaning political leaders in recent years to abandon attacks on concentrated wealth and inequality has been disastrous for progressive causes and for the common people whose interest these leaders purport to represent. To begin with, attempts to bring about reforms that would help those lower down the ladder are bound to fail as long as the economic power of the wealthy is left intact, since the wealthy will inevitably use their clout to block progressive change. The kinds of reforms that Dalton Conley proposes are tiny drops in the bucket, even if they were to be widely enacted. Matching political donations six to one—or even sixty to one—won't counter the massive and pervasive power of the wealthy elite, who don't just exert their influence through political donations but through countless other direct and indirect means.

There are many stages of the political process, each one with many opportunities for influence to be exercised: the selection of political candidates, the drafting of party platforms, the financing and organizing of political campaigns, the drafting and amending of legislation, the input of interest groups, the shaping of public opinion through media and think tanks. The wealthy aren't just adept at influencing one stage of this process but each and every stage. Indeed, even when they aren't directly trying to influence the political process, they manage to, because politicians are constantly anticipating their demands, anxious to curry their favor and fearful of doing anything that might offend them. As one congressional assistant noted: "You can't run for the Senate in Arkansas if the Waltons oppose you."[5]

It might seem logical to assume that when the wealthy are particularly prosperous, they are more likely to feel generous and support policies that help the poor. But the record shows the opposite, that the poor fare worse when inequality is most pronounced. Economic historian Peter Lindert, who has studied redistributive policies in England and the United States over three centuries, describes a phenomenon he calls the "Robin Hood paradox": the more unequal a society becomes, the less it adopts redistributive policies favoring those at the lower end. Lindert speculates that the answer to the apparent paradox "must lie in the relationship of income distribution to political voice. . . . Highly skewed societies are ones in which the wealthy elite retains a high share of political power as well as of wealth and income."⁶ Evidently, the bigger the share of income the rich enjoy at any given time, the more clout they have to enact policies in their own interests—and the more they do so.

By declining to protest the concentration of income and wealth, progressives have conceded important ground. At the center of their case should be a strong moral argument about the illegitimacy of a small number of people gaining control over too large a share of society's resources and, with it, undue control over society. Conservatives have their own moral argument, about the legitimacy of private property and the illegitimacy of taxes imposed on what they regard as justly acquired riches. There is much ground for debate here between the two sides, but progressives have largely folded their tent and gone home. This has allowed the conservative antitax argument to dominate, even as the concentration of income and wealth at the top has become ever more extreme. The conservatives' use of a morally charged narrative has enabled them to be effective in making their case—a case that only serves the interests of a very small group and that, without some creative moral embellishment (by a lot of high-priced talent), would be intuitively unappealing to most people.

The disastrous effects of abandoning the moral high ground to conservatives can be seen in the uncertain fate of the federal estate tax, which has been the backbone of progressive taxation in the United States since 1916. It is the one tax that exclusively hits the very rich, taxing them once a generation on their accumulated wealth. Traditionally, the tax has only applied to the top 1 to 2 percent of estates; fully 97.7 percent of all the adults who died in 1999 were able to leave all their holdings to their heirs without triggering a penny in estate taxes. The only people who pay the tax are members of the wealthiest and most powerful families in America (in 1999, nearly a quarter of the estate tax revenue came from just 550 estates, all containing wealth exceeding $20 million). Even so, the amounts collected by the tax are substantial: roughly $25 billion a year, more than twice the annual size of the federal grants given to help American students attend college.[7] Furthermore, the tax has little negative effect on economic activity in the country, and is considered largely benign by public finance economists. In other words, it is a levy that appears to do little or no economic damage while doing much good; economist Robert H. Frank describes it as "the closest thing to a perfect tax that we have."[8]

And yet, astonishingly, over the course of the past decade, the U.S. estate tax has been largely gutted, and its future is highly uncertain. Its gutting was part of the Bush tax cuts of 2001. Under the Bush plan, which was phased in over a ten-year period, the estate tax got gradually smaller and applied to fewer and fewer rich people. So, while it applied to about 2 percent of all estates in 1999, it applied to only 0.9 percent of estates in 2006, and to only 0.6 percent by 2009.[9] By then, an estate had to be worth $3.5 million (or $7 million in the case of a couple) before it was required to pay tax at all in 2009.

The gutting of the estate tax has not only been deep, but it took on a strange form, due to the bizarre schedule of fluctuating rates and exemptions—part of a congressional reconciliation over the bill. So, for instance, the schedule included the complete repeal of the estate tax in the year 2010, and then its revival in 2011. Economist Paul Krugman noted the weird and perverse implications of this schedule: "If your ailing mother passes away on December 30, 2010, you inherit her estate tax-free. But if she makes it to January 1, 2011, half the estate will be taxed away. . . . Maybe they should have called it the Throw Momma from the Train Act."[10] Similarly, Paul Caron, a tax professor at the University of Cincinnati College of Law, pointed out that an elderly widow with $10 million would be able to leave her heirs either $6.4 million, $7.1 million, or $10 million, depending on exactly when she died during a 367-day period straddling the end of 2009 and the beginning of 2011.[11]

When the estate tax reappeared in 2011, it came back as a mere wisp of its former self, with an exemption of $5 million ($10 million for couples) and a flat rate of merely 35 percent (compared to 50 percent in 2002). This meant that there would be little serious tax imposed on intergenerational wealth transfers—despite the fact that the wealth of America's richest families is at a historic high.

The gutting of the estate tax has been accomplished through a masterful political campaign, funded and ultimately orchestrated by powerful wealthy interests. Caron reports that eighteen extremely wealthy families alone contributed more than $500 million to the campaign to repeal the tax.[12] But this is not only a story of behind-the-scene machinations by wheelers and dealers buying off politicians with political contributions. Rather, the repeal of the estate tax was ultimately accomplished because those running the campaign figured out how to sell their case to the public by presenting it in a morally powerful way.

They dubbed the estate tax a "death tax," implying there was something inherently cruel about levying a tax at death. They also portrayed it as the enemy of hard-working citizens trying to live the American Dream. A morally powerful counterargument never really appeared; progressives had long since abandoned attacks on concentrations of wealth, thinking it strategically better to focus on making the case for helping the poor. So no effort was made to articulate a strong, principled argument along the lines of the one advanced by President Theodore Roosevelt in 1906 when he advocated a tax whose "primary objective should be to put a constantly increasing burden on the inheritance of swollen fortunes, which it is certainly of no benefit to this country to perpetuate."

The absence of this sort of moral critique in recent years has given conservatives virtual free rein to shape public opinion on the issue. In a comprehensive account of the estate tax battle, academics Michael J. Graetz and Ian Shapiro note that the campaign for repeal, which is a key part of a larger Republican antitax crusade, was able to gather steam with little opposition: "The antitax movement has built up a powerful philosophical attack on the very concept of progressive taxation. . . . An opposing philosophical case was never made."[13] As a result, a fundamental philosophical debate over progressive taxation—a debate that had apparently been settled nearly a hundred years ago and been considered uncontroversial for many decades—was suddenly thrown wide open. A new debate was abruptly staged, but this time only one side showed up to make its case, and won by default.

Of course, taxes are not the sole solution for the extreme inequality that plagues our society. As social justice advocates have been insisting for decades, tremendous gains in equality could be accomplished through more generous social assistance programs, as well as through improvements in our public education system, in more accessible child care, in more affordable university and college programs, in greater investment in public housing, and so on. We agree that there is a pressing need for all these reforms. But we also believe that the key to any solution involves making our tax system considerably more progressive. While reforms in education, child care, housing, and other areas would all contribute to the overall quest for a more equal society, their impact is likely to be gradual and slow-moving at best. The tax system, with its huge and comprehensive reach, has the capacity to reduce inequality much more quickly and decisively (while interfering minimally with the operation of the market economy, as Henry Simons noted). Furthermore, progressive taxation provides a key source of income to pay for reforms in all these other areas.

In stressing the need for a more progressive tax system, we are not suggesting that the rich alone should bear the burden of paying for public services. On the contrary, we believe that we should all be willing to contribute to the costs of such services, given their importance to the quality of our lives and the vibrancy and cohesiveness of our communities. A willingness to pay for them collectively through the tax system—even to regard this as an important aspect of citizenship—reflects a sense of society as a shared project that benefits us all and imposes responsibility on us all.

In the Scandinavian countries, where there is strong appreciation of public services, there is little popular resistance to paying taxes, even though taxes are much higher. In fact, the social welfare systems in Scandinavia and northern Europe are primarily financed through sales and payroll taxes, not through progressive income taxes that take a big bite out of the rich. In other words, the working populations of these countries value their public programs and are willing to pay for them. But then these are much more egalitarian countries, with pretax income spread far more evenly throughout the population.

But the need for progressive taxation goes beyond simply revenue needs. Just as (if not more) important is its role as a vehicle for reducing inequality. The problem of inequality is not simply a problem of too little money at the bottom, but also of too much money at the top. In recent years, we've been led to believe that the fortunes of those at the summit are benign, that any disgruntlement we have about their wealth is simple jealousy. But, as noted, there is compelling evidence that these vast fortunes pose a threat to the health and well-being of the rest of society. They significantly impair the functioning of democracy—a fragile enough institution at the best of times, but one that is seriously undermined by the presence of an extraordinarily rich elite controlling the political agenda, often in highly destructive ways.

Indeed, the consequences of this undermining of democracy are huge. It not only means that we are disempowered as citizens—which would be bad enough—but that we are effectively blocked from enacting policies that are necessary to protect our most vital interests. The capacity of billionaires to imperil the public interest becomes ever more menacing as the human capacity for destruction grows ever larger. Wealthy interests have been the key stumbling block— really the only true stumbling block—to efforts to mount an organized global campaign to tackle climate change. The oil lobby's relentless campaign to deny the validity of the climate science has succeeded in creating enough apparent controversy around the climate change issue to enable governments to get away with doing little. Given this willingness of the wealthy to use their clout to prevent collective action on this and other pending environmental disasters, the negative effects of such extreme concentrated economic power appear to be beyond calculation.

•    •    •

Here then are a few key tax reforms that could go a long way to addressing the egregious overconcentration of income, wealth, and power in the hands of the few.

*The income tax system should be made more progressive.* We propose adding a new rate of 60 percent to be applied to incomes above $500,000, and a new top rate of 70 percent for incomes above $2.5 million.

Our proposed higher rates are clearly much higher than the present top income tax rate, which is 35 percent and kicks in at $379,150. That rate should remain, but the two rates we suggest, which would apply to much higher levels of income, should be added to the rate scale. These rates might seem unrealistic in view of the fact that there is a huge political battle over whether the present top rate should be raised back to 39.6 percent (where it was before the Bush tax cuts). But, taking a longer view over the past seventy years, it is a top rate of 35 percent rate—not our proposed top rate of 70 percent—that is anomalous.

Before President Reagan began the assault on progressive taxation in the 1980s (reducing the top rate to 50 percent and then to 28 percent), the top rate had been 70 percent or above for five decades. Indeed, throughout the period from 1940 to 1963, the top rate averaged about 90 percent. Thus, all we are suggesting is that the top rate be returned to what it was during the Golden Age of Capitalism, that early postwar period of widely shared economic prosperity. And now, as then, these higher rates would apply only to a relatively small number of people with very high incomes, who can easily afford to bear a heavier share of federal taxes. In 1966, for instance, when the top marginal rate was 70 percent, it only applied to incomes above $200,000, which in today's dollars would be about $1,385,000, substantially lower than the threshold to which we are suggesting the top 70 percent rate should be applied.

It bears repeating that the five-decade period in recent American history when the top rate averaged 80 percent was not only a period of increasing equality but also a period of one of the highest rates of economic growth and lowest rates of unemployment. There is no evidence that the high income tax rates stifled entrepreneurial activity or caused mass malingering on Wall Street. Throughout this period, the financial sector was able to perform its important function of allocating capital efficiently, even if boringly.

A recent study by Peter Diamond and Emmanuel Saez in the *Journal of Economic Perspectives* concludes that the optimal marginal tax rate on the highest earners should be in the vicinity of 70 percent. The study takes into account the fact that, at some level, high rates would cause top earners to work less or to hide earnings underground. Thus a top tax rate of 100 percent would be counterproductive. But, the authors conclude, a top rate in the range of 70 percent would be ideal, collecting the maximum revenue from those with the highest incomes.[14]

It is sometimes suggested that, although the top rates were high in the 1950s and '60s, there were so many loopholes that the rich seldom paid tax at these high rates. But the evidence is to the contrary. If we look at what tax was actually paid—as opposed to what the rates were—we see that in 1960, the top .01 percent actually paid 71.4 percent of their income in federal taxes. By comparison, in 2004, the top .01 percent paid only 34.7 percent of their income in federal taxes, indicating that there are many more loopholes in the present income tax code than there were during the 1950s and '60s.[15] Looking only at the income tax, and the very richest Americans, in 1955 the top four hundred Americans made on average $13.3 million (in 2008 dollars) and paid 51.2 percent of it in income tax. In 2008, the top four hundred made on average $270.5 million each—a staggering twenty times more than the richest four hundred made only a half-century ago—and yet they paid only 18.1 percent of their total income in federal income tax.[16]

Even if they only affect a small number of people, high rates are important. They not only would collect significant additional revenue, but would also send a message that society regards extreme inequality as a danger to the public good and as something that, in the words of Henry Simons, is inherently "unlovely."[17]

*Close the loopholes and remove the tax preferences that now riddle the income tax system and almost exclusively benefit the rich.* Many of the loopholes in the income tax system are now widely referred to as "tax expenditures," since, economically, they are the same as direct spending programs. Whether the government writes an individual a check, or simply allows an individual to pay less tax than would otherwise be owed, the government is effectively providing a subsidy—a subsidy paid for by other taxpayers. The income tax code contains over two hundred of these federal spending programs that are administered by the Internal Revenue Service. Their estimated annual cost is well over $1 trillion. They include measures that benefit most taxpayers but disproportionately benefit the well-to-do, such as the deduction for mortgage interest on owner-occupied residences and the exclusion of employer contributions for health care and health-insurance premiums. But they also include a good number of measures that almost exclusively benefit the rich, such as the reduced rate on capital gains, the deduction for business meals and entertainment, and the deduction for charitable contributions. There are many more provisions that almost exclusively benefit the rich, and they all should be repealed. For illustrative purposes, however, we briefly discuss just these three.

**1.** High-income individuals currently pay income tax at a top rate of 35 percent on their salaries and business income. But on long-term capital gains or dividends, their tax rate is only 15 percent. In 2011, this much lower rate resulted in a loss of revenue to the U.S. Treasury of $84.2 billion.[18]

An astonishing 75.1 percent of this tax saving was received by the top 1 percent of income earners, and 55.4 percent is received by the top 1/10th of those, the top 0.1 percent (for an average benefit of $356,895). By contrast, the middle 20 percent of income earners receive only 0.9 percent of the tax savings (for an average benefit of $23).[19]

Providing these enormous tax savings to the richest citizens—who do not labor for their income but realize it simply by holding investments—is profoundly unfair. Nobel laureate Joseph Stiglitz pointed to the absurdity of favorable tax treatment for capital gains: "Why should those who make their income by gambling in Wall Street's casinos be taxed at a lower rate than those who earn their money in other ways?"[20] Such tax treatment not only is highly inequitable, but provides an incentive for high-income people to come up with complex schemes to categorize their income as capital gains. Removing the special tax treatment for capital gains would eliminate a whole raft of tax avoidance opportunities, including, of course, the "carried interest" loophole that hedge fund and private equity managers use to keep taxes unconscionably low on their multimillion-dollar incomes.

Defenders of this tax concession argue that taxing capital gains at favorable rates is necessary to encourage entrepreneurial activity. But there is little evidence for this proposition. Experience has shown that entrepreneurs will generate good ideas whether they receive $5 million or $50 million. Furthermore, only a small fraction of the capital gains received by high-income taxpayers are realized by entrepreneurs, somewhere on the order of 3 percent. Most capital gains are realized by speculators in real estate and secondary securities markets—individuals who perform services of very little social value and whose income is largely determined by luck and other factors completely beyond their control.

**2.** Businesspeople are able to deduct 50 percent of the costs of business-related meals and entertainment. At a time when there is congressional pressure to reduce spending on food stamps and school breakfasts for America's neediest children, it is a moral outrage that the U.S. government is subsidizing, to the tune of $11 billion a year, the meals and entertainment consumed by the wealthiest citizens at the most luxurious restaurants and the most exclusive sporting events. It's impossible to know whether these activities are even related to business at all. It is likely that there is more outright fraud being committed by those claiming these tax-deductible meal and entertainment expenses than there is in any welfare office in the country. But even if some snippets of business are discussed during meals at five-star restaurants or in skyboxes at baseball games, this "business entertainment" provides immense personal benefit to the participants. Such indulgence should be enjoyed to the fullest. But it should not be subsidized by other taxpayers, who in many cases can only afford to eat at fast-food outlets or very occasionally to take their kids to a sports event, and sit in the back row.

Businesspeople often fly first or business class and stay in the most lavish hotels while traveling. Americans would appear to be gaining little competitive advantage by subsidizing this extravagance. As has been observed, the back of an airplane arrives about the same time as the front end. For tax purposes, business travel expenses should be limited to economy fares and reasonable accommodation expenses.

One of the plutocrat's most treasured status symbols, along with oversized yachts, is the private jet. More than six hundred private jets converged on Dallas for Super Bowl XLV. As well as providing one more avenue for the super-rich to isolate themselves from the community, private jets impose enormous costs on the environment (ten times more carbon dioxide is typically emitted per passenger in a private jet than a commercial airline) and the air-traffic infrastructure.[21] Yet private business jets and their personal use by corporate executives receive generous tax subsidies. All of these subsidies should be removed. When President Obama suggested, during a 2011 speech, that one of these subsidies be removed, he was bitterly attacked by the corporate jet manufacturers who accused him of class warfare. They also argued that removing the favored tax treatment would result in the loss of thousands of jobs in their industry. It's true that removing a subsidy for private jets would likely result in fewer jets being purchased. Instead of wasting funds on private jets for executives, corporations might invest their profits on more productive activities, perhaps research and development, where jobs of a higher value would be created.

These two tax expenditures—the special low rate for capital gains and dividends, and the business meals and entertainment deduction—benefit a tiny minority of citizens, basically the top 1 percent. Asking the 99 percent to subsidize these activities strikes at the fairness and integrity of the tax system.

**3.** At first sight, the tax deduction for contributions to charitable organizations appears to be in the public interest. But this is deceiving. The first thing to notice about this tax expenditure is that, like most tax expenditures, it takes the form of a tax deduction, an amount taxpayers can deduct from their earned income in arriving at their income for tax purposes. A tax deduction is necessarily worth more to a taxpayer in a higher tax bracket than a taxpayer in a lower bracket; that is to say, it provides a larger subsidy to a rich taxpayer than a middle-income taxpayer, even when both claim the same amount as a deduction.

Thus, a rich person in the 35 percent income tax bracket will receive a subsidy (save in taxes) $35 for each $100 contributed to a charity. A middle-income family in the 15 percent income bracket will only receive a $15 subsidy for contributing the same $100 to a charity. And perversely enough, a low-income person below the threshold for tax liability will receive no subsidy at all if she can manage to contribute $1 or $100 to a charity.

In 2011, the deduction for charitable contributions cost the U.S. government $34.5 billion in lost revenue.[22] The top 1 percent received 34.2 percent of these tax savings (or an average benefit of $11,474), and the top 0.1 percent received 20.9 percent of the tax savings (or an average benefit of $68,577), while the middle 20 percent received just 3.3 percent of the tax savings (or an average benefit of $40).[23]

The tax deduction for charitable contributions also allows wealthy individuals to decide how the public's money is spent, since they get to direct where the money they are saving in taxes will go, whether it will, for instance, be directed to their alma mater or their favorite hospital, museum, or concert hall. This allows the wealthy to direct the spending of billions of dollars of government money, over which the government has no control, and for which there is no public accountability or transparency. In addition, they get enormous public recognition and adulation for their charitable donations, often in the form of having important public buildings named after them, which gives legitimacy to their concentrated economic power and their indifference, in many cases, to the public good.

At the very least, the tax deduction for charitable contributions should be restructured so that all individuals who give money to charities receive the same subsidy for contributions of the same amount. The simplest way to do this would be to convert the tax deduction into a tax credit. For that matter, every tax expenditure should either be repealed or converted from a deduction to a credit. Converting all tax expenditures into tax credits would make this system of hidden tax subsidies much fairer. It would also simplify the tax code.[24]

*Support the international implementation of a financial transaction tax (sometimes referred to as the "Tobin Tax" or the "Robin Hood Tax").* The idea of curbing financial speculation by imposing a tax on financial transactions was first proposed by John Maynard Keynes in 1936 during the Great Depression. Following the collapse of the Bretton Woods system for stabilizing international currencies in 1972, Nobel Prize–winning economist James Tobin proposed a similar "currency transaction tax" for the purpose of reducing the volatility of currency trading. Several countries enacted financial transaction taxes (FTT) with this goal in mind. In recent decades, the idea of enacting an international financial transaction tax—which would also provide substantial revenue for international development—has gained wide support among a diverse group of reformers.

The idea of an FTT is brilliant: impose a tax so small (as little as a 0.05 percent, or 50 cents per \$1,000) that it would have no impact on serious investors making long-term investments, but would amount to a million pinpricks in the flesh of those engaging in high-volume, quick-turnover, speculative activities—like the ones that have turned financial markets into wildly gyrating, high-risk casinos. Therefore, the tax wouldn't affect long-term investors (middle- or low-income investors tend to hold on to stocks and bonds for long periods). It would only hit people, mostly wealthy investors, who trade stocks and other financial instruments on a daily or hourly basis.

So it's hard not to love the FTT: it could raise billions of dollars globally each year from financial speculators while leaving genuine investors unharmed—like a miracle cancer drug that leaves the healthy surrounding tissue undamaged. But if the idea of a financial transaction tax has always been a crowd-pleaser, these days it has the potential to go viral, given the extent of the public anger over reckless financial speculation in the wake of the Wall Street meltdown.

Long resisted by Wall Street, the FTT has recently been winning approval in the corridors of power. German chancellor Angela Merkel, French president Nicolas Sarkozy, and European Commission president Jose Manuel Barroso have all indicated support for an FTT-type tax. There has even been some high-level support for it in the United States, particularly after former Federal Reserve chair Paul Volcker emerged as Obama's leading advisor on financial reform, in 2009. In the spring of 2010, Obama himself is reported to have said during a high-level discussion of the tax, "We are going to do this!" However, Lawrence Summers, director of Obama's National Economic Council, apparently disagreed.[25] Treasury Secretary Tim Geithner, with his close ties to Wall Street, was also opposed. As a result, a proposal for the tax was never brought forward by the Obama administration.

The tax is resurfacing on the global agenda largely through the efforts over the past decade of nongovernmental organizations such as Oxfam, Friends of the Earth, Christian Aid, and the Salvation Army. In the spring of 2011, over a thousand economists, including a number of Nobel Prize winners, signed a letter to G20 finance ministers urging them to adopt an FTT. In the summer of 2011, the International Monetary Fund issued a report concluding that, although other taxes might be better suited for revenue raising and mitigating the risk of financial market failures, an FTT was administratively feasible.[26] On

September 28, 2011, the European Commission formally proposed a broad-based financial transactions tax in all twenty-seven member states of the European Union, beginning in 2014, at a rate of 0.1 percent on transactions of stocks and bonds and 0.01 percent on derivatives. The commission estimates it will raise the equivalent of $80 billion a year.[27]

A number of industrialized countries, such as the United Kingdom, Hong Kong, and Singapore, currently impose a small financial transaction tax. It has been estimated that if the United States imposed a 0.5 percent tax on stock transactions and a tax of 0.01 percent on other financial transactions, the tax would raise up to $175 billion a year, even if the total number of trading transactions were cut in half.[28] Naturally, if international agreement could be reached on the imposition of such a tax, the revenues could be enormous.

*Support international measures for a clampdown on tax avoiders and evaders.* When all the other arguments fail, the fallback position argued by people opposed to higher taxes on the rich is simply this: they will cut and run, moving their assets out of the country to a low-tax jurisdiction. Those pointing to this threat of "capital flight" typically treat it as an unsolvable problem.

It is estimated that wealthy U.S. citizens have hidden over $1 trillion of assets offshore, evading $40 billion to $70 billion in taxes a year. However, as we note in chapter 8, over the past few years the Obama administration has substantially cracked down on U.S. tax evaders using tax havens. By 2014, the Foreign Account Tax Compliance Act will require financial institutions in every country in the world, including tax havens, to provide automatically all information relating to the income earned by their U.S. depositors. In the summer of 2011, Senator Carl Levin and five cosponsors introduced the Stop Tax Haven Abuse Act, the result of ten years of committee hearings and investigative work. It contains a number of recommendations that if implemented would make it almost impossible for rich tax evaders to avoid paying their legal share of tax by moving their money offshore.

Although the U.S. government has been aggressive in attempting to prevent U.S. citizens from evading tax by moving their money to secrecy jurisdictions, it has been strangely complacent about allowing its own financial institutions to benefit by storing the financial assets of tax evaders from other countries. Washington does not require U.S. financial institutions to automatically report the investment income earned by nonresidents. More than $3 trillion in assets have been stashed in U.S. financial institutions by tax evaders from other countries—an astonishing fact that was revealed in a letter to the Obama administration from the Florida congressional delegation, which strongly opposes any effort to increase the transparency of U.S. banks.[29]

As a result of inaction by the U.S. government, the tax revenue lost to foreign countries, including some of the poorest in the world, amounts to at least $50 billion a year—twice the size of the total U.S. official development assistance. In addition to international tax evaders, the beneficiaries of this inaction have been U.S. banks, particularly Florida-based banks, which store huge amounts of hot money from Latin America. Attempts to clamp down on this egregious tax avoidance have been effectively blocked by the U.S. banking industry.

Washington should take the initiative in winning international cooperation to completely close down all tax havens, including the use of its own financial institutions by nonresident tax evaders. It would be easy to prevent all offshore tax evasion by setting up an international system for reporting bank payments—a system (described in chapter 8) that would be no more complicated than the international system of passports.

*Strive to bring about a change in social attitudes toward taxation and its essential role in a democracy.* The conservative movement has been successful in recent decades in directing public anger toward taxes. It will only be possible to rebuild a properly progressive tax system once the self-serving arguments of the antitax zealots have been exposed, and an appreciation of the importance of taxation in a democracy is restored. The Occupy Wall Street movement has begun this task.

It involves not so much creating a new way of thinking as reviving long-established notions of justice and democracy. While these notions have come under attack in recent years, they were originally championed by some of the leading thinkers of the modern age—including Adam Smith, John Stuart Mill, and Oliver Wendell Holmes Jr.—and were widely accepted in America in the early postwar years. In essence, taxes are about collectively creating things of value in a democracy. As Holmes, a former U.S. Supreme Court justice, succinctly put it, "Taxes are the price we pay for civilization." It could be added that they are also the price we pay for membership in the community and for citizenship in a democracy.

So those who try to cheat their way out of paying them should be treated with disdain, as antisocial members of the community. In recent years, tax avoidance and even evasion have become socially acceptable. There's been a growing industry of tax professionals who push the envelope, coming up with ever more creative ways for clients to get around or subvert the law, including by hiding assets offshore. What's striking is the lack of public outrage over this blossoming industry and its participants—both the professionals and the clients—who defraud the community of badly needed revenues.

While we're considering the need to change social attitudes, here's another attitude badly in need of change: the social acceptance of excessive greed. Part of the credo implanted by the conservative business revolution of the last few decades has been a tolerance for—indeed an encouragement of—unlimited personal acquisitiveness. Rather than seeing extreme selfishness as boorish and antisocial, there's been a tendency to treat the most acquisitive among us as heroes and leaders, people to be featured admiringly in the media and celebrated on Who's Who lists of the rich and famous. This approval of greed has given corporate boards the green light to award ever larger bonuses to executives, and it has encouraged legislators to provide ever more generous tax savings at the upper end, with the idea that the tax system should reward these high-fliers.

And yet, such encouragement of greed—supposedly based on Adam Smith's notion that the pursuit of individual self-interest benefits all—is in fact a gross distortion of the broader vision of Smith, who saw danger in excessive inequality and was highly suspicious of the self-serving nature of business interests. Conservatives have latched onto and promoted certain aspects of Smith's thinking, while ignoring others, such as his forceful indictment of the rich and powerful. As Smith wrote in *The Theory of Moral Sentiments:* "This disposition to admire, and almost to worship, the rich and the powerful, and to despise, or, at least, to neglect persons of poor and mean condition . . . is . . . the great and most universal cause of the corruption of our moral sentiments."[30] Reviving a healthy contempt for excessive greed and extreme inequality—along the lines of Adam Smith's critique—would help restore a saner approach to unwarranted wealth concentration, and provide an important social restraint on corporate boards and legislators.

While conservatives have done their best to erase the notion of society as a community, and taxes as a mark of citizenship, it is essential that we revive these potent ideas.

Here for instance are two personal commentaries—one from a successful American businessman and one from billionaire author J. K. Rowling—that reframe the issue of taxation in a compelling way.

Martin Rosenberg, a New York–based software entrepreneur, explains why he is a supporter of the campaign to preserve the U.S. estate tax:

> My wealth is not only a product of my own hard work. It also resulted from a strong economy and lots of public investment, both in others and in me.
>
> I received a good education, and used free libraries and museums paid for by others. I went to college under the GI bill. I went to graduate school to study computers and language on a complete government scholarship, paid for by others. While teaching

at Syracuse University for 25 years, my research was supported by numerous government grants—again paid for by others.

My university research provided the basis for Syracuse Language Systems, a company I founded in 1991 with some graduate students and my son Larry. I sold the company in 1998 and then started a new company, Glottal Enterprises. These companies have benefited from the technology-driven expansion—a boom fueled by continual public and private investment. . . .

I was able to provide well for my family. Upon my death, I hope taxes on my estate will help fund the kind of programs that benefited me and others from humble backgrounds: a good education, money for research and targeted investments in poor communities. I'd like all Americans to have the same opportunities I did.[31]

And here's J. K. Rowling, who came from modest roots, explaining why she hasn't left high-tax Britain:

I chose to remain a domiciled taxpayer for a couple of reasons. The main one was that I wanted my children to grow up where I grew up, to have proper roots in a culture as old and magnificent as Britain's; to be citizens, with everything that implies, of a real country, not free-floating ex-pats, living in the limbo of some tax haven and associating only with the children of similarly greedy tax exiles.

A second reason, however, was that I am indebted to the British welfare state; the very one that [Prime Minister David] Cameron would like to replace with charity handouts. When my life hit rock bottom, that safety net, threadbare though it had become under John Major's government, was there to break the fall. I cannot help feeling, therefore, that it would have been contemptible to scarper for the West Indies at the first sniff of a seven-figure royalty cheque. This, if you like, is my notion of patriotism.[32]

To these powerful commentaries, let's add a third. Here's John C. Bogle, founder of the Vanguard Group, nicely capturing the pointlessness of excessive greed:

> At a party given by a billionaire on Shelter Island, the late Kurt Vonnegut informs his pal, the author Joseph Heller, that their host, a hedge fund manager, had made more money in a single day than Heller had earned from his wildly popular novel *Catch 22* over its whole history. Heller responds: "Yes, but I have something he will never have . . . *Enough.*[33]

*Repeal the estate tax, and replace it with a serious inheritance tax that will reduce wealth inequalities.* As unequal as the distribution of income is in America, the distribution of wealth is even more unequal. Whereas the top 1 percent of Americans capture about 21 percent of all income, they hold over 35 percent of American wealth. And the concentration of wealth has increased in recent years. From 1983 to 2009, the wealthiest 1 percent of households obtained over 40 percent of all the nation's gains in wealth, with 80 percent going to the wealthiest 5 percent. By contrast, during this same period, the bottom 60 percent of households actually saw a decline in their net wealth. The wealthiest 1 percent now has net wealth 225 times greater than the net wealth of the typical American household. This is the largest gap in wealth holdings on record.[34] The situation is particularly acute for African American families; fully 39.9 percent have zero or negative net worth. Indeed, while the median net worth among white households was $97,900 in 2009, it was a measly $2,200 for black households—the lowest level ever recorded.[35]

The United States has an estate tax that levies a tax on the transfer of wealth between generations. One purpose of this tax is to reduce wealth inequalities and to promote equality of opportunity. From 1935 until 1981, the tax was highly progressive and applied a top rate of 70 percent on large wealth transfers. In 1981, this top rate would have applied to estates over about $12 million (in 2012 dollars). The estate tax undoubtedly contributed to the long-run decline in wealth concentration over this period. However, in recent years it has been gutted.

As late as 2001, the top rate was 55 percent and applied to estates over about $850,000 (in 2012 dollars). Under the Bush tax cuts, by 2009 the exemption level had been raised to $3.5 million and the rate reduced to a flat 45 percent. As described earlier, as a result of a bizarre political compromise between the Obama administration and the Republican-controlled Congress, in 2010 the estate tax was repealed for one year. It returned in 2011 with a $5 million exemption ($10 million per family) and a flat rate of 35 percent. If no further congressional action is taken, the estate tax exemption will be reduced to $1 million in 2013. Thus, it is very likely that the fate of the estate tax will be a major political issue over the next two years. Just as they did in promoting the Bush tax cuts, the wealthy will be pouring millions of dollars into a political campaign to have the estate tax repealed.

Any hope of limiting the dynastic power of enormously rich families requires that they pay tax on inherited wealth. This could be accomplished through the present estate tax, if substantially progressive rates were reintroduced. But it could also be accomplished through an inheritance tax, which would impose the tax not on the donor but on the recipient. For reasons of equity and political salability, and because it is more effective for redistributing wealth, we advocate an inheritance tax.

But before getting into why we recommend this change, let's emphasize the importance of maintaining some form of tax on inherited wealth.

The case for taxing inheritances is similar to the case for a more progressive income tax, except even stronger. As we've argued, the way the market distributes income is quite arbitrary. But at least income received in the marketplace is in some way connected to the individual's effort, labor, and skill. This is not true with inherited wealth, which allows individuals to become incredibly rich by doing nothing more than being born into the right family.

The circumstances of one's birth are always a key determinant of a person's financial well-being. Warren Buffett has dubbed this the "Ovarian Lottery." Here's how he describes it:

> Imagine there are two identical twins in the womb, both equally bright and energetic. And the genie says to them, "One of you is going to be born in the United States, and one of you is going to be born in Bangladesh. And if you wind up in Bangladesh, you will pay no taxes. What percentage of your income would you bid to be the one that is born in the United States?" . . . The people who say, "I did it all myself," and think of themselves as Horatio Alger—believe me, they'd bid more to be in the United States than in Bangladesh. That's the Ovarian Lottery.[36]

Buffett also notes that if he had been born in some different epoch of human history, he (and, for that matter, Bill Gates) might well have ended up as some other animal's lunch, because both he and Gates have poor vision and can't climb trees well. Buffett also observes that his particular talent—knowing how best to allocate capital—would have been useless in many other eras and geographical locations. His point is that people lucky enough to be born with appropriate talents for their time and place are winners in the Ovarian Lottery.

But those who inherit wealth are particularly big winners in the Ovarian Lottery. The circumstances of their birth mean that they don't have to do anything at all to thrive materially. The money just falls into their hands. And then, in case this great blind luck isn't enough, the government tops it up by exempting up to $10 million of their inheritance from taxation. This allows these real lucky duckies to be spared paying tax the way they would if they'd earned the money, like other Americans, by actually working for a living.

With the rise of a new class of billionaires in recent years, much has been made of the fact that many of them acquired their fortunes themselves, rather than through inheritance. In the rush to celebrate these "self-made" billionaires, one might be left with the impression that inherited wealth is declining in importance. In fact, inherited wealth is still holding its own. Five of the top ten on the 2011 *Forbes* list of wealthy Americans have inherited substantial fortunes. David and Charles Koch each inherited hundreds of millions of dollars and a thriving oil business, which they turned into multibillion-dollar fortunes. And three of the top ten spots on the *Forbes* list are taken up by the heirs of retail baron Sam Walton. Indeed, the combined wealth of these heirs—Christy, Jim, and Alice Walton, the jackpot winners in the Ovarian Lottery—totals $66.4 billion. Together, they control more wealth than any family in America, none of it the product of any particular skills, effort, or perseverance on their parts.

So, taxing large inheritances is vital to any plan seeking to diminish the power and influence of extraordinarily wealthy families and prevent their entrenchment as a kind of permanent aristocracy—something that surely sits uneasily with the notion of "equality of opportunity" and the American Dream.

We think, however, that this can be better accomplished through an inheritance tax than an estate tax. The key difference is who the tax applies to. In the case of the estate tax, the levy is imposed on the estate of someone who's just died. This has allowed opponents to label it a "death tax"—a levy that appears to punish someone for dying or at least is associated with someone's demise. An inheritance tax, on the other hand, imposes the levy on the heirs. It's logical to impose it on them, because they are in fact the beneficiaries, and to them it is not a tax on assets long held, but rather on newfound gains—some lucky bounty that will enhance their financial situation through no effort of their own. In this sense, it becomes, in the words of New York University law professor Lily Batchelder, not a tax on death but a tax on "privilege."[37] Privilege is the very negation of the American Dream and the idea that everyone starts out with an equal chance in life. The notion of privilege acknowledges that some people start the race ten yards ahead of the rest, or in some cases almost at the finish line. Applying a tax on this special status seems not only intrinsically fair, but appears far more likely to resonate with the American public.[38]

This is not the place to elaborate on the precise design features of such a tax, but the rates should be set at least high enough to restore the revenue-raising potential and redistributive effects of the tax on wealth transfers to what they were in the early postwar years. During the 1950s and '60s, the estate tax raised revenue equal to about 0.5 percent of gross domestic product (GDP) and generally made up over 2 percent of total federal government revenues. Over the last few years, in its shriveled form, it has been collecting revenues equal to only about 0.2 percent of GDP and 1 percent of total revenues. And in its 2011 form, it will collect even much less—a paltry $10 billion. If its taxing power were restored to the level of the 1950s and '60s, the estate tax (or an inheritance tax) would easily yield $75 billion a year.

In designing an inheritance tax, we propose a lifetime exemption for heirs of up to $1.5 million (in inheritances and gifts) before any tax is applied. This means that for the few who are lucky enough to inherit money at all, the vast majority would be spared paying any tax whatsoever on their inheritance. For those exceptionally fortunate individuals who receive lifetime inheritances above $1.5 million, taxes would be applied at progressive rates. A top rate of 70 percent would apply to inheritances over $25 million. While 70 percent might seem like a high percentage, let's not lose sight of the fact that we are talking about applying it to amounts in excess of $25 *million*—an amount far greater than any individual, no matter how wildly extravagant, can reasonably dream of spending in a lifetime. There need be no fear that privilege would disappear in America.

*With the extra money raised from this more progressive inheritance tax, educational trust funds could be established for every American child.* Let's just pause for a moment to savor this idea, and what it would mean to the lives of hundreds of millions of young people, and how it would change the very nature of American society. The revenue collected from the inheritance tax would be sufficient to create individual trust funds so that all Americans, on their sixteenth birthday, would receive $18,000. The money would be deposited into an individual trust, which could be used exclusively to cover costs of education or training.[39] This would mean that very large fortunes previously accumulated would be taxed so that children in the next generation would have a greater chance to develop their talents and skills to the fullest. It would amount to a direct transfer of wealth, taking from the very richest families and giving improved educational possibilities to all American children as they prepare to enter adulthood.

There would clearly be many benefits. Improving the education and skills of young people would greatly enhance their future work prospects, contributing to their own development and, ultimately, to the nation's productivity. It would also enhance the democratic nature of the country by taking concrete steps toward realizing "equal opportunity"—a concept that is almost universally admired and celebrated, but which in practice has diminished further and further in recent decades as inequality has reached grotesque proportions in America. Moving closer to the goal of "equal opportunity" would send a powerful signal to young Americans, many of whom have become withdrawn and cynical, that their country is serious about democracy and about their participation in it.

This would be Robin Hood in grand style, achieving in one swoop a transfer of wealth from the very richest families to the next generation of Americans, helping them in the most fundamental way. And it would in no way interfere with the push for other urgently needed reforms—such as enhancing assistance to the poor, making health care accessible to all, strengthening retirement security—which are funded out of other revenues. This proposal involves new revenues from a new tax, and would be handled separately. Such a clear relationship between the new inheritance tax and the new education trust funds would allow the public to see a direct connection, establishing a strong moral case for the inheritance tax as a vehicle for enhancing the prospects of young Americans while creating a more democratic and egalitarian society.

It strikes us that this proposal fits very well with the values of Americans, who respect hard work and effort and support the notion that individuals should earn their own way. Large inheritances are clearly unearned income—a gift that only a very few individuals, as a result of their lucky draw in the Ovarian Lottery, will ever be fortunate enough to receive. So imposing a limit to how much of this unearned income remains tax-free seems well in keeping with the moral principles and sense of fairness held by most Americans. It would also bring the United States a little closer to the Swedish-style level of wealth distribution that Americans apparently prefer.

Of course, there have been similar ideas aimed at using revenues from the rich to finance broad-based programs. One that generated a lot of discussion and interest came from Yale University law professors Bruce Ackerman and Anne Alstott. Their idea was to provide every American, upon reaching adulthood, with a grant of $80,000, paid for by an annual wealth tax of 2 percent and a "payback" from recipients at death. The Ackerman-Alstott plan stipulated only that recipients complete high school and stay away from crime. If they did this, they would receive their $80,000 in four annual installments and be free to spend it how they wished—on college, on saving for a house, or on a gambling spree in Las Vegas. It was their stake in life, and they were free to be as responsible or irresponsible with their life's chances as they chose to be.[40]

There are intriguing aspects to the Ackerman-Alstott plan, but we think a plan involving educational trusts offers more advantages. Why tempt young people with such huge amounts of money, possibly enticing them to spend it frivolously at a time in their lives when they likely haven't fully thought out their long-range needs? For that matter, why tempt people at any age with such large sums of money—rather than ensuring that the funds are invested in a way most likely to improve their futures? Our plan gives them considerably less money, but enough—especially if combined with earnings from a part-time job—to allow them to complete a university degree, a college diploma, or work-related apprenticeship or training program. It wouldn't by any means level the playing field in America, but it would give millions of young Americans, who are currently effectively barred from the field, a chance to take their place on it.

Ackerman and Alstott make a lovely point when they note that the idea of taxing wealth in order to provide benefits for all is really a way of ensuring that inheritance is something we all share in as part of our democracy, not just a privilege enjoyed by the rich: "The time has come to create a world in which inheritance is not merely a function of family but of *citizenship*—where all members of the commonwealth have a right to inherit a fair share of the material endowment created by previous generations and are not merely forced to rely on the luck of inheriting wealth from a rich family."[41]

This is certainly an idea we endorse. The fortunes amassed by the rich represent an enormous legacy from humanity's past. As we've argued in this book, the vast sums that the rich have been accumulating, particularly in recent decades, are based on the technological, scientific, and cultural advances achieved over many centuries due to the work of countless scientists, innovators, and thinkers (and those who helped them, taught them, and nurtured them). The contribution of any one innovator or entrepreneur to the overall development of today's products is actually minuscule in the grand scheme of things. Furthermore, it is only because of copyright and licensing laws—part of our manmade system of rules—that these individuals have been able to lay claim to such a large proportion of the benefits of this legacy.

It seems utterly appropriate then to use another manmade system of rules—the tax system—to ensure that the benefits are distributed much more widely, so that this vast inheritance ends up, not in the hands of a privileged few but in the hands of many.

The American Dream, despite its iconic stature, has sadly become more myth than reality in recent years. As it risks fading further into mythology, educational trust funds could put real heft behind the notion that society is a community and that all in the community should have a chance to live their dreams.

# Acknowledgments

We'd like to thank a number of people for generously giving their time and expertise to help with this project, particularly Michael Wolfson, Daniel Wright, Barbara Nichol, Harry Lengsfield, Doug Peters, and David Peters, as well as Thaddeus Hwong, who provided helpful research assistance on a few key points.

A special thanks goes to Joanna Green at Beacon Press, whose insights and thoughtful editing are greatly appreciated, and certainly improved the book. Others at Beacon who also contributed enormously include Pamela MacColl, Tom Hallock, Helene Atwan, Beth Collins, Susan Lumenello, and Marcy Barnes.

The talented crew at Penguin Books did a terrific job. Right from the beginning, Diane Turbide showed enthusiasm for the subject and a keen sense of how to make it work. It was also a real pleasure working with Barbara Bower, Yvonne Hunter, Sandra Tooze, and Justin Stoller. Freelance copy editor Scott Steedman did great work on the manuscript. Our agent, Chris Bucci, was always helpful.

Linda also thanks Peter Langille, for being supportive and wonderful.

# Notes

## Chapter 1: Return of the Plutocrats

1. Jonathan Larsen and Ken Olshansky, "Memo: DC Lobbying Firm Spells Out Plan to Undermine OWS," MSNBC-TV website, November 20, 2011.

2. Julian Glover, "Shaken Survivors of Economic Blast Ask: What Went Wrong?" *Guardian,* January 30, 2009.

3. Terry Bisson, letter to the editor, *New York Times,* February 4, 2009.

4. Data on international inequality from the *World Factbook* 2010 (Washington, DC: Central Intelligence Agency, 2010).

5. David Cay Johnston, "9 Things the Rich Don't Want You to Know about Taxes," Association of Alternative Newsmedia, April 14, 2011. Johnston's calculations, using pretax, inflation-adjusted 2008 dollars, are based on data compiled by economists Emmanuel Saez and Thomas Piketty, the leading scholars in the field of income inequality data. See also A. B. Atkinson and T. Piketty, eds., *Top Incomes: A Global Perspective* (Oxford, UK: Oxford University Press, 2010).

6. Johnston, "9 Things the Rich Don't Want You to Know about Taxes."

7. Matt Taibbi, "The Big Takeover: How Wall Street Insiders are Using the Bailout to Stage a Revolution," *Rolling Stone,* March 22, 2009.

8. In Andrew Clark, "Top Hedge Funds Boom Despite Recession," *Guardian* (UK), March 25, 2009.

9. Calculations from Sam Pizzigati, ed., *Too Much* newsletter (Washington, DC: Institute for Policy Studies, October 10, 2011).

10. Adapted from Austan Goolsbee, "For the Super-Rich, Too Much Is Never Enough," *New York Times,* March 1, 2007. See also Marjorie Mader, "How School Districts, Towns Share Pain of Ellison Refund," *Almanac Online: Menlo Park, Atherton, Portola Valley, Woodside,* April 9, 2008. (On the 2011 *Forbes*'s list, Ellison's fortune had risen to $33 billion, making him the third-richest American.)

11. Jon Bakija, Adam Cole, and Bradley Heim, "Jobs and Growth of Top Earners and the Causes of Changing Income Inequality: Evidence from U.S. Tax Return Data," working paper, November 2010, table 1, p. 49.

12. "The Few," *Economist,* January 20, 2011.

13. Chrystia Freeland, "The New Rise of the New Global Elite," *Atlantic,* January-February 2011.

14. Bakija et al., "Jobs and Growth of Top Earners and the Causes of Changing Income Inequality."

15. Comments by John C. Bogle are from an interview with him September 21, 2011, and are also drawn from his book, *The Battle for the Soul of Capitalism* (New Haven, CT: Yale University Press, 2005), p. xx.

16. Bogle, *The Battle for the Soul of Capitalism,* p. 15. See also Kurt Anderson, "Ovitz and Eisner: A Kid's Story," *New York,* May 21, 2005.

17. Bogle, *The Battle for the Soul of Capitalism,* p. xxii.

18. Warren E. Buffet, letter to Berkshire Hathaway shareholders, February 28, 2006, pp. 18–19 (italics in the original).

19. Ibid.

20. Bogle, interview, September 21, 2011.

21. Ibid.

22. Dave Kansas and David Weidner, "Volcker Praises the ATM, Blasts Finance Execs, Experts," *Wall Street Journal,* December 8, 2009.

23. Chuck Collins, Alison Goldberg, and Sam Pizzigati, "Shifting Responsibility: How 50 Years of Tax Cuts Benefited the Wealthiest Americans," *Wealth for the Common Good,* April 7, 2010.

24. Michael Hiltzik, "McCourts Pitch a Shutout on Taxes," *Los Angeles Times,* February 24, 2010.

25. Bakija et al., "Jobs and Growth of Top Earners and the Causes of Changing Income Inequality."

26. One of the best-known attempts to reconstruct the distribution of income in preindustrial societies relates to England and Wales in 1688. Prepared by seventeenth-century English civil servant Gregory King, it was based on confidential government information. Recently, economic historians, led by Peter Lindert, have revised King's data and used additional data to provide a fuller picture of income distribution in the seventeenth, eighteenth, and early nineteenth centuries. See Peter Lindert, "Revising England's Social Tables 1688–1812," *Explorations in Economic History* 19, no. 4 (October 1982): 385. See also Branko Milanovic, Peter Lindert, and Jeffrey Williamson, "Measuring Ancient Inequality," policy research paper #4412, World Bank (2007) online.

27. Interestingly, people confined to lunatic asylums had somewhat better incomes, averaging 30 pounds a year by 1801; see Lindert, "Revising England's Social Tables 1688–1812."

28. We have calculated the heights in this American parade based on reported incomes for 2010, or for the most recent year available.

29. Average income is the total income of all the individuals in a group, divided by the number of individuals. Median income, on the other hand, is simply the income of the person exactly in the middle of all the income earners, with half earning more than that middle person and half earning less.

30. Outer space usually is deemed to begin at 62 miles (100 kilometers) above sea level.

**Chapter 2: Why Pornography Is the Only True Free Market**

1. John Arlidge, "I'm Doing 'God's Work.' Meet Mr. Goldman Sachs," *Sunday Times* (UK), November 8, 2009. See also Helia Ebrahimi, "Goldman Sachs Teams Could Quit the City over Taxes and Regulations," *Telegraph* (UK), January 4, 2010.

2. The marginal tax rate is the rate applied to any extra income received by an individual. By raising the top marginal rate, the government is raising the rate of tax to be collected above a certain income threshold.

3. Iain Martin, "Britain Is Going to Need Far More People Like Sir Michael Caine," *Daily Telegraph* (UK), April 27, 2009.

4. Liam Murphy and Thomas Nagel, *The Myth of Ownership: Taxes and Justice* (Oxford, UK: Oxford University Press, 2002).

5. For an excellent discussion of the theories of Robert Hale, see Barbara Fried, *The Progressive Assault on Laissez-Faire: Robert Hale and the First Law and Economics Movement* (Cambridge, MA: Harvard University Press, 1998).

6. See Dean Baker, "The Reform of Intellectual Property," *Post-Autistic Economics Review* 32 (July 5, 2005).

7. Murphy and Nagel, *The Myth of Ownership.*

8. Hindery, Frankfort, and Weill are all quoted in Louis Uchitelle and Amanda Cox, "The Richest of the Rich, Proud of a New Gilded Age," *New York Times,* July 15, 2007.

**Chapter 3: Millionaires and the Crash of 1929**

1. Ferdinand Lundberg, *America's 60 Families* (New York: Vanguard Press, 1937), pp. 102–3.

2. Ron Chernow, *The House of Morgan* (New York: Atlantic Monthly Press, 1990), p. 130.

3. Anna Rochester, *Rulers of America* (New York: International Publishers, 1936).

4. Matthew Josephson, *The Robber Barons* (New York: Harcourt, Brace and World, 1934), p. 449.

5. Louis D. Brandeis, *Other People's Money and How the Bankers Use It* (New York: Harper & Row, 1967).

6. Lundberg, *America's 60 Families*, p. 95.

7. Chernow, *The House of Morgan*, p. 129.

8. Ibid., p. 130.

9. Lundberg, *America's 60 Families*, p. 147

10. Ibid., p. 177.

11. Robert S. McElvaine, *The Great Depression: America, 1929–1941* (New York: Times Books, 1984), p. 23.

12. Louis Eisenstein, *The Ideologies of Taxation* (New York: The Ronald Press Company, 1961), p. 65.

13. Lundberg, *America's 60 Families*, p. 166.

14. Ibid., pp. 167–68.

15. John Kenneth Galbraith, *The Great Crash 1929* (Boston: Houghton Mifflin, 1961), p. 7.

16. Lundberg, *America's 60 Families,* pp. 231–35. See also Chernow, *The House of Morgan,* pp. 308–9.

17. Lundberg, *America's 60 Families,* p. 221.

18. Cited in Chernow, *The House of Morgan,* p. 365.

## Chapter 4: Billionaires and the Crash of 2008

1. Paul Krugman, *The Conscience of a Liberal* (New York: W. W. Norton, 2007), pp. 7–9, 46.

2. Harold Ickes, "Lawless Big Business Must Be Controlled to Save Democracy," *Progressive,* January 8, 1938.

3. Thomas Piketty and Emmanuel Saez, "How Progressive Is the U.S. Federal Tax System? A Historical and International Perspective," *Journal of International Perspectives* 21, no. 1 (Winter 2007).

4. Quoted in Josephson, *The Robber Barons,* p. 441.

5. Chernow, *The House of Morgan,* p. 508.

6. David Moss, "An Ounce of Prevention: Financial Regulation, Moral Hazard, and the End of 'Too Big to Fail,'" *Harvard Magazine,* September–October 2009.

7. Federal Deposit Insurance Corporation, "Bank Failures and Assistance Transactions," *Historical Statistics on Banking,* http://www2.fdic.gov/hsob/.

8. Simon Johnson and James Kwak, *13 Bankers* (New York: Pantheon Books, 2010), p. 35.

9. Recently, there's been a new appreciation in some circles for this post-war dullness. Following the wildly volatile events of September 2008, Mervyn King, governor of the Bank of England, urged a group of British bankers "to join me in promoting the idea that a little more boredom would be no bad thing. The long march back to boredom and stability starts tonight." Quoted in Kelly Fiveash, "Bank of England Prescribes 'Boredom,'" *Register* (UK), October 22, 2008.

10. Nick Baker, "Ajay Kapur Quits Citigroup, Plans Hong Kong-Based Hedge Fund," Bloomberg.com, February 28, 2007.

11. James Livingston, "Income Shares and Bubbles, part 2," *The Economist's View,* blog, October 18, 2008.

12. Gregory Zuckerman, *The Greatest Trade Ever* (New York: Broadway Business, 2009), p. 14.

13. Chernow, *The House of Morgan,* p. 716.

14. Simon Johnson, "The Quiet Coup," *Atlantic Monthly,* May 2009.

15. Taibbi, "The Big Takeover."

16. Connie Bruck, "Angelo's Ashes," *New Yorker,* June 25, 2009.

17. Johnson and Kwak, *13 Bankers,* p. 7.

18. McElvaine, *The Great Depression,* pp. 49–50.

19. Branko Milanovic, "Two Views of the Cause of the Global Crisis, Part 1," *Yale Global Online,* Yale Center for the Study of Globalization, Yale University, May 4, 2009.

20. James Livingston, "Their Depression and Ours, Parts 1 and 2," *History News Network,* October 7 and 13, 2008.

## Chapter 5: Why Bill Gates Doesn't Deserve His Fortune

1. The story of IBM's early dealings with Gary Kildall and Bill Gates is re-counted in Harold Evans, *They Made America* (New York: Little Brown, 2004), pp. 402–19. See also Steve Hamm and Jay Greene, "The Man Who Could Have Been Bill Gates," *BusinessWeek*, October 25, 2004.

2. Evans, *They Made America*, pp. 402–19.

3. James Essinger, *Jacquard's Web* (Oxford, UK: Oxford University Press, 2004), p. 37.

4. Ibid., p. 249.

5. Thierry Bardini, *Bootstrapping: Douglas Engelbart, Coevolution, and the Origins of Personal Computing* (Stanford, CA: Stanford University Press, 2000), pp. 81–102.

6. Gar Alperovitz and Lew Daly, *Unjust Deserts* (New York: The New Press, 2008), p. 58.

7. Ibid., pp. 59–61.

8. Ibid., p. 60.

9. Cited in ibid., p. 63.

10. Robert M. Solow, "Growth Theory and After," Nobel lecture, December 8, 1987, http://www.nobelprize.org.

11. Herbert A. Simon, "UBI and the Flat Tax," *Boston Review*, October/November 2000.

12. Cited in Alperovitz and Daly, *Unjust Deserts*, p. 36.

13. Ibid., p. 96.

14. John Stuart Mill, "Land Tenure Reform," *Collected Works*, vol. 5 (Toronto: University of Toronto Press, 1967), p. 691.

15. John Stuart Mill, *Principles of Political Economy*, vol. 2, book 2, chap. 1, section 3, p. 208.

16. L. T. Hobhouse, *Liberalism and Other Writings*, ed. James Meadowcroft (Cambridge, UK: Cambridge University Press, 1994), pp. 91–92.

17. Frank E. Manuel and Fritzie P. Manuel, *Utopian Thought in the Western World* (Cambridge, MA: Belknap Press, 1979), p. 466.

18. Bardini, *Bootstrapping*, pp. 6–14.

19. Alperovitz and Daly, *Unjust Deserts*, p. 144.

## Chapter 6: Why Other Billionaires Are Even Less Deserving

1. Quoted in Zuckerman, *The Greatest Trade Ever*, p. 192.

2. Ibid., p. 95.

3. Ibid., pp. 3 and 8.

4. Martin Wolf and Simon Johnson, online interview, Yahoo Originals, April 21, 2010.

5. This analogy is an adaptation of one made by Phil Angelides, head of the federally appointed Financial Crisis Inquiry Commission and cited in Dean Baker, "Goldman's Scam #5476, Yes, It Can Get Even Worse," *Guardian* (UK), April 19, 2010.

6. Wolf and Johnson interview.

7. As noted earlier, Henry Paulson is not related to John Paulson but is a former CEO of Goldman Sachs.

8. In fact, Goldman bought more of this insurance from AIG than any other bank. See Richard Teitelbaum, "Secret AIG Document Shows Goldman Sachs Minted Most Toxic CDOs," Bloomberg.com, February 23, 2010.

9. Les Leopold, "The Preposterous Reality," Alternet.org, April 10, 2010.

10. Joseph Stiglitz, "Skewed Rewards for Bankers, CEOs," *Korea Herald,* March 30, 2010.

11. Evans, *They Made America,* pp. 413–14.

12. *World Wealth Report 2007,* Merrill Lynch.

13. Cited in Anatole Anton, Milton Fisk, and Nancy Holmstrom, eds., *Not for Sale: In Defense of Public Goods* (Boulder, CO: Westview Press, 2000), p. 3.

14. Ibid., p. 14.

15. Robert Nozick, *Anarchy, State, and Utopia* (New York: Basic Books, 1974), pp. 177–80.

## Chapter 7: Hank Aaron and the Myths about Motivation

1. After 1971, there was a separate, higher top marginal rate for "unearned income"—that is, income not derived from employment, but rather from dividends, rents, or interest payments. For most of the 1970s, the top marginal rate on this unearned income was 70 percent, while the top marginal rate on earned income (from employment) was 50 percent.

2. Joel Slemrod and Jon Bakija, *Taxing Ourselves: A Citizen's Guide to the Debate over Taxes* (Cambridge, MA: MIT Press, 2004), p. 116.

3. Ibid., p. 118.

4. See A. B. Atkinson, "The Welfare State and Economic Performance," *National Tax Journal* 48 (1995): 171.

5. Lawrence Mishel, Jared Bernstein, and Heidi Shierholz, *The State of Working America 2008/2009* (Ithaca, NY: Cornell University Press, 2009), pp. 26–27.

6. Dan Andrews, Christopher Jencks, and Andrew Leigh, "Do Rising Top Incomes Lift All Boats?" IZA DP No. 4920, Institute for the Study of Labour, April 2010.

7. Michael S. Derby, "Trickle-Down Economics Fails to Deliver as Promised," *Wall Street Journal,* digital edition, June 30, 2009.

8. Robert E. Lane, *The Market Experience* (Cambridge, UK: Cambridge University Press, 1991).

9. Robert H. Frank, *Luxury Fever: Money and Happiness in an Era of Excess* (New York: The Free Press, 1999), p. 65.

10. Ibid., p. 73.

11. Lane, *The Market Experience,* p. 345.

12. Hindery, Weill, and Griffin quoted in Uchitelle and Cox, "The Richest of the Rich, Proud of a New Gilded Age."

13. Quoted in Frank, *Luxury Fever,* p. 122.

14. Ibid., p. 120.

15. Richard A. Posner, "Are American CEOs Overpaid, and If So, What If Anything Should Be Done about It?" *Duke Law Journal* 58, no. 1023 (2009).

16. Ibid., p. 102. See also Sanjai Bhagat and Bernard Black, *The Non-Correlation Between Board Independence and Long-Term Firm Performance,* 27 J. CORP. L. 231, 263 (2002).

17. Interview with John C. Bogle, September 21, 2011.

18. Calvin H. Johnson, "Stock and Stock Option Compensation: A Bad Idea," *Canadian Tax Journal* 51, no. 3 (2003): 1269.

19. Arthur Levitt, "Arthur Levitt's Crusade," *BusinessWeek,* September 30, 2002. Excerpted from Arthur Levitt, *Take On the Street: What Wall Street and Corporate America Don't Want You to Know* (New York: Pantheon, 2002).

20. Ibid.

## Chapter 8: Taking the Fun out of Tax Havens

1. U.S. Senate Permanent Subcommittee on Investigations, *Tax Haven Abuses: The Enablers, the Tools and Secrecy,* staff report, August 1, 2006.

2. The details of the Wyly case are reported and analyzed in ibid., pp. 113–348. See also David Segal, "In S.E.C. Fraud Suit, Texas Brothers Stand Firm," *New York Times,* August 22, 2010.

3. "Robust Response of Executive Stock Option Initiative," press release, Internal Revenue Service, November 7, 2005.

4. U.S. Senate Permanent Subcommittee on Investigations, *Tax Haven Abuses,* p. 167.

5. Ibid., p. 113.

6. Oddly, the Wyly lawyers argued that the offshore entities were independent, arm's-length operations. But if so, the Wylys would have been required to pay tax on the stock options at the time they were transferred, which they did not.

7. U.S. Senate Permanent Subcommittee on Investigations, *Tax Haven Abuses,* p. 113.

8. Ibid., p. 125.

9. Ibid., p. 1. More recent estimates put the tax evasion figure at about $100 billion a year.

10. See studies referred to in Ronen Palan, Richard Murphy, and Christian Chavagneux, *Tax Havens: How Globalization Really Works* (Ithaca, NY: Cornell University Press, 2010), pp. 61–62.

11. U.S. Senate Permanent Subcommittee on Investigations, *Tax Haven Banks and U.S. Tax Compliance,* staff report, July 17, 2008.

12. Neil King Jr. and Elizabeth Williamson, "Business Fends Off Tax Hit," *Wall Street Journal,* October 14, 2009.

13. Michael J. McIntyre, "How to End the Charade of Information Exchange," *Tax Notes International* 56, no. 4 (October 26, 2009).

14. If countries refused to cooperate, the cooperating countries might agree to impose defensive measures on them, perhaps modeled on the U.S. treatment of Cuba: any connection between business in the cooperating countries and the

noncooperating countries would be barred. That would mean no banking and business deals, and no tourists. Surely, preserving the integrity of the tax systems in both the industrialized and developing world is no less important than whatever it is the United States is trying to accomplish by imposing these sorts of sanctions against Cuba.

## Chapter 9: Why Billionaires Are Bad for Your Health

1. John Kormos and Benjamin Lauderdale, "The Mysterious Stagnation and Relative Decline of American Heights after c. 1960," *Social Science Quarterly* 88, no. 2 (2007): 283.

2. Thorvaldur Gylfason, "Why Europe Works Less and Grows Taller," *Challenge*, January–February 2007.

3. Richard Wilkinson and Kate Pickett, *The Spirit Level: Why More Equal Societies Almost Always Do Better* (London: Penguin Books, 2009), p. 18.

4. Michael Marmot, *Status Syndrome: How Your Social Standing Directly Affects Your Health and Life Expectancy* (London: Bloomsbury, 2004), p. 39. The first Whitehall study examined only male civil servants; Whitehall II included female civil servants as well.

5. Donald A. Redelmeier and Sheldon M. Singh, "Survival in Academy Award–Winning Actors and Actresses," *Annals of Internal Medicine* 134, no. 10 (2001): 955–62.

6. Marmot, *Status Syndrome*, p. 1.

7. Dennis Raphael, ed., *Social Determinants of Health: Canadian Perspectives*, 2nd ed. (Toronto: Canadian Scholars' Press, 2009).

8. Marmot, *Status Syndrome*, pp. 114–18.

9. S. S. Dickerson and M. E. Kemeny, "Acute Stressors and Cortisol Responses: A Theoretical Integration and Synthesis of Laboratory Research," *Psychological Bulletin* 130, no. 3 (2004): 355–91.

10. Wilkinson and Pickett, *The Spirit Level*, pp. 51–53.

11. Ibid., p. 65.

12. James Gilligan, *Violence: Our Deadly Epidemic and Its Causes* (New York: Putnam, 1996), p. 110.

13. UN Crime and Justice Information Network, *Survey on Crime Trends and the Operation of Criminal Justice Systems* (New York: United Nations, 2000).

14. Danny Dorling, "Prime Suspect: Murder in Britain," in *Criminal Obsessions: Why Harm Matters More Than Crime*, eds. P. Hillyard et al. (London: Crime and Society Foundations, 2005).

15. Frank, *Luxury Fever*, pp. 1–5.

16. Wilkinson and Pickett, *The Spirit Level*, p. 223.

17. Jo Blanden, Paul Gregg, and Stephen Machin, *Intergenerational Mobility in Europe and North America* (London: Centre for Economic Performance, London School of Economics, 2005).

18. Mishel, Bernstein, and Shierholz, *The State of Working America 2008/2009*, chapter 2.

19. See studies cited in Neil Brooks and Thaddeus Hwong, *The Social Benefits and Economic Costs of Taxation* (Ottawa: Canadian Centre for Policy Alternatives, 2006).

20. Reto Foellmi, Tobias Wuergler, and Josef Zweimuller, "The Macroeconomics of Model T," Institute for Empirical Research in Economics, University of Zurich, Working Paper Series, no. 459, December 2009.

## Chapter 10: Why Billionaires Are Bad for Democracy

1. Jonathan Alter, "A 'Fat Cat' Strikes Back," *Newsweek*, August 15, 2010.

2. Alan Feuer, "New York's Resolutions," *New York Times*, December 31, 2009.

3. "Policy Options to Raise Revenue by Eliminating or Reducing the Tax Subsidies for Wealthy Individuals and Profitable Businesses," press release, Citizens for Tax Justice, September 19, 2011.

4. Warren E. Buffett, "Stop Coddling the Super-Rich," *New York Times*, August 14, 2011.

5. Alan S. Blinder, "The Under-Taxed Kings of Private Equity," *New York Times*, July 29, 2007.

6. John C. Bogle, interview, September 21, 2011.

7. Tom Bawden, "Buffett Blasts System That Lets Him Pay Less Tax Than Secretary," *Times* (London), June 28, 2007.

8. Steve Wamhoff, private correspondence with authors.

9. Figures from the Congressional Budget Office and the Center on Budget and Policy Priorities reported in "Policy Changes Under Two Presidents," graphic, *New York Times*, July 24, 2011. Also, Nicholas Kristof, "Taxes and Billionaires," *New York Times*, July 6, 2011.

10. Ezra Klein, "Obama's and Bush's Effects on the Deficit in One Graph," *Washington Post*, July 25, 2011.

11. CNBC quote in Reuters, "Blackstone Boss Calls for Flat Tax for U.S.," September 7, 2011.

12. Harvey Golub, My Response To Buffett And Obama," *Wall Street Journal*, August 22, 2011.

13. Robert A. Dahl and Charles E. Lindblom, *Politics, Economics and Welfare* (Chicago: University of Chicago Press, 1976).

14. Robert A. Dahl, Ian Shapiro, and Jose Antonio Cheibub, *The Democracy Sourcebook* (Cambridge, MA: MIT Press, 2003), p. 385.

15. Task Force on Inequality and American Democracy, *American Democracy in an Age of Rising Inequality* (Washington, DC: American Political Science Association, 2004), p. 1.

16. Jacob S. Hacker and Paul Pierson, "Abandoning the Middle: The Bush Tax Cuts and the Limits of Democratic Control," *Perspectives on Politics* 3, no. 1 (March 2005): 33–53.

17. Quoted in ibid., p. 40.

18. *Too Much* newsletter, December 7, 2009.

19. Martin Gilens, "Inequality and Democratic Responsiveness," *Public Policy Quarterly* 69, no. 5 (2005): 794.

20. Larry M. Bartels, *Unequal Democracy* (Princeton, NJ: Princeton University Press, 2008), p. 5.

21. Jacob S. Hacker and Paul Pierson, *Winner-Take-All Politics* (New York: Simon and Schuster, 2010), p. 149.

22. Ibid., p. 153.

23. Mark Ames and Yasha Levine, "Exposing the Rightwing PR Machine," Playboy.com, February 27, 2009.

24. "Public Interest Comment on the Environmental Protection Agency's Request for Comment on a Petition: Control of Emissions from New and In-Use Highway Vehicles and Engines," press release, Regulatory Studies Program, Mercatus Center of George Mason University, 2001.

25. Quoted in Andrew Goldman, "The Billionaire's Party," *New York,* July 25, 2010.

26. Jane Mayer, "Covert Operations," *New Yorker,* August 30, 2010.

27. Kim Phillips-Fein, *The Invisible Hand* (New York: W. W. Norton, 2009), p. 9.

28. Quoted in H. W. Brands, *Traitor to His Class: The Privileged Life and Radical Presidency of Franklin Delano Roosevelt* (New York: Anchor Books, 2009), p. 447.

29. Ibid., p. 416.

30. Ibid., pp. 401–5.

31. Quoted in Phillips-Fein, *The Invisible Hand,* p. 119.

32. Dwight D. Eisenhower, in *The Papers of Dwight David Eisenhower,* eds. L. Galambos and D. van Ee, volume XV, "The Presidency: The Middle Way," doc. 1147.

33. The Powell Memo, dated August 23, 1971, also known as the Powell Manifesto, is available online at ReclaimDemocracy.org.

34. Phillips-Fein, *The Invisible Hand,* p. 165.

35. Lee Edwards, *The Power of Ideas* (Ottawa, IL: Jameson, 1997), p. 9.

36. Phillips-Fein, *The Invisible Hand,* pp. 169–72.

37. Quoted in Hacker and Pierson, *Winner-Take-All Politics,* p. 54.

38. Yasha Levine and Mark Ames, "Charles Koch to Friedrich Hayek: Use Social Security!" *Nation,* September 27, 2011.

39. Harry G. Frankfurt, "Reflections on Bullshit," *Harper's Magazine,* February 1987. Frankfurt later developed his theory into a best-selling book, *On Bullshit* (Princeton, NJ: Princeton University Press, 2005).

40. Special Inspector General Neil Barofsky reported to Congress in 2009 that some fifty initiatives and programs set up by the Bush and Obama administrations to help the financial sector through the crisis cost $4.7 trillion.

### Chapter 11: The True Badge of Citizenship

1. Quoted in Frank Rich, "The Axis of the Obsessed and the Deranged," *New York Times,* February 27, 2010.

2. Seth Lubove and Oliver Staley, "Schools Find Ayn Rand Can't Be Shrugged as Donors Build Courses," *Bloomberg Markets Magazine,* May 5, 2011.

3. Kris Hundley, "Billionaire's Role in Hiring Decisions at Florida State University Raises Questions," *St. Petersburg Times,* May 9, 2011.

4. Hugh Stretton and Lionel Orchard, *Public Goods, Public Enterprise, Public Choice: Theoretical Foundations of the Contemporary Attack on Government* (New York: St. Martin's Press, 1994), p. 20.

5. Karl Polanyi, *The Great Transformation* (Boston: Beacon Press, 1957), p. 163.

6. For a discussion of the political views of Gerrard Winstanley and the Diggers, see Christopher Hill, *Liberty against the Law: Some Seventeenth-Century Controversies* (London: Penguin Books, 1996), pp. 48–49.

7. R. H. Tawney, *Religion and the Rise of Capitalism* (Toronto: Penguin Books, 1990), p. 73.

8. Henry Simons, *Personal Income Taxation* (Chicago: University of Chicago Press, 1938), p. 29.

9. Henry Simons, *Economic Policy for a Free Society* (Chicago: University of Chicago Press, 1948), p. 6.

10. Adam Smith, *The Wealth of Nations* (London: Penguin Books, 1999), p. 725.

11. Ibid., p. 842.

12. Ibid., p. 857. Interestingly, while Smith appears to support a progressive income tax, Karl Marx thought the idea was rather lame and that it fell considerably short of the kinds of changes needed. "Tax reform is the hobbyhorse of every radical bourgeois, the specific element in all bourgeois economic reforms," Marx wrote, along with Friedrich Engels. "From the earliest medieval Philistines to the modern English free-thinkers, the main struggle has revolved around taxation. . . . The further it slips from his grasp in practice, the more keenly does the bourgeois pursue the chimerical ideal of equal distribution of taxation. . . . The reduction of taxes, their more equitable distribution, etc., etc., is a banal bourgeois reform." Karl Marx and Friedrich Engels (1850), "Review: Le Socialisme et L'Impot, par Emile de Girardin," in K. Marx and F. Engels, *Collected Works,* 1978 ed., vol. 10 (London: Lawrence & Wishart), p. 326; pp. 330–31.

13. Editorial, "Their Fair Share," *Wall Street Journal,* July 21, 2008.

14. Rachel M. Johnson and Jeffrey Rohaly, *The Distribution of Federal Taxes,* 2009–12 (Washington, DC: Urban-Brookings Tax Policy Center, August 2009).

15. Martin A. Sullivan, "Is the Income Tax Really Progressive?" *Tax Notes,* December 14, 2009.

16. Chuck Collins, Alison Goldberg, and Sam Pizzigati, "Shifting Responsibility: How 50 Years of Tax Cuts Benefited the Wealthiest Americans," *Wealth for the Common Good,* April 7, 2010.

## Chapter 12: Revamping the Ovarian Lottery

1. Dalton Conley, "Don't Blame the Billionaires," *American Prospect,* December 15, 2009.

2. Benjamin Page and Lawrence Jacobs, *Class War? What Americans Really Think about Inequality* (Chicago: University of Chicago Press, 2009).

3. William Yardley, "Oregon Voters Approve Tax Increase," *New York Times,* January 27, 2010.

4. Michael I. Norton and Dan Ariely, "Building a Better America—One Wealth Quintile at a Time," *Perspectives on Psychological Science* 6, no. 9 (2011).

5. Quoted in Michael J. Graetz and Ian Shapiro, *Death by a Thousand Cuts: The Fight over Taxing Inherited Wealth* (Princeton, NJ: Princeton University Press, 2005), p. 241.

6. Peter Lindert, "Three Centuries of Inequality in Britain and America," in *Handbook of Income Distribution,* vol. 1, eds. A. B. Atkinson and F. Bourguignon (North Holland: Elsevier, 2000), p. 167.

7. Graetz and Shapiro, *Death by a Thousand Cuts,* p. 6.

8. Robert H. Frank, "The Estate Tax: Efficient, Fair and Misunderstood," *New York Times,* May 12, 2005.

9. Steve Wamhoff, "State-by-State Estate Tax Figures: Number of Deaths resulting in Estate Tax Liability Continues to Drop," Citizens for Tax Justice, October 20, 2010.

10. Paul Krugman, "Throwing Momma from the Train," *The Conscience of a Liberal* blog, New York Times.com, December 16, 2009.

11. Paul L. Caron, "The Costs of Estate Tax Dithering," *Creighton Law Review* 43 (2010): 644, http://papers.ssrn.com/.

12. Ibid., p. 646.

13. Graetz and Shapiro, *Death by a Thousand Cuts,* p. 10.

14. Peter Diamond and Emmanuel Saez, "The Case for a Progressive Tax: From Basic Research to Policy Recommendations," *Journal of Economic Perspectives* 25, no. 4 (Fall 2011): 165–90.

15. Piketty and Saez, "How Progressive Is the U.S. Federal Tax System?" 3–24.

16. Chuck Collins et al., "Shifting Responsibility," p. 4.

17. Henry Simons, *Personal Income Taxation* (Chicago: University of Chicago Press, 1938), pp. 18–19.

18. Joint Committee on Taxation, *Estimates of Federal Tax Expenditures for Fiscal Years 2010–2014* (Washington, DC: U.S. Government Printing Office, 2010), p. 41.

19. Urban-Brookings Tax Policy Center Microsimulation Model.

20. Joseph Stiglitz, "Scarcity in the Age of Plenty," *Guardian* (UK), June 15, 2008.

21. See Chuck Collins et al., "High Flyers: How Private Jet Travel Is Straining the System, Warming the Planet, and Costing You Money," Institute for Policy Studies, 2008.

22. Joint Committee on Taxation, *Estimates of Federal Tax Expenditures,* p. 47.

23. Urban-Brookings Tax Policy Center Microsimulation Model.

24. In the American Jobs Act, proposed by the Obama administration, a somewhat similar proposal was made that would limit the tax savings for each dollar of tax expenditures claimed by rich persons to 28 cents. The administration estimates that this provision would raise $400 billion over ten years and would affect only the top 5 percent of taxpayers; 75 percent of the increased revenue would be raised from the top 1 percent.

25. See Ron Suskind, *Confidence Men: Wall Street, Washington, and the Education of a President*, 2nd ed. (New York: Harper, 2011), p. 365.

26. John D. Brondolo, "Taxing Financial Transactions: An Assessment of Administrative Feasibility," working paper, International Monetary Fund, August 2011.

27. European Commission, "Proposal for a Council Directive on a Common System of Financial Transaction Tax and Amending Directive 2008/7/EC," Brussels, September 28, 2011.

28. Dean Baker et al., "The Potential Revenue from Financial Transaction Taxes," working paper #212, Center for Economic and Policy Research, December 2009.

29. "CF&P Praises Florida Delegation's Leadership in Seeking Withdrawal of Destructive IRS Interest-Reporting Regulation," press release, Center for Freedom and Prosperity Foundation, March 4, 2011.

30. Adam Smith, *The Theory of Moral Sentiments* (1759), part 1, chapter 3.

31. Quoted in Chuck Collins, Mike Lapham, and Scott Klinger, *I Didn't Do It Alone: Society's Contribution to Individual Wealth and Success* (Boston: United for a Fair Economy, 2004), pp. 1–2.

32. J. K. Rowling, "The Single Mother's Manifesto," *Times* (UK), April 14, 2010.

33. John C. Bogle, commencement address, Georgetown University, May 18, 2007. Bogle later expanded his thoughts into a book, *Enough* (Hoboken, NJ: John Wiley & Sons, 2009).

34. Sylvia A. Allegretto, "The State of Working America's Wealth, 2011: Through Volatility and Turmoil, the Gap Widens," Economic Policy Institute, March 2011, p. 2.

35. Ibid., p. 9.

36. Warren Buffet has described his concept of the Ovarian Lottery on a number of occasions, including in a lecture at the University of Florida School of Business, October 15, 1998.

37. Lily L. Batchelder, "Taxing Privilege More Effectively: Replacing the Estate Tax with an Inheritance Tax," discussion paper, Hamilton Project, Brookings Institution, June 2007.

38. A further advantage of an inheritance tax is that it would strengthen the case, particularly politically, for taxing the accrued gains on capital property at death. Under the present law, if a taxpayer holds an investment when she dies with $3 million of accrued gain (assume she purchased the investment for $1 million and it has a value of $4 million on her death), bizarrely enough, this gain is never subject to income tax. Instead, for income tax purposes, when she dies, she is deemed to have disposed of the investment at its cost, and her heir is deemed to acquire it at its fair-market value. This provision has been characterized as one of "the most serious defects in our federal tax structure." It violates every precept of a fair tax system and leads to serious economic distortions, since rich individuals know that if they retain their existing investments until death, their income will escape tax. Over the next three years, it is estimated that this exemption of capital gains on death will amount to a gift to the richest

Americans of between $40 to $50 billion a year. Politically, it has been somewhat difficult to tax these accrued income gains, since to some it appears that the taxpayer is being taxed twice on death—on her accrued capital gain and on the value of her wealth. These are, of course, quite separate taxes. But this is made more evident with an inheritance tax. The decedent is required on death to pay tax on the income that she has earned but has not been required to pay tax on while she was alive, including her accrued capital gains, while the heir is required to pay tax on the income he inherits.

39. If anything, an inheritance tax, similar to what exists in some other Organisation for Economic Co-operation and Development countries, would enable a larger amount to be deposited in each trust fund, so the bequests could become larger over time.

40. Bruce Ackerman and Anne Alstott, "Why Stakeholding?" *Politics & Society* 32, no. 1 (March 2004): 41–60.

41. Ibid., pp. 55–56.

# Index

BAKER COLLEGE LIBRARY

3 3504 00573 4514

HC 110 .W4 M42 2012
McQuaig, Linda, 1951-
Billionaires' ball

DATE DUE

DEMCO, INC. 38-2931

Property of
Baker College
of Allen Park